The Compleat Guide to Film Study

The Compleat Guide to Film Study

G. HOWARD POTEET, EDITOR/ESSEX COUNTY COLLEGE/NEWARK, NEW JERSEY
COMMITTEE ON FILM STUDY/NATIONAL COUNCIL OF TEACHERS OF ENGLISH

CONSULTANT READERS FOR THIS MANUSCRIPT Leo P. Ruth, University of
California, Berkeley/David A. Sohn, Evanston Public Schools, Evanston, Illinois/NCTE
COMMITTEE ON PUBLICATIONS Robert F. Hogan, NCTE Executive Secretary, Chairman/
Robert Dykstra, University of Minnesota/Walker Gibson, University of Massachusetts,
Amherst/Robert E. Palazzi, Burlingame High School, Burlingame, California/Eugene C. Ross,
NCTE Director of Publications/EDITORIAL SERVICES Linda Jeanne Reed and Mary
McCormick, NCTE Headquarters/BOOK DESIGN Norma Phillips Meyers, NCTE
Headquarters

Library of Congress Catalog Card Number LC 74-171577
ISBN 0-8141-4481-0
NCTE Stock Number 44810

Acknowledgments

George Stevens, Jr., "The Mass Media in a Liberal Education." © 1965 by the American Council on Education. Reprinted by permission.

Larry Cohen, "The New Audience: From Andy Hardy to Arlo Guthrie." ©1969 Saturday Review, Inc. Reprinted by permission of the author and Saturday Review, Inc.

Roy Huss & Norman Silverstein, "Film Study: Shot Orientation for the Literary Minded." ©1966 by the National Council of Teachers of English. Reprinted by permission of the authors.

Frank Manchel, "The Archetypal American." Copyright, Media & Methods, April 1968. Used with permission.

Rodney E. Sheratsky, "Freaking Around with Film." Copyright, Media & Methods, November 1970. Used with permission.

Elenore Lester, "Shaking the World with an 8-mm Camera." © 1967 by The New York Times Company. Reprinted by permission.

Howard Poteet, "Film as Language: Its Introduction into a High School Curriculum." © 1968 by the National Council of Teachers of English. Reprinted by permission of the author.

Sister Katherine McKee, S.S.N.D., "Film Aesthetics in the Curriculum." Reprinted by permission of Today's Speech.

Adele H. Stern, "Using Films in Teaching English Composition." ©1968 by the National Council of Teachers of English. Reprinted by permission of the author.

James F. Scott, "Film as an Academic Subject: Reservations and Reminders." Reprinted by permission of the author and The Speech Communication Association.

Robert W. Wagner & David L. Parker, "A Filmography of Films about Movies and Movie-Making." Reproduced with the permission of Eastman Kodak Company.

Photo Credits

p. 66/*The Virginian.* Photo courtesy of MCA, Inc.

p. 68/From *My Darling Clementine.* © Copyright 1947. 20th Century-Fox Film Corporation. All Rights Reserved.

p. 69/*High Noon.* United Artists Corporation.

p. 70/*Cat Ballou.* Reprinted by permission of Columbia Pictures Industries, Inc.

p. 74/*Metropolis.* Photo courtesy of The Museum of Modern Art/Film Stills Archive.

p. 77/*Alphaville.* Reprinted by permission of Contemporary Films/McGraw-Hill.

p. 80/*2001: A Space Odyssey.* © Copyright 1968. Reprinted by permission of Metro-Goldwyn-Mayer, Inc.

p. 84/*Gone with the Wind.* © Copyright 1939. Reprinted by permission of Metro-Goldwyn-Mayer, Inc.

p. 85/*Bataan.* © Copyright 1943. Reprinted by permission of Metro-Goldwyn-Mayer, Inc.

p. 89, 91, and 95/*Morgan!* Photos courtesy of Cinema 5.

p. 129/*Summertree.* Reprinted by permission of Columbia Pictures Industries, Inc.

p. 130/From the motion picture *The Learning Tree* by Warner Brothers, Inc. Copyright© 1969.

p. 133/*The Naked Prey.* Copyright©1964 by Paramount Pictures Corporation and Theodora Productions, Inc. All Rights Reserved.

p. 140/*Shane.* Copyright©1959 by Paramount Pictures Corporation. All Rights Reserved.

p. 141/*Julius Caesar.* © Copyright 1953. Reprinted by permission of Metro-Goldwyn-Mayer, Inc.

p. 142/*The Red Badge of Courage.* © Copyright 1951. Reprinted by permission of Metro-Goldwyn-Mayer, Inc.

p. 143/*The Red Balloon.* Reprinted by permission of Contemporary Films/McGraw-Hill.

p. 152/From *Sunrise.* © Copyright 1927. Fox Film Corporation. All Rights Reserved.

p. 155/From *Three Bad Men.* © Copyright 1926. William Fox. All Rights Reserved.

p. 156/From the film *The Bride of Frankenstein.* Courtesy of Universal Pictures.

p. 157/*Mr. Deeds Goes to Town.* Reprinted by permission of Columbia Pictures Industries, Inc.

p. 164/*The Seventh Seal.* Reprinted courtesy of Janus Films.

p. 167/*Ballad of a Soldier.* Still courtesy of Audio Brandon, the distributor of the film in 16mm.

p. 168/From the motion picture *Rebel without a Cause* by Warner Brothers Pictures, Inc. Copyright©1954.

p. 172/*A Raisin in the Sun.* Reprinted by permission of Columbia Pictures Industries, Inc.

p. 173/*Nobody Waved Goodbye.* Still courtesy of Audio Brandon, the distributor of the film in 16mm.

p. 174/*The Pawnbroker.* Still courtesy of Audio Brandon, the distributor of the film in 16mm.

p. 175/*Hud.* Copyright©1962 by Paramount Pictures Corporation, Salem Productions, Inc., and Dover Production, Inc. All Rights Reserved.

p. 192/*A Man for All Seasons.* Reprinted by permission of Columbia Pictures Industries, Inc.

p. 193 and 194/*Black Orpheus.* Reprinted courtesy of Janus Films.

Table of Contents

Introduction

G. Howard Poteet
Newark, New Jersey

It is agreed that this book is not "compleat"; no book written about film will ever be. Rather than serving as an example of content analysis, the archaic word in the title is more of an attempt to hint at the need for students of film to rely on the art forms of the past, the intellectual heritage to which students and teachers must pay homage in order to understand a new art form. At the risk of offending those who believe that everything must be relevant (whatever *that* means) I should like to point out that movies are not really "now" after all, because they owe a debt to many art forms and their traditions. For this reason, I have tried to include articles of interest to the teacher or student of film who has a traditional academic background.

It is unacceptable to many people to suggest that since the English teacher is anxious to facilitate communication, he should help students examine all media. To some people, the film is simply the movie—a synonym for mere entertainment. We must remind them, of course, that the stage play and the novel were also once thought of as mere entertainment. The purpose of this book is to help teachers and students learn how to explore the art form of film and to help them derive some bases for understanding it. The English teacher need have no monopoly on this aspect of education—it can be done as well by other teachers of the humanities. Nor must the institution which we call the school have a monopoly on this instruction; education takes place outside the classroom as well as in.

Film study has frequently been disorganized, and there are those who say that since life is sloppy and chaotic, so be it. Indeed, much of the argument of those people engaged in the teaching of film has been between those who see film as a medium demanding new modes of teaching and learning and those who simply apply traditional learning processes to film study. What this book attempts to do is not to present a single process or procedure for film study, but, rather, to suggest to the reader ways to explore the ecology of film: the study of the effect of environment upon film, the effect of film upon the environment, and the effect of film on film. The book is not intended as a revolutionary handbook; its organization suggests that the student and teacher of film build on the pedagogical systems and procedures of the past—not destroy them without replacement. It is somewhat in the style of *The Whole Earth Catalog*—listing alternative systems as McLuhan-like probes.

Film study encompasses a wide range of diversified ideas and concepts which work and interact with one another just as plants and animals interact in nature. In *The Log from The Sea of Cortez* John Steinbeck points out that we change the Sea of Cortez by wading in it, that shrimp boats change the ecological balance of that region, that bombs falling in Europe change mankind. And, agreeing with Steinbeck that all of it is important, we concur that "we shall take something away from it, but we shall leave something, too."

G.H.P.

Rationale

Why do we teach film, anyway? A lot of people still think of film study as a frivolous part of the curriculum. The following article discusses the role of film in the curriculum.

The Mass Media in a Liberal Education

George Stevens, Jr.

Will Rogers said, "there is only one thing that can kill the movies, and that is education. . . . Some say, what is the salvation of the movies? I say, run'em backwards. It can't hurt'em and it's worth a trial."

Some may claim that humor has stood still since Will Rogers left the scene, but it would be difficult to argue that motion pictures have stood still. The medium that once was merely the nickelodeon is today being described as "the art of the present," "the great global educator," "the whole of art in one art," and "the central and characteristic art of our age."

The film is many things—art, education, entertainment, record of history, a dominant form of communication, and perhaps even a language in itself. Yet it seems that even though the motion picture was born and raised in the United States in this century, it is only beginning to acquire the public esteem in America that it has long possessed in other countries of the world.

Plato said, "What is honored in a country will be

Reprinted from *The Educational Record* 46:1 (Winter 1965) 68-71.

cultivated there," and the obvious importance of the film medium to our nation's culture gives reason to question the American attitude toward the motion picture and brings cause for an examination of the potential of this medium as a positive force in our national life.

In the event that there be question over the proposition that films have been less respected in the United States than overseas, we can look to a number of examples:

1. The film medium has long been regarded as an art form in the countries of Western and Eastern Europe, and the makers of motion pictures have been subjects of the study and respect accorded creators in other art forms. In England picture makers are knighted; in France they are in the ranks of the esteemed Académie Française; on the other side of the iron curtain they receive the respect which might be expected for participants in the medium which Lenin, Stalin, and Khrushchev each described as "the most important of all the arts." By contrast, America is a country with a film vocabulary stifled by the word "movie" and garbled by persistent use of the noun "Hollywood" as an adjective and with a cinema literacy generally centered on the names, faces, and personal lives of film stars. As far as national acknowledgment to creators of films, there is little or none. America's Freedom Awards have been directed to writers, composers, sculptors, performers, and painters, but never to film makers, with the single exception of Walt Disney, who, I fear, was singled out more for his amusement park than for his great contribution to the art of filmmaking.

2. However unlikely in the nation to which the film is an indigenous art form, both the Lincoln Center in New York and the Kennedy Center in Washington were planned without thought for the medium of motion pictures. The Lincoln Center discovered its error and the New York Film Festival has proved to be one of its few unanimous successes. The Kennedy Center concept was that no hall be set aside for the showing of films, and only cursory thought was given to film presentation of any sort. It is pleasing to note that study is now being given to the proper role for films in the center.

3. In a country with an intellectual elite concerned with development of the arts, the charitable foundations steadfastly turn away from sorely needed assistance to the development of film talent, while generously supporting experiments in other art forms. The first foundation interest in cinema came last year [1964] from the Ford Foundation in the form of twelve grants totaling $118,500. This is commendable, but relative importance may be judged by the traditional absence of any other foundation interest in films and also by comparing this to the Ford allocation to the ballet—$7,750,000.

4. Basic to the preceding three situations, and perhaps the most serious, is an attitude among a large segment of well-educated Americans who offer a ready confession of ignorance about the cinema ("Oh, we

hardly ever go to the movies.") while proudly claiming erudition in the more fashionable intellectual exercises such as opera, symphony, ballet, and drama. Disdain for motion pictures is at its most dangerous on university faculties, where men accustomed to being indifferent or condescending to the film medium frequently fail to encourage the curiosity and interest that today's students have in films.

Most problems can be solved by education, and this, I believe, is true of the cinema gap in the United States. There are two aspects to this educational requisite: (1) means must be provided for young people to study the film art, and (2) equally important, but more difficult, there must be opportunity for young people to be trained in the art of making films.

Taking the latter first, it should be considered that film, in addition to being an art form, is one of the basic modern means for teaching and recording history. This includes film in its motion picture form, film as projected on television, and also live television and video tape, which draw all their fundamental techniques from the medium of motion pictures. The teaching of science, art, medicine, language, and so many other subjects is more and more to be done through film techniques. The recording of civilization—presumably initiated by the caveman on his wall at Altamira and since then the province of writers, sculptors, painters, and, in recent times, still photographers—is more and more coming to depend on the motion picture medium.

This demands men and women who are capable of using the medium effectively. Emerson said, "We infer the spirit of the nation in great measure from the language." And it must follow in our age that the grammar and style of film will reflect our culture. Consider just one aspect, the legacy of history. It is said that civilizations are remembered more for their arts than for their statesmen. And, in fact, statesmen are often remembered because of the arts. Napoleon owes much to painters; the reign of many kings would be the less in history were it not for the mastery of Shakespeare's drama; the Italian Renaissance is a civilization remembered over others because painting and sculpture flourished and its artists left a legacy; and the brilliance of the early Greeks endures by virtue of greatness in the written word and architecture.

So in a large measure will the civilizations of our time be judged by that which survives on celluloid. And history teaches us that that which is most artful resists being obscured by the passing of time. Therefore, it seems both obvious and reasonable that in America we should have a deep concern over the development of creative talent in a medium of communication so fundamental to our culture and our civilization. Certainly we would not leave to chance the training of our scientists, our teachers, our musicians, our statesmen, and our physicians. How then can we be so casual, even careless, about the training of our filmmakers.

In France, Italy, the USSR, Czechoslovakia, and Poland there are elaborate, well-staffed, and well-equipped national institutions for the teaching of all phases of filmmaking. Yet in the United States the acquisition of these skills is left largely to chance, despite the enormous annual output of film and television products and the countless man-hours devoted to the witness of this output.

I believe it fair to say that there is no more complicated and demanding activity than filmmaking. True mastery of the medium requires understanding of writing, photography, sound, music, optics, architecture, editing, and acting. All of this plus stamina, a facility for transcending difficulties, and, of course, the artist's wisdom and vision.

Claude Debussy once wrote, "I feel myself free only because I went through the mill of a complete schooling. If I can go beyond the fugue it is because I know how to write it." If it is true that the arts are close to the center of a nation's purpose and that the quality of our expression will be a measure of our civilization, then it would seem essential that attention be directed to eradicating the poverty of American film training and education.

The demands of his audience are the artist's stimulant, and nothing is more likely to raise his sights than an informed and discerning public. Unlike painting, in which a world of experience may be owned to leaf through the volumes of one's own library, the understanding and appreciation of cinema is physically more complicated. Where one book can give an illustrated comprehension of the work of Van Gogh, only hours of theatergoing can provide a similar survey of Chaplin. As America comes to accept the film as art, more high schools and colleges will develop curricula for the study of cinema classics; yet this should be preceded by the training of teachers. *Time* magazine was more than clever when it suggested that a modern man must be

Tammy and the Bachelor

"cinemate" as well as literate. For future generations this will require hundreds of hours plus guidance and opportunity.

To provide this opportunity, greater care will have to be given to the preservation of film classics, which in the United States tend to disappear or to be sold for mutilation by television. Ironically, the preservation of American screen art has largely been left to the Europeans.

There must also be leadership in the training of teachers and in the planning of curricula. A liberal education should include viewing of screen classics—film series on the great directors, the great eras—from silent films to neorealism, from Garbo to Guinness, from Eisenstein to Chukrai, from Biograph to New Wave, and onward. Only by providing the opportunity to view and study can we promise ourselves future generations that will make the right choice when confronted with *Godzilla* and *Greed* or *Tammy* and *Tom Jones*.

The opportunity for film makers to learn and the opportunity for young audiences to develop a taste for excellence are two aspects of American life which will have considerable effect on the quality of our culture.

In his remarks at the ground-breaking of the Kennedy Center, President Johnson stressed that opportunity must be provided for young artists. In so doing he specifically mentioned film makers. This special mention of the motion picture art by a president of the United States is as unique as it is welcome. And it is perhaps an indication that the problems of film study in liberal education are meant to be tackled in the Great Society.

There are in this country signs of action: the New York Film Festival and its related seminars and work groups; the survey of the American Council on Education and the Motion Picture Association of America on the teaching of films in colleges; the worthwhile studies at the film conferences at the Aspen Institute; the progress being made by the American Federation of Film Societies; and the foundation leadership provided by Ford with the

Tom Jones

first grants to the field of cinema. Yet these and other similar endeavors are fragments and no match for the enormous challenges we face.

But they are, indeed, beginnings and must be buttressed by far greater support and leadership than has yet been forthcoming. The foundations should take a new look at their involvement, or lack of it, in the field of motion pictures. The academic community has a responsibility toward film communication. The film industry should examine its future with respect to filmmaking talent and the film audience of tomorrow. State and local governments will very likely play a role, and if the legislation proposed for a National Foundation for the Arts is passed by the Congress, support for film education could be one worthwhile result [the National Foundation on the Arts and Humanities was founded in 1965].

These are formidable and important challenges. And the success and the speed with which they are met will have a strong bearing on our nation and, in a larger sense, our civilization.

The great French marshal Lyautey has been quoted as once saying to his gardener: "Plant a tree tomorrow." And the gardener said, "It won't bear fruit for a hundred years." "In that case," Lyautey said to the gardener, "plant it this afternoon." That is how I feel about these challenges.

George Stevens, Jr., is the director of the American Film Institute.

History

What can you say on the history of teaching about film? It started at the turn of the century and stopped. It started up again in the late twenties and then stopped at the beginning of World War II. It started again in the early sixties and maybe it will stop again. And maybe it won't.

The New Audience: From Andy Hardy to Arlo Guthrie

Larry Cohen

According to the headline of an article that appeared . . . in the *New York Times*, buried with the film advertisements, . . . "Young Writers Say They Don't Read." The five interviewed authors, all of whom were respectably under thirty, announced that they rarely if ever opened a book. "It's just easier to go to a movie and let it all wash over you," one of them said.

There were, of course, prominent exceptions to this impatient rule. Hermann Hesse and J.R.R. Tolkien both have large youthful followings. So does Kurt Vonnegut, Jr., who was singled out because "he writes cinematically." But most authors met a grimmer, much less cordial fate. Reading was regarded as an academic pastime, and most books were relegated to the level and enthusiasm of a chore. The article came to an abrupt close with one of those statements that must have chilled the warmest hardbound heart. One of the young writers, Sally Grimes, who had previously spent some time composing obituary

Reprinted from *Saturday Review* 52(December 27, 1969) 8-11, 36.

notices for the *Philadelphia Bulletin,* committed her own cool piece of manslaughter by concluding: "I find I'm reading less and less. I really don't know why."

It occurs to me that the content of such a remark is less important than the tone with which it appears to have been said. Just think about what she's announcing. The death of literature? Hardly. The temporary disaffection of a substantial cross section of young writers (and young readers) with books? Maybe, despite the fact that the paperback marketplace is currently a veritable gold mine and new softcover publications such as *New American Review* and *US* have whopping, young readerships.

But listen to the statement rather than just its meaning. What resounds is something casual and half-shaded, something innocent and perhaps even unconscious. The remark sounds like an afterthought, as if the speaker was deaf to any echo. There is nothing guilty about such a confession, no sense that the Furies of literature are about to swoop down upon her for heresy. It is the nonchalance that says everything, the pronouncement itself relatively little. For the mood to which Miss Grimes and the other young writers are subscribing may well be an accurate expression of a *new* sensibility, one which is defined in part by its very lack of guilt about not being well-read and, on the other hand, by its overtly positive enthusiasm about film. In its openness and bluntness, "I really don't know why" reflects 1969 and a large new audience.

These changes in emphasis are so recent that it's extremely difficult to pin down their source with any real exactitude. There are clues, however, and a quick personal flashback to four years ago, around the time I graduated from high school, brings to mind a different picture. The kids with whom I grew up were avid readers; some of them even lay awake late at night and sweated out plans for writing the "great American novel." Vietnam and a pervasive drug scene were not substantial issues yet; like us, they were in their pubescent stages, and the day they would be taken for granted as realities seemed a long way off. Literature still had its grip on us and we on it. For, McLuhan and television notwithstanding, the primary frame of reference from which we derived our formal tastes and plans for the future was still verbal. Our own "great expectations" used writers like Ken Kesey, Thomas Pynchon, J.D. Salinger, and Nathanael West as models and sources of passionate discussion.

Significantly mitigating this classical orientation was a film course I took in my senior year with about thirty other kids. We spent the first part of a fall semester staring at supposedly familiar objects—a leaf or our thumb, for example—and discovered the hard way what Joseph Conrad meant when he argued that his purpose was to make us *see.* With our thumbs out of our mouths, we then began looking at films by Griffith, Chaplin, Eisenstein, and Welles. *Potemkin* and *Citizen Kane* served as textbooks; we dissected their sequences frame by frame and assimilated a new vocabulary, learning how a movie was put together and why it still worked decades later. While most of our friends were surrendering themselves to term papers on Milton or even to diagraming the perennial sentence, we were reading the late James Agee's movie criticism and screenplays, using Arthur Knight's *The Liveliest Art* to gain a historical context, and worrying about montage and nonlinear structures. In retrospect, we already were taking films personally and seriously.

By 1969, what has happened is simply this: the young audience for books has not so much shrunk as the young audience for motion pictures has appreciably grown and become more vocal. As a breed, the kids of the late fifties and early sixties—the ones who had avidly attended university creative writing courses or earnestly imagined themselves as editors for a New York publishing house— were now generally anachronistic. For that matter, almost no one I knew at college read anything beyond the required classroom texts. Students were now crowding and overfilling smoky lecture halls to see and "rap" about films—their theory and history—and in more than a few instances this new breed was also making 8mm and 16mm movies despite the cost of equipment.

One crucial difference between movies and the other arts was simple accessibility. Even in the cultural provinces of the Middle West, it was possible to see as many as a half-dozen films a week. (Francis Ford Coppola, the thirty-year-old director of *You're a Big Boy Now* and *The Rain People*, predicts that "movies will be sold like soup in the future," that "you'll be able to buy it in cartridges for three dollars and play it as you would a record at home.") In addition to sheer availability, films were answering the lusting college cry for "relevance," taking both their raw celluloid material and subject matter from today rather than the day before yesterday.

In this regard, *Blow-Up* functioned as the pivotal film; it radicalized the way in which many college students responded to film. More than three years after it first appeared, it remains a significant milestone in this country's awareness of motion pictures. Antonioni's tour of mod London was one of the first movies young people saw more than once. Its ambiguities, its mysteries, and its technological breakthroughs brought them back to the theater again and again, converting them to the language of film. (Curiously and ironically, it even inspired some kids to become photographers.) Rather than just being one more foreign film, *Blow-Up* was a primer in technique.

In the process of this shift of focus off the writer and onto the film maker, the literary gods lost many of their aspiring novices to a medium that was itself in a state of relative infancy. There was and is, of course, a set of both happy and notorious exceptions. Nabokov's *Ada* and John Fowles' *The French Lieutenant's Woman*—works of

Blow-Up

matters for young people today is the number of campus literary successes now being made into motion pictures. We already have witnessed several: Peter Brook's grainy 1963 adaptation of William Golding's book *Lord of the Flies;* Larry Peerce's pushy but humorous sixties transplant of Philip Roth's 1959 novella, *Goodbye, Columbus;* and the soon-to-be-released film version of John Barth's *The End of the Road* [released in 1970]. Even the indomitable classroom Shakespeare found himself ruthlessly pruned and feverishly revitalized for a young audience as the literally teenage Leonard Whiting and Olivia Hussey became Romeo and Juliet. If the results in this latter case were a trifle goofy, seeing the star-crossed lovers played by kids against the background of director Franco Zeffirelli's lush visual imagery almost justified any irreverence.

As we enter a new decade, the possible list of properties based on collegiate favorites increases. A new company, United Screen Arts, has optioned Hesse's *Steppenwolf,* and Conrad Rooks, whose hallucinatory film-nightmare on drugs, *Chappaqua,* was released several years ago, is rumored to be preparing the same author's *Siddhartha* for the screen. Hillard Elkins, the producer of *Oh! Calcutta!,* is readying a movie version of *Cat's Cradle,* and other works by Vonnegut—including *Player Piano* and *Sirens of Titan*—are also scheduled. Some of these are tentative projects and may never make it to the screen. Their mere presence on the boards,

genius in my opinion—would be quickly purchased in spite of their prohibitive costs in hardbound editions. Similarly, there would be large campus audiences for such national best sellers as *Portnoy's Complaint, Myra Breckinridge,* and *Couples.* The big money and larger audience, however, now belonged to film, and it is not surprising that all of these novels (with the understandable exception of *Ada*) are headed for the screen.

One key sign of film's evolution as the form that

however, suggests a different contextual base for American films in the future. With Tolkien's *Lord of the Rings* soon to go into production, can Richard Fariña's *Been Down So Long It Looks Like Up to Me* [released in 1971] be far behind?

One industry journal recently estimated that "at least seventy percent of box-office revenue comes from young people between sixteen and twenty-nine," a statistic that indicates that the economy of motion pictures is quantitatively a matter of age. Thought of five years ago *only* as an entertainment form—with a separately delineated category for "art" house imports—movies are now *in* and regarded as a legitimate pursuit in America. In contrast, the more traditional arts such as theater and opera are shaky if not altogether ready to enter an old age home. The lines at the box office are a proof of sorts that film and film alone is attracting kids. Just as it is inconceivable that anyone would stand in line for two hours to see a play or purchase a book, it is taken for granted that one will wait this long to see *Midnight Cowboy* in a city like New York. Legitimate theater, with the exception of such youth-geared musicals as *Hair* and *Salvation,* exerts little if any appeal. And the one-week performance by the Who of their rock-media opera *Tommy* at the Fillmore East is the closest anyone under thirty will get to a tier at the Metropolitan.

To understand the kind of age polarization that has occurred, one has only to glance quickly at the lyrics of two songs: the title number from *Hello, Dolly!* and "Go to the Mirror" from *Tommy.* "It's so nice to have you back where you belong," sing the waiters in the long-running Broadway musical, articulating a nostalgia and a red-carpeted style of life that seems altogether foreign if not indulgent to the kids who witnessed Woodstock, the Vietnam moratorium, and the march on Washington. In sharp contrast, the psychologically deaf, dumb, and blind Tommy sings, "See me, feel me, touch me, heal me" from the heavily amplified stage of the Fillmore, and the generations neatly split themselves right down the middle. One has fake cotton-candy dumplings in its mouth, while the other speaks of irresistible pinball wizardry from an electronically vibrant stage.

This polarization has been widely publicized, and the evidence is staggering in its abundance. It is now virtually impossible to pick up a national magazine without stumbling across a prominent article that discusses the "youth market" and the "new American film." One of the November issues of *Look,* for example, featured Daria Halprin and Mark Frechette, the two young nonprofessionals chosen by Antonioni for his first film in America, the soon-to-be-released *Zabriskie Point* [released in 1969].[1] Earlier last fall *Newsweek,* with Arlo Guthrie gracing its cover, featured a story on Arthur Penn's *Alice's Restaurant.*[2]

If the age bracket of the audience has been widely covered and debated in the press, it is also no secret that the major studios are in deep trouble and that Hollywood is running scared. Clearly, the old sorts of investments—the heavily insured, multimillion-dollar dinosaurs such as *Paint Your Wagon*, *Sweet Charity*, and *The Madwoman of Chaillot*—cannot hope to recoup their budgets at the box office and are suffering tremendous losses. Like the Norma Desmond of Billy Wilder's *Sunset Boulevard*, these films are now in a revealing close-up at the end of their staircase. They simply can't survive against the relatively low-budget, personal wave of films that *Easy Rider* typifies: a movie made for less than $500,000 that may well gross as much as fifty million dollars in foreign and domestic sales.

Amid corporate power struggles, massive overheads, and the infusion of somewhat younger management, the studios are trying frantically to cater to this new audience. They are floundering because the only real precedents for youth films are the packages of American International Pictures—everything from the motorcycle and beach party formulas to *Wild in the Streets* and *Three in the Attic*—movies that were commercially successful and immune to critical reception. But a good film—and, to some degree, that is what is being demanded today—doesn't lend itself to readily identifiable denominators. The pseudo-politics of *Medium Cool*—the Democratic convention, the awkward restaging of Kennedy's assassination—make Haskell Wexler's film a work of serious intentions in spite of my strong reservations

Dont Look Back

about its success. Used in Agnes Varda's *Lions Love*, the same issues are inane, if not in appallingly poor taste.

As a result of the youth craze, we are due for a series of films—some good, some bad—that reflect a Hollywood in transition. The year 1970 will witness the release of a mixed bag of pictures that are genuinely topical as well as those that will be lamentably foolish. MGM has completed *The Magic Garden of Stanley Sweetheart* from a screenplay by twenty-three-year-old Robert Westbrook based upon his own novel. The same studio is also preparing a screen version of James Simon Kunen's *The Strawberry Statement*. With its locale shifted from Columbia College to Oakland, the screenplay is an interesting blend of fiction and documentary by thirty-year-old playwright Israel Horovitz.

Joseph E. Levine, head of the company that released the phenomenally successful *The Graduate*, has dubbed Avco-Embassy's future banner as "New Faces of the '70s" and turned over the filming of the plague-ridden *Ski Bum* (from Romain Gary's novel) to three young graduate film students from UCLA. Haskell Wexler is readying production of *A Really Great Movie*, which Paramount describes as a film about two young college filmmaking students who are given the opportunity to make a major motion picture. Universal has the Berkeley-set *The Activist* in release. And only last month Radio City Music Hall, known for its tourists, kicking Rockettes, and tradition of Walt Disney fare, showed *Hail, Hero!*, perhaps the worst example to date of a film that tries to appeal to both pacifists and militants and rightfully pleases neither.

If *Blow-Up* was instrumental in attracting young people to film, the equivalent American landmark was Mike Nichols' *The Graduate*. Holden Caulfield, his worried future, identity crisis, and traumas fairly intact, found a close screen ally in the person of Benjamin Braddock as played by Dustin Hoffman. Both characters assert the same basic appeal, a nervy and youthful cry against hypocrisy and false values that are captured lucidly by one word: *plastics*. What seems to me to be vital about the movie is that it signifies a phenomenon of rapport rather than a purely aesthetic triumph; that it functions as a sociological replacement for Salinger despite its own confusions and impurities of self-conscious camerawork; that its score is by Simon and Garfunkel rather than Max Steiner.

This alliance with contemporary music has a great deal to do with the new look of American films and their success with a young audience. The Grateful Dead, Big Brother and the Holding Company, and John Barry's superb orchestrations contributed heavily to the impact of *Petulia*. And the two intentional or coincidental imitations of Nichols' film—the previously mentioned *Goodbye, Columbus* and *I Love You, Alice B. Toklas*—respectively used the Association and Harper's Bizarre for their title songs. When the team responsible for writing the latter movie made their directing debut this year with *Bob & Carol & Ted & Alice*, they appropriately ended what is in essence a middle-aged comedy with Dionne Warwick singing "What the World Needs Now Is Love."

There is a special category of movies in which the music and performer mean everything, and craft is less of a concern. D.A. Pennebaker's *Dont Look Back* opens with Bob Dylan holding placards for "Subterranean Homesick Blues" as the song is played on the soundtrack; it is a fresh, ingenious, and indelible image. But in spite of Pennebaker's attempts to have the camera be more than a passive recorder of a rock concert, the only interest in *Monterey Pop* is the roster of "stars": the Jefferson Airplane, Janis Joplin, and the Who. One feels inclined to reserve formal criticism because it somehow seems irrelevant, even in a simple exploitation film such as *Popcorn,* in which the audio performances by the Rolling Stones and Joe Cocker are virtually scuttled by the abysmal color visuals and self-conscious, intrusive camerawork. At this point, there is simply no conjecturing

Alice's Restaurant

what the upcoming release of *Woodstock* by Warner Brothers will be like, but it clearly represents a much needed departure from the primitivism of its predecessors [*Woodstock* was released in 1970]. It is described as a full-length color entertainment that makes use of split-screen techniques with up to six multiple images.

So much for the survey of the change, its physical and financial appearance. To borrow from the title of one of Richard Lester's early short subjects, the American cinema and its audiences are now running, jumping, and standing still—all at the same time. Some of this youthful insistence on relevancy has been invigorating and valuable in that it reflects an outcry against what is truly dated. It has brought us a vital (if not slightly late) awareness that film is primarily a director's medium. Consequently, kids and adults are becoming familiar with the names and works of Arthur Penn, Stanley Kubrick, Sam Peckinpah, and, of course, Mike Nichols. It has led to an appreciation of criticism. One spectator at this year's San Francisco Film Festival even asserted that the writings of critic Pauline Kael will survive the films of Sidney Lumet.

If we are lucky, this positive education will not stop with the director but will be extended to include an awareness of the components that define filmmaking: Nicholas Roeg's cool, alienating camerawork for *Petulia* (as well as the cinematography of such men as Lucien Ballard, Conrad Hall, William A. Fraker, Laszlo Kovacs,

Pasquale de Santis, and Michael Nebbia); Dede Allen's major contribution as editor in *Rachel, Rachel* and *Bonnie and Clyde;* and Lawrence Marcus's brilliant screenplay of lacerated nerves and casual violence for *Petulia.*

Similarly, we are discovering just how a film maker like Peter Yates can straddle two theoretically divided kinds of films—the entertainment and the so-called art movie. Superficially a cops-and-robbers film, *Bullitt* on closer examination yields a complicated and fascinating set of structural parallels between the policeman and the killer. And his new film, *John and Mary,* transforms the banalities of an updated romance by complementing them with incisive visual details. By showing, for example, how Dustin Hoffman cracks his soft-boiled egg and eats it scooped out in the cup while Mia Farrow cracks and eats hers from the shell, by taking an overused device like the freeze-frame and showing how it can still be used humorously and originally, the British director draws attention to simple, illuminating bits of action instead of leaving the viewer to rely on dialogue to get his bearings.

On a more profound level, this youthful impact at the box office, if allied with a willingness to suspend old expectations and easy solutions, can lead to an appreciation of a film such as the current *Tell Them Willie Boy Is Here* [1970]. The second movie to be written and directed by the politically blacklisted Abraham Polonsky is remarkable (as was his 1948 *Force of Evil*) for its density of formal and moral texture and in its eloquent union of image and sound. In its uncompromising attitude toward film and vision of a country that compromises its inhabitants, *Willie Boy* is a stunning achievement. The support of a new generation of filmgoers hopefully will elevate Polonsky to his rightful position as a unique force in American cinema—a man of ideas.

Young people's demands on the medium *can* take us in this direction. Yet there is an equal if not greater chance that we are moving toward a mere embracing emphasis of today for the sake of today and a real irrelevancy. As Kunen puts it in *The Strawberry Statement,* "To say that youth is what's happening is absurd. It's always been happening. Everyone is nineteen, only at different times. This youth-cult scene is a disservice to everyone." His is a good, prematurely wise statement that foresees an inevitable and endless rash of "youth" films, imitations of some intangible quality that exists, after all, only in the mind. Like a Ponce de León in search of the magic fountain, the studios currently are equating being young with being talented with being profitable. I only hope the logic of this direction is reversed before the studios learn the hard way all over again that making bad films—young, old, or middle-aged—is no way at all.

The pair of films that I think genuinely reflect the end of this decade and the start of another are *Easy Rider* and *Alice's Restaurant.* As companion pieces of styles, attitudes, and approaches, they form a composite blow-

Easy Rider

ner's song, "We Can Be Together," by visually demonstrating that "we are all outlaws in the eyes of America." More than any film in recent memory, it generates its own pulse into the heartbeats of its predominantly under-thirty audience. The spirit of the movie is personal, even conversational. It says yes, it has been to this wave length of the United States before, and to prove that its age is ours, the soundtrack makes intensive use of contemporary rock—Steppenwolf, the Band, and Jimi Hendrix, among others. When Roger McGuinn sings "It's Alright Ma (I'm Only Bleeding)" near the end of the film, the audience and the movie have a viselike grip on each other. They go back a long way together, and I'm not altogether certain that anyone who wasn't weaned on Bob Dylan—whether three or thirty—can share the journey. Sometimes, the film says about itself, you just have to be there to understand.

Alice also utilizes music as its integral base but directs it toward a more complicated, trickier, and eventually subtler end. Some of the soundtrack is simply music, like the appropriate and evocative "Songs to Aging Children Come," by Joni Mitchell. It is used as a quiet, melancholic background for a funeral sequence in the snow, a scene that owes a formal and emotional debt to the final part of François Truffaut's *Fahrenheit 451*. There are other songs including Pete Seeger's renditions of "Pastures of Plenty" and "The Car Song." The traditional hymn "Amazing Grace" becomes a generational link be-

up of what is happening in this country. They both take drugs for granted as a part of the grass ethic, and they are both possessed with a sense that we are becoming our own films. They are also intrinsically interesting in what they tell us about the interaction between audiences and movies, in the way the former sees itself on the screen.

Of the two, *Rider* works more obviously and is the more immediate film, applying the lyrics of Paul Kant-

tween a revival meeting and a youthful and communal Thanksgiving Day at Ray and Alice's church. And then there is the title song itself, the best expression of what the movie is really about. It articulates a cartooned life-and-death style, a giving and a taking, the good and bad times of a country in its logical but paradoxical youth. "You can get anything you want," says the song, "*excepting* Alice," suggesting the peculiar light and dark moods of an America and a film whose final shot will literally mimic this tension between lament and celebration.

The two films are similar in other ways. Both use non-professionals as well as trained actors; both are framed by the geography of late-sixties America. *Rider* goes cross-country on its fateful cycle journey to a whorish New Orleans, and along the harrowing way shows us places where the word police has a long *o*, a vowel stretched out so far that it almost whistles like a rubber band. It is a land of motels with quickly turned on "No Vacancy" signs as soon as its turned-on, long-haired riders arrive. And inevitably, it is a mental landscape full of crewcut goons with murderous aim if not intent.

Alice documents a lighter but hardly less scary America: a country of induction boards in which a young black veteran of the war has a hook instead of a hand; in which Arlo is violently abused for his hair and called a "hippie perversion"; in which Vietnam is pronounced "Veetnam"; and in which a solitary billboard from the

Little Big Man

Johnson administration still says "Keep America Beautiful! Cut Your Hair."

The crucial differences between the two films are not raw material but age and tone. For all intents and purposes, *Rider* is the first work of a young man (although Dennis Hopper is thirty-three and goes back to the days of James Dean in the fifties), and *Alice* is the sixth movie by a middle-aged man sincerely trying to bridge the considerable "great divide." Hopper's vision is obsessed with death and prostitution from its very first minute on the screen; it senses persecution all around it, and it invites us to join in with our personal nightmares and experiences, our collective paranoia. It says that this is the way this country is, and, cleverly, it shows us the devastating fire and explosions in advance of their actual, sequential appearance that ends the film.

Undeniably, the movie is horribly effective; its own confusions even add a terrifying and inescapable logic. When the lawyer George Hanson (played brilliantly by Jack Nicholson) is killed, the loss is acute. The movie misses him. It came alive when he appeared, and in a curious way it seems to die when he does. Fonda's and Hopper's destruction elicits a strong response by virtue of the brutality of the act rather than by feelings for the individuals. Ours is a purely visceral reaction to murder, a response we even indulge in. But we have no time to think, no time to sort out the differences between the deaths. Despite whatever Hopper claims were his intentions, the film lurches out of control and so does the audience. There is a distinction that demands time to be thought out: namely, that Hanson was worth more alive than dead, and Wyatt and Billy become emotionally more valuable to us precisely *because* they die. It is a distinction few if any of us are able to make while still in the theater.

Alice also has its share of deaths: the passing of Woody Guthrie, of Shelley, of a whole way of life personified by the reconsecrated church. But unlike the brutal murders of *Rider*, both the man and boy die off-screen here. Their deaths are presented as a part of life rather than an end to it. Penn's film is vitally and compassionately interested in life and in a sense of humor as a style for coping, for living in Moratorium America without paranoia. Arlo's songs and manner are those of mild ridicule despite the disasters that shroud the film; the music and the style seem healthy and they wear well.

In effectively suggesting these youthful but polar responses to domestic life, the two films are expressive landmarks for a medium and a country that are suffering growing pains. Hopper's seems more important right now because it slams in the gut, it is frequently right by sheer instinct, *because* it lacks subtlety. Penn's complex work—with its neat geometrical triangles, both religious and secular—strikes me as the more masterful and enduring motion picture. In its own way, *Alice* is a remake of the fifteen-year-old *Rebel Without a Cause* by Nicholas Ray. Yes, Arlo's hair is longer than James Dean's, he doesn't wear white socks, and the girls aren't as heavily lipsticked as Natalie Wood. But what Penn is attempting is a translation into a late-sixties style of the earlier film's anguish, vulnerability, and groping search for a surrogate family. And in linking Arlo with Dean's different but nonetheless similarly transcendent sort of articulateness, *Alice* suggests not only a way of being young in

Love Finds Andy Hardy

America, but also a possible way of being older. Arlo's grace takes us a long way from Andy Hardy.

Notes

1. "Antonioni's America," *Look* 33(November 18, 1969), p. 36.
2. "Alice's Restaurant's Children," *Newsweek* 74(September 29, 1969), p. 101.

Larry Cohen has written a number of screenplays and is a contributing editor to "Show" magazine.

Language

If you try to talk about the language of film, most people are puzzled. To be sure, they have noticed the quick back and forth cuts in *Easy Rider* which are used as a means of making transitions from scene to scene. They might even remember how Pare Lorentz did some clever stuff in *The River* when he used shots of smoke and steam to make transitions. But, most people think that these things are accidental, or that they were done because they looked pretty. It is interesting to find that these shots are often used purposely for aesthetic reasons. Roy Huss and Norman Silverstein discuss film language in general terms; Ernest Callenbach and Eileen Wall use specific films for their applications.

Film Study: Shot Orientation for the Literary Minded

Roy Huss &
Norman Silverstein

The serious filmgoer who would elevate cinema study to the realm in which art, music, and literature are taught in American colleges is open to the charge of frivolity. Even with the cinema of ideas of the fifties and sixties—represented by Antonioni, Fellini, Kurosawa, Bergman, and Godard—movies are regarded merely as a popular art, still considered to be an industry on a par with comic strips and potboilers. Even when given the authority of a single mind, as in the phrase *un film de* . . ., implying that an individual, not a company of technicians, is responsible for the movie product, a film seems not to be more than an entertainment, rarely capable of initiating new ideas that will move men to serious action or elevate their spirits, as great art can do. For the literary-minded filmgoer the movies remain another bit of ephemera like yesterday's newspaper or the political cartoon.

When classicists, historians, philosophers, professors of art and music, and the like, praise films, they also do not want them taught, fearing the destruction, through

Reprinted from *College English* 27:7 (April 1966) 566-568.

pedanticism, of naivete and spontaneity that will be likely if films are subjected to the discipline of college courses. Put a movie in a syllabus, make it an assignment, allow the professor to dissect it, and its spontaneity is gone. Movies provide us with fictions to which we make free responses. They share with our dreams the private world that, once "tapped" by the professor, becomes public, exposing the emotional concord of movie goer and movie, and, perhaps, stripping away his delight.

Bad analytical criticism destroys the movie organism. At their best, good analytical movie critics destroy the life of a work of art and, with luck, can, like Dr. Frankenstein, bring it back to life, but risk its being monstrous. The wise movie critic, according to this theory, does not "murder to dissect," leaving responses to art, especially the movies that relax him, in an uncritical paradise. Professional intellectuals—including art faculties that one would suppose to be conscious of the pictorial—prefer the literary element of a film and desire that movies remain a pastime of pleasure.

The result of this obscurantism is that a filmgoer prefers to be ignorant about how a film is made. He accepts a good "bad" film like *Frankenstein* as a "just" movie experience, unpretentious and proper to the film medium. Remaining a passive observer, an instrument to be played upon by the film maker, who plucks various strings that induce emotion, the literary-minded, intellectual filmgoer ignores the language of film aesthetics and film-making—*shot, cut, jump cut, intercut, wipe, iris, dissolve, back projection, squeeze, "tintype," low angle.* He remains unaware of directional lines of movement and form cuts, the multitude of pictorial accords and oppositions that create cinematic harmony, preferring "story." Remaining literary-conscious rather than shot-conscious, the intelligent moviegoer who *relaxes* at the movies ends by looking at a window as if it were a wall. Whenever "pictures," or "photography," overshadow story in importance—as they should—the bored, literary-conscious intellectual is likely to accuse the movie maker of being pretentious, a charge frequently leveled at Antonioni and Godard.

Consider for a moment the ways in which the art of the film is both similar to and different from certain literary genres. Since cinema seems to be counted among the performing arts (except for animated films and certain kinds of documentary and experimental films), and since actors and directors often come to it from the theater, a commonplace view is to regard the film as a branch of dramaturgy. To this one usually adds the observation that the camera can broaden the scope of the stage by being able to film "on location."

But the differences between the stage and the film are more crucial than the matter of spatial range. In the theatre the basic division of action is the scene, whether determined by a particular setting or time span or, as in the French style, by the number of characters on stage.

In a film, however, the fundamental unit of action is the "shot," or single camera operation, a great number of which may actually combine to form a "sequence," that is, a scene in the stage sense. For example, in the theater two men talking in a law office might comprise a scene of twenty minutes. In a film, on the other hand, this same scene might consist of a sequence of fifty shots. The first might be a middle-shot of the two men in profile facing each other; the second might focus on the face of the first man and on the back of the second; the third might be a close-up of a coffee cup on the desk; and so on.

Good film makers compose sequences out of such a variety of shots not merely, as many believe, for the sake of giving a continual flow of fresh sensations to the eye of the spectator. Their main aim is to heighten visual perceptions of meaning, feeling, and form. In the scene just mentioned, the camera cuts to the face of the speaker or listener whose outward emotional reaction is more dramatic, and then to the image of the cup to stress an important—possibly symbolic—detail. Furthermore, the camera may "look down" upon one character from above and "look up" to the other from below—one of the many simple ways in which the film maker, unlike the dramatist, can directly intrude an "attitude" towards his subject.

Indeed the possibility of constantly varying the position and focus of the camera plus the ability to cut

Great Expectations

rapidly from shot to shot is what most distinguishes the art of the film from the theater and places it closer to the novel. D.W. Griffith, as a matter of fact, admitted that he was able to devise these two most vital elements in the grammar of film art only after a careful study of Dickens. One need merely glance at the opening pages of *Great Expectations* to see that a fluid "camera point of view" is operative: a middle-shot of the cemetery becomes a long-shot pan of the landscape, then a close-up

Great Expectations

of the gravestones, and later a "subjective" camera view of the swinging church steeple when Pip is turned upside down. Since craftsmanship delimits emotion, such devices in both Dickens and Griffith often actually control what appears, on the mere narrative level of their work, to be undisciplined sentimentality.

Like any novel, the film is free to manipulate time as well as distance and space. Violating normal time sequences, as in the "flashback," and alternating between parallel actions are of course possible in the theater, but protracting or compressing a scene by restructuring its fragments is not. Let us say it takes an actor in reality ten seconds to cross a room (or stage). A film editor can condense this to three seconds by "jump-cutting" from the initial segment of the action to its concluding segment. Or he may prolong the time by joining together a series of "overlap" shots, that is, each of several shots of the action (from different angles) will repeat part of the distance covered in the previous shot. Another way of extending time is to represent serially the simultaneously occurring details of an action, as Eisenstein does in the famous Odessa Steps sequence in *Potemkin*. Each of these methods imposes a view and rhythm of experience quite different from the order of actuality, or that of the stage.

From this it can be seen that the further one delves into the heart of cinematic structure and movement the nearer one comes to discovering something that is very much like poetry. Rhythm and tempo are generated by the combinations of the movement of object, background, and camera, and an overall metrics is produced by variations in the lengths of shots. The technique of intercutting or juxtaposing shots of different material (what Eisenstein calls "montage") allows for the setting up of visual similes and metaphors, as in a poem. A famous example is the way in which Eisenstein in *Strike* intercuts shots of a bull being slaughtered with details of the brutal handling of a mob. Sometimes a close-up of an object can elevate it to a poetic symbol, as the focus on hands tends to do in *David and Lisa*, and the repetition of a device, like the "zoom-freezes" of the face of the dead father in *The Loneliness of the Long Distance Runner* or of the "wanted" posters in *The 400 Blows*, institutes a type of rhyme or refrain.

The quest for these kinds of poetic essences in a film is ultimately the only valid way for a moviegoer to be "literary-minded." When he praises the story of *The Last Laugh*, he must point out how the old doorman's tragedy is enhanced by the gradual shift of the camera angle from a low one to a high one or how photographing him through the hotel's perpetually revolving door beautifully reveals the fast tempo of the world which will crush him. When a film buff praises Lorentz's *The River*, he misses the mark if he cites merely the beauty of Virgil Thompson's score together with the excitement of the verse commentary and the competence of the photog-

The 400 Blows

raphy. He must realize that the real "poetry" of the film lies in such devices as a series of "form cuts" to circular masses and objects in order to indicate the uninhibited rolling quality of the Mississippi—that the cuts to billowy clouds above the water, then to the wheels of a turbine engine on the bank, and then to logs tumbling into the stream and bales of cotton being rolled onto the wharves all suggest an undulating motion, even at points where the river itself appears to be placid and undramatic in its progress.

Since 1945, the year of the advent of television, all of us consume almost as many pictures as we do words. Every movie sequence is a deck of picture cards, as every sentence is a collection of words, and their arrangement has some significance. Film teaching ought to change a student from story orientation to shot orientation. It ought to make him aware of moving forms and moving cameras, of angles, of contrasts between foregrounds and backgrounds, of playing areas of the screen in which actors are placed. Above all, the student of film ought to know the unseen force behind the film, the mind that orders the fragments of film into a unified aesthetic organism, discouraging him from stressing stars or dialogue or story. As he learns to recognize cinematic excellence, i.e., pictorial movement artfully presented, he will return to past film *auteurs*, eager to preserve the work of earlier decades, now decomposing for want of funds to process them. He will distinguish film *kitsch* from film culture, becoming an active moviegoer who observes the visual structure of a film.

The chief argument against teaching appreciation of films in college lies in their being largely a part of popular culture. If films, why not courses in comic-strips, rock 'n' roll, advertising appreciation, or the lyrics of Lorenz Hart? The literary-minded Harold Rosenberg defines film aestheticism as "vigorous unculture developed at the expense of books." He disdains film aesthetics for spending time in praising Bogart smoking a cigarette.

Yet film art, like literature, has its highly sophisticated *Poetics* in the theoretical writings of Sergei Eisenstein, who, unlike Aristotle, actually created monumental examples of the art about which he philosophized. For those who remain skeptical that films can be a high art form, the only remedy is to discover that even the most run-of-the-mill films are primarily a collection of shots rather than a story.

Roy Huss and Norman Silverstein are Associate Professors of English at Queens College of the City University of New York.

Seeing Style in Film (With Some Notes on <u>Red</u> <u>Desert</u>)

Ernest Callenbach

The first problem about seeing style in film lies simply in *noticing* style. It is much harder to observe and discuss style in film than in literature. In any art which has a strong "content" side, of course, our initial exposure is apt to be overwhelming; we are far too caught up with the destiny of the Brothers Karamazov to pay much detailed attention to Dostoevsky's style; we perceive it with the fringe vision of our minds. Only in music and abstract painting, perhaps, do we normally and consistently behave as if the style were the main thing. And if a film is any good at all, it grips our perceptive processes in an extremely possessive way. For myself, I have learned not to try to write more than a few words about a film I've only seen once, and in class assignments, at least of any substance, I ask students to write at length only about films they can see twice.

One of the difficulties is permanent and is also the source of one of the main fascinations of the medium—the immense specificity and literalness of film. If we mean by style the manner in which the materials of the medium are organized, the film maker labors under certain problems very different from those of the novelist, which is also to say he is presented with opportunities different from the novelist's. The novelist can write, "He sat wearily down in front of the fire." So long as the novel as a whole has prepared us for the existence of a fire—say as part of a Victorian household—he need be no more specific about physical aspects of the scene and may proceed with his dialogue or character analysis or internal monologue. The film maker who is operating in any more or less realistic mode must be far more concrete (and by *film maker* I mean not only the director, but a shorthand for those responsible for the film—usually also the writer and sometimes the cameraman or producer or whatnot). He must specify a vast number of detailed facts in the scene: the way the room is laid out, the kind of furnishings it has, its lighting, even the sort of fire that is burning—for all these matters bear upon the effect the scene will have. And they bear upon it *obligatorily;* they cannot be dealt with by omission. Moreover, the film maker in practice must specify his viewpoint within the scene in an actual, literal, physical way—he must put the camera somewhere or move it in such-and-such a way, and his choice will have an immense influence on how we perceive the scene. Here, obviously, we come to one of the basic descriptive elements of film style—for it is possible to photograph and edit even a simple scene in an astonishing variety of ways, and only a considerable experience with the works of different good film makers can sensitize us to these differences.

This brings me to a second, and I think diminishing, reason for the difficulty of seeing style in films—namely the unfortunate fact that for many decades commonly experienced variations in film style were not nearly as wide as the comparable variations in literature: up until the great invasion of foreign films after World War II, our feature films had plenty of Dickens-type style or Hemingway-type style but not much Faulkner or Joyce. And our nonfiction films, either documentaries or experimental films, seemed to most moviegoers freakish sideshows. Now, with a much more diverse experience of films behind them, the younger generation, both here and in film-mad countries like France, has a far clearer eye; and films which seem problematic in style to me sometimes seem perfectly perspicuous to students. But even we who are over thirty have now seen, after *Breathless*, that the geographic continuity cutting of the Hollywood feature, which took care to preserve the unity of apparent time within every scene, was only one convention among many. After *Rashomon*, we know that a film need not be based upon a single narrative point of view. After *Last Year at Marienbad*, we know that a film need not indeed be a reflection of some given or constructed reality but may instead body forth wholly self-contained fantasy, with no less shame than a Romantic poem. On the other hand, after the almost fetishist realism of the *cinéma-vérite* documentaries, such as *Titicut Follies* or *Warrendale*, we also know the gulf that yawns underneath even the canniest of acted performances.

Even people who seldom go to movies now know, in short, that film is an art capable of many styles—an art in which the individual impress of the film maker is a major factor to reckon with. Thus, film is an art that can be talked and written about in more than generalities; we have learned our Arnheim[1] and our Lindgren,[2] and the problem now is criticism. That is to say, the resources of the art are well enough known; what we need to do is to see how contemporary artists are employing them.

Our students, it is clear, are intensely interested in film. They see it still as a free art—one not yet culture-bound and sterilized; they know that film makers fight an unending and bloody battle for self-expression, enmeshed in a large and voracious industry which nevertheless cannot get along without artists. And, although to my observation they are not very curious about aesthetic generalities, they definitely wish to know how it is done. They are not much interested in that hoary topic, "the essence of cinema," but they are willing to talk, and talk intently and personally, about practically any decent film.

There is something about film as a medium which especially fits with the way young people now feel about the relation of man and environment (physical and social environment). By contrast, the stage drama seems to isolate man artificially; even though it has many charms now that it has escaped from naturalism, it seems confining. Prose fiction, in the postwar years, has not brought forth much that really impresses young people. When it is complex and sophisticated, like Saul Bellow's, it strikes them as tired and academic; when it is undisciplined and personal, like Mailer's or Baldwin's, it strikes them as a branch of Rhetoric. Poetry has been much livelier since the incursions of the Beats and its turn back to the spoken word. Experimental film makers are fond of poets, and some of them also write poetry themselves; but, with the exception of Ginsberg and Lowell, poets are not often felt to be on the artistic firing line in the real world.

Now I do not presume to say the foregoing judgments are accurate, or that in twenty years they may not seem wildly wrong. What we do know at present is that film seems alive to many intelligent and sensitive young people in a way that no other art, and certainly not TV, can approach.

The chief key to this, again, seems to me to lie in the nature of film style—which can be impassive yet purposive, which can conceal the artist's intentions without the risk of bad faith, which can deal with an apparently self-moved physical reality and yet operate by the forms and tensions of art.

Film is opaque, so to speak. It is what it presents. A good film has no ideas showing, in the sense that Thomas Mann or Dostoevsky have ideas showing. When we look at a film, unless we are critics or other unnaturally self-conscious persons, we look at it much as we look at our own experiences. (This is much less true, of course, on second viewing.)

This opacity has increased in recent decades, with the demise of the well-made, Hollywood-plot film. Indeed it is practically a mark of the best postwar films that they resist paraphrase; and they give grievous trouble to critics who still believe that it is obligatory to have characters with simple, powerful motivations, acting out plots in which the causational line is straightforward, leading to a sensible conclusion, from which we could draw a coherent moral. Coherent morals in recent films are generally only expressed in interviews given out by the director, and they usually turn out to be misleading. Or, as in the case of what Antonioni has said about *Red Desert*, directors speak so generally as to be of little help in understanding how the film is really put together. Even Godard, who is the most ideational of major directors at present, alternates between inscrutability and what often seems chic nonsense.

Yet clearly the films themselves do have structure. They have beginnings, middles, and ends; you can chart the fortunes of their characters as you can those of a tragedy. They evidently have meaning in the sense of presenting emotional coherence and bodying forth an attitude and feeling which we as spectators somehow grasp and are pleased or anguished or infuriated by.

The question is, if films have abandoned dramaturgy, as Pauline Kael and other critics complain, then how are they getting through to us?

I submit that this is the central problem of film criticism today, and I don't propose to answer it in a few pages. We can, however, turn it over in our minds as we consider *Red Desert*, a rather typical contemporary film and one which, incidentally, I do not rate nearly as high as Antonioni's *L'Avventura, Blow-Up, Le Amiche*, or even the somewhat related *Il Grido*.

The trouble is that style is everything, just as it is in the novel or poetry; it has to be talked about minutely if talked about at all. We may observe, first of all, that *Red Desert* is a widescreen film. The frame-line establishing the screen shape is perhaps the fundamental aesthetic convention of the film. And the widescreen shape is far more than a commercial gimmick; as writers such as André Bazin[3] and Charles Barr[4] have established, the wide screen is associated with a pronouncedly different style of shooting and cutting than was the old-format screen. Actually Antonioni, like Renoir and Stroheim before him, was working in a widescreen style in *Le Amiche* before CinemaScope was introduced. He is interested in integrated scenes with great spatial solidity in most of his films—although in *Red Desert* he often modifies this with a special and exceptional plane-of-focus technique. In general, he abstains from the conventional "montage" resources of film—the quick cut, the scene assembled from tiny bits, mosaiclike in time, each bit kicking the film along with its little impulse, creating scenes that could never really quite exist. Antonioni seldom resorts to the two-shot, over-the-shoulder method that was the staple of talkie technique, because he feels the rapid alternation of point of view is mechanical and distracting. He wants to build up fluid, interconnected space-time entities. And this is true too of *Red Desert*, even though the unity here is that of a troubled girl's perceptions, which, psychologically speaking, are shallow, out of focus, and interpersonally almost vapid. The film communicates to us much more by the interrelations of things *within* shots than by the relations *between* shots; the camera captures images, of course, but it too participates *in* the scene, and its position and its movements are expressive.

Next we may observe that the film is not constructed with a strong story tension. Its time sense is vague; it "makes time into stagnant pools." We are introduced to no burning issue whose resolution we await, although we are soon curious whether Corrado will seduce Giuliana. But this is not a sufficient or interesting criterion of relevance, of what, in detail, is to be included or cut out—it cannot provide the businesslike economy of, say, a thriller like *Rififi* or *The Killing*. Yet we know that Antonioni is much concerned with artistic economy; in fact, he talks of wanting every square centimeter of every shot to be essential. Well then, how in such a film does

he know what is essential? I submit that he is after the expression of certain feeling-states, loosely organized in a certain psychic development, and he wishes to make these hang, so to speak, between us and the world. Thus many kinds of image material, besides plot material, can serve his purposes—for instance that shot out the window as Giuliana begins to make love with Corrado and sees the round building, the bollards, and the old man walking.

In *Red Desert*, Antonioni goes further in the direction of the abstract film than any other feature director, for instance, the somber shots of Giuliana wandering along the dock at the end, through a series of abstract-expressionist backgrounds; or the strange heaving abstract shape of Corrado's back in the seduction scene. These shots do not *tell* us anything, in the plot sense; nor do they help us to understand character or establish any important fact about the scene. They are in ordinary Aristotelian terms inexplicable and superfluous. Yet they are clearly very close to the central concerns of the film. And to Antonioni at the time they seemed of great importance as a departure from the realism of the widescreen image with sharp focus in depth—the great tradition stretching back to *Citizen Kane* and beyond. (Let me add parenthetically that this departure hardly seems momentous to experimental film makers, who have been using images this way since the twenties.)

Third, *Red Desert* is a film in which color is consistently used for expressive rather than naturalistic purposes. Antonioni was quite bold in painting things—trees and bushes and pipes, as well as walls and the famous grey cart full of grey fruit. Much of this is not technically different from what is done in any carefully planned color film, though it is carried further; what is novel is that it is used subjectively in a frank and explicit way. Many cameramen might darken a green, and costumes are always color cues, but no ordinary art director would let a grey wall change to pink.

Now I would like to turn my topic about, and speak of style in film as literally *a way of seeing*. We must be willing to be quite concrete and literal about this, just as in discussing style in fiction we must ultimately question how one word follows another. You may have noticed that in *Red Desert* one of the basic units of Antonioni's photography and editing is to start with a shot that is empty of humans: a landscape, a sludgy pond, a room wall, a window, or an area of vague colors —shot slightly out of focus, as, indeed, is the whole introductory credit sequence. Then, into this area, usually from the left or below, there intrudes a figure or a head or a foot, as in the shack scene. You will remember there that the people have been milling about outside in the cold which permeates the whole movie. The colors are bluish and greenish. Then suddenly—with a simple cut rather than the Hollywood dissolve (which Antonioni declares "expresses nothing")—we see a vaguely glowing red area, and then a female foot stretches out into the shot, toward what we realize is a fire. This is not, of course, the only way of proceeding, or indeed the usual way, whereby scenes are introduced through a general shot so that the viewer can become oriented. The difference is like that between writing

> The embers glowed in the grate—Mili stretched her stockinged leg toward them.

and

> Mili stretched her stockinged leg toward the embers in the grate.

The comparative weight of the film usage is much greater than in the prose examples, because the soft focus makes the embers unrecognizable yet emotively hot at the beginning of the shot; because we are startled to realize that they *are* embers in a stove; and above all because, by restricting the plane of focus, here as in many scenes of *Red Desert*, Antonioni is forcing us to perceive, to *see*, in a way analogous to the shifting, erratic, partial perception of Giuliana. We see things that are often beautiful, but also unnerving—and sometimes recognizing them is in itself unnerving. So we know to some extent, after a time, what Giuliana means when she says she is frightened of everything, after which she names a succession of *visible things*, not events or feelings.

Now film style has "person" in its point of view, just as prose does, although it is not so neat and unambiguous and although the strict first person, in which the camera is identified with the eyes of a character, poses what seem to be insoluble problems. (We are also realizing, of course, that film has tense—not all film scenes are necessarily in the present tense or simple past tense, and this can apply to an ambitious commercial entertainment like *Point Blank* as well as to *Marienbad*.) In *Red Desert*, examining the camera work soon brings us to questions of perspective and narrative point of view.

Above all, we must ask whether Antonioni is mostly observing Giuliana or mostly giving us a view which, although it is not literally hers since the camera always observes her objectively and in focus, is nonetheless a parallel to hers. Antonioni talked to interviewers as if he were doing the first: a kind of clinical study of a person who is trying to live by "rhythms that are out of date" in the modern technological environment. Yet surely, if the film is really an external account of her, intended to analyze the source of her troubles in an unresolved relationship with the world, it would situate her rather exactly in some kind of personal and social history, as Antonioni is careful to do with the characters in *L'Avventura*. But he doesn't give us that.

And, if we study how the film is shot, we find that to some extent the point of view spreads over to Corrado. This weakens the film, in my opinion. For instance, in the opening sequence of Ugo showing Corrado the factory, Giuliana's presence is not maintained strongly enough to keep us "with her" throughout, so we veer off into a kind of documentary, and this happens again in the scene when Corrado speaks with the workers about going to Patagonia. In general, Corrado seems to me such a nullity that Harris simply seems beyond his depth; and perhaps he was. But it is at least possible that Antonioni—who keeps a rigid control over his actors—*made* Corrado a pale and shallow character because that is the way Giuliana sees him.

However, Antonioni is obviously not trying to be rigorous in this, as a French director might be—Resnais or Robbe-Grillet. The story is being told by the camera. But the camera is in the hands of a man who loves Monica Vitti. He is, I surmise, here using her to personify certain troubled aspects of his own character, and hence the problem of point of view becomes, in fact, a very subtle and personal thing. The film is, so to speak, how he sees her seeing for him. It is silly, of course, to attribute real-life parallels to the fantasies directors embody in their films; but it is equally silly to ignore the developments in a man's fantasizing about a woman he both lives and works with. In *L'Avventura*, and also *La Notte*, Vitti is the moral center about which the dissatisfactions and corruptions of the story revolve. In *The Eclipse*, she becomes more ambiguous, more unsure. In *Red Desert* she gives way entirely. And in *Blow-Up* the focus is on a male figure who is, in his way, adjusted to the modern environment, even though it proves a deceptive surface only. We may wonder whether the Vitti persona, which, despite Antonioni's opinions about acting, transcends the roles he has given her, will ever again be able to serve as a unifying point, the vital center to which his camera constantly orients.

Now obviously there is a great deal more that could be said about *Red Desert*, but I hope I have said enough to indicate the kind of analysis I think is needed if we are genuinely to understand how modern film makers are working: the *explication* that needs to accompany interpretation and evaluation. Once we know that, we can more legitimately speculate on what lies behind the opaque images they have presented to us. In the case of *Red Desert*, for instance, some kind of psychological doctrine is probably implicit; for Giuliana has regressed to a point where she is obsessed with water—the primordial womb, a means of "returning" to the mystic infantile state, through suicide or the story she tells her son. And Corrado *does* "help her," evidently. Moreover, Antonioni is some sort of Marxist, and no doubt Giuliana's weird attempt to start a shop is a petty, bourgeois fantasy; similarly, the transformations of contemporary capitalism are such that few workers are necessary, and when they go on strike, their leaders arrive in Fiats and use electronic bull-horns; they are by no means eager to go to Patagonia. In general, of course, the industrial life trains people (even Italian people) to live with big spaces, both emotional and physical, between them, for anything else interferes with the smooth transactions of the cash nexus. To the extent the film is successful, it makes us feel these underlying factors through the world it temporarily places us in.

Notes

1. Rudolf Arnheim, *Film as Art* (Berkeley and Los Angeles: University of California Press, 1957).
2. Ernest Lindgren, *The Art of the Film* (New York: The Macmillan Company, 1963), revised edition.
3. André Bazin, *What Is Cinema?* (Berkeley and Los Angeles: University of California Press, 1967).
4. Charles Barr, "CinemaScope: Before and After," *Film Quarterly* (Summer 1963), pp. 4-24. Reprinted in abridged form in *Film: A Montage of Theories*, Richard Dyer MacCann, ed. (New York: E. P. Dutton & Co., Inc., 1966).

Ernest Callenbach is the founder and editor of "Film Quarterly," published by the University of California Press. This article is based on a talk given before the Modern Language Association.

How to See a Film

Eileen Wall

One Sunday morning I began to consider how to use *Requiem for a Heavyweight* in the classroom, and I found an answer while talking with my five-year-old niece, who was watching television as I pondered. During our discussion, I began to notice that she was chipping away at the superiority complex I had developed after taking one course in film. Not only was she surprised that I had never heard of Sonny Fox, but she seemed to find inconceivable the fact that I had never before seen the new "crawling baby," which creeps along after the magic pocketbook. When I later commented with some surprise on the fact that the Flintstones were taking a vacation on Mars—a fact which they and my niece seemed to consider ordinary enough—she asked, "When you were a little girl, did they have television?" Now she had done it. My superficial feeling of superiority merely disguised a deep inferiority complex. Here I was, rooted in a print-oriented culture but trying to make it in a visual medium. Actually, this is my starting point about using film in the classroom. Most of us, whether we have had a course in film or not, have a lot to learn about the visual world, and one of the ways we may learn is by listening to our students when they talk about what they have seen in a film.

The advent of *student superiority* in the classroom is new in education, and I believe it is healthy. Too often the school, comfortable enough for the teacher who can think English all day because he likes it, is uncomfortable for the student, who is programmed to think Algebra from 8:25 to 9:35, Spanish from 9:35 to 10:45, and so on. As bad as this is, perhaps the most damaging thing that could be said about school is that it is often only an extension of the parent-child conflict, so alive in the teenager, because the teacher's answers are always right and the students' are invariably wrong. But the visual sophistication of the students over that of the teacher himself demands a lesson that will not only turn the classroom around, but one that will really turn the teacher around. It is called the unstructured lesson. Although the teacher has to do as much preparation for this lesson as he would for a conventional lesson, he is in the discussion as a consultant, a resource person; the students create discussions around questions and comments the teacher has thrown in.

Perhaps the first question asked by the teacher after a showing of *Requiem for a Heavyweight* would be, "Did you enjoy the movie?" I would imagine that one of the first answers would be something like this: "I liked the film because I liked that first scene where Mountain was knocked out. It was great the way they showed how Mountain said things when he was regaining consciousness." If the class has done any film work at all, somebody would be bound to talk about this scene and mention that it was done by use of what is called "subjective camera." The focus of the camera was Mountain's eyes, and the distortions and blurred surroundings were visualizations of how Mountain saw things. In one issue of *Newsweek,* a movie review mentioned this scene:

> The camera takes a beating in the opening scene. Fighter Cassius Clay, attacking the lens, goes blurry, comes back into focus and jabs again. The overhead lights swim dizzily, and the referee's count has a dream-like clarity of enunciation. Staggering back to the dressing room, the camera's eye, still groggy, notices a flash-bulb here, a gesture of a belligerent fan there, as it makes its way down a long, bleak corridor. Outside the dressing room the camera passes a mirror and suddenly beholds itself, Anthony Quinn, bloodied and scarred. The sequence is electrifying.[1]

Of the film reviews I have read, this one is unique. Reviews rarely mention the film as something visual; more often than not, you can read a film review and wonder whether it is reviewing a play or perhaps even a book. The critics seem to suffer, with few exceptions, from our problem: they are print- and stage-oriented people. But

not so the students. I think they would be able to comment on more things than even *Newsweek*. Someone would mention, I'm sure, the seemingly unattached flashbulbs that were recording Mountain's defeat as crassly as the press hunts down a story, irrespective of how it invades privacy or grief or even shame. I'm sure someone would have heard Cassius Clay, the victor, being interviewed on the sound track, even as the semiconscious Mountain, the loser, leaves. They would see the cheering crowds that follow Clay with applause and the few spectators that remain with the loser. Shot as the sequence is, from below, someone would say how dominating Maisch is in the screen when he is seen—how dominating he is in the life of Mountain. The manager's flabbiness is moral as well as physical. Then there is Army, played by Mickey Rooney, who is also shown first in this scene. Next to Maisch, he is physically very small, and this is a clever visualization, because next to Maisch, in the eyes of Mountain, he really *is* much smaller. You will also notice that Rooney is most often shot at an unflattering angle. Usually the camera, up on Maisch, is down on him. Army is a bigger man than Maisch, for sure, selfless and loving instead of selfish and conniving. But then, things are shown as Mountain sees them. Even in the wonderful card-playing scene between Army and Maisch, the angle of the camera is up on Maisch the victor, in both cards and in manipulating Mountain into wrestling, and down on Army, the loser. Very often

fights in films are shot like this; camera angles up on the victor, down on the loser. In this film the angle is continually up on Maisch, suggesting the idea that evil will triumph.

Someone, too, would have noticed the sign Mountain passes on his long walk to the mirror where he first sees himself. It has Clay in the top position and Riveria on the bottom, a preview of the odds against Mountain. Later on, too, a new sign is plastered up on the wall of St. Christopher Arena, replacing the advertisement of the Clay-Riveria fight. Mountain sees it done as casually as people are destroyed in this racket.

But if the students were given a copy of the *Newsweek* review, I think they could come up with a correction. Actually this electrifying scene was not the first scene in the movie. There is a pan shot of the men in the bar room watching the Clay-Riveria fight on TV. The focus in this scene, shot in the "Graveyard," as the place is later identified, is also on the men's eyes, something to be considered again. In this bar there's a dream, like Mountain's "fifth in '52, I was almost the heavyweight champion of the world" on every stool. The scene fits, but it probably is in the film chiefly for the projectionist in the commercial theater. Can you imagine what the projectionist might have done if the knockout scene were first, and he suspected his projector was out of focus. One of Hollywood's best cinematic moments could have been killed. Now, stepping away from a discussion that

I can say is almost one that students would have to begin with on this film, you can see that they will begin with the visual.

English teachers should never begin a review with characters, theme, or symbol, words dear to all of our hearts, unless we prove that what we have come to has visual foundations. In short, we have to start with a film as something chiefly seen and heard. Believe me, this was hard work for me, for I was a novel-turned-filmed teacher. I was ready only to mention what the camera did last and so were most of the people in the class. Here we had to begin with the camera.

For instance, take the whole beginning sequence. It establishes much about the film. Chiefly, this is a boxer's world, a world like the western, the war picture, or the waterfront world where milieu is very easy to capture. Mountain's initial defeat takes place in the ring. You probably notice, too, that very often the pictures were shot at a corner of the room, emphasizing the top ledge of the room so that you have the effect of the rectangular prize fighting ring. This is the way the scene in Miss Miller's office was shot. Mountain stands in the corner; already he has begun his life in a corner. The usher's suit didn't fit him any more than the job would have. Going down in the elevator from Miss Miller's office, he clings to the rail as if it were the ring. The boxing world is never forgotten even in the scenes away from it. But most of the picture is set in this boxing world. It is in

Requiem for a Heavyweight

this ring that Maisch gets beaten up and is made to dance by Ma Grundy and her gang. His problem is that he lacked Mountain's power to withstand, a pretty good foreshadowing of the end, too. Even in Mountain's apartment there are pictures of the boxer's world, the world of one-night cheap hotels and pulsing neon lights, a world that has no security except success. Then there is the scene in Jack Dempsey's restaurant and the marvelous touch when Army, whom Maisch had gotten out of the way, takes the sandwiches he was sent for and slams them angrily on the table—a visual economy for sure. But Jack Dempsey, in contrast to Mountain, wasn't fifth; he was *first* for a significant length of time, and he invested wisely, using his name, his money, and the American love of the boxing atmosphere.

The final scene of *Requiem* (to be talked of later) also takes place in the ring. In all, the picture visualizes a good old American thought about a film—it should create an atmosphere, a milieu. And what a milieu this is, the world of boxing, perhaps a microcosm of many of the problems modern man feels. When boxing finishes with the fighter, there is no guaranteed annual wage, no social security, no pension plan. This is a spectator sport, the gladiator is still in an inhuman racket, and when he's done, there's only the memory, often of the "has been." (The whole pattern of American society in the last thirty-five years has established the fact that there are some indignities to which a man should not be subjected.) When Willie Loman is fired from his job in *Death of a Salesman*, he cries out desperately, "You can't eat the orange and throw the peel away—a man is not a piece of fruit!"[2] Mountain asks the movie's central question, "Why, what I gonna do now? I mean, all I know to do is fight." Even Maisch comments to the doctor who suggests Mountain get a scrap book, "You think he's a cow. You can put him out to pasture."

Say what you want, this picture of man, the victim, either because of his own fault or because he has been used up, manipulated, is still something that arouses us. Outliving usefulness, what we call today the problem of geriatrics, is very much the human situation. Add to this Mountain's ineptness because of what boxing had done to him physically and his lack of education, and you see how unfit he is for another phase of society. But that long scene indicates something major about Mountain. His central problem throughout the film concerns vision. Mountain doesn't seem to know Maisch, to see him for what he is. Miss Miller, who has only heard of him, seems to see Maisch more clearly than Mountain. She asks him why he has put Maisch in a shrine for seventeen years. Mountain answers innocently, "When I was knocked out, I looked up and he was crying." But then think of all the things Maisch has done in the seventeen years that Mountain hasn't seen or has viewed, at best, out of focus. Nor can Mountain see that Army is really his friend and, most tragically, that there can never be anything between Miss Miller and him, since they are from two different worlds.

But then Miss Miller has a problem with her vision, too. Not just by chance is she shown in the employment office wearing glasses. Later, when she comes to the "Graveyard," she takes the glasses off to tell Mountain about the job as counselor and his appointment at the Saint Moritz, a world we can see at a glance is not Mountain's. Does Miss Miller see herself as we do? Here is a good girl but a predestined old maid, a girl flustered by the blustery, loquacious Mr. McNulty, who, in a beautiful touch, precedes inarticulate, almost nonverbal Mountain into her office. Both Mountain and Miss Miller dream of a better life than they have been living, but reality shows them that their life as lovers is an impossibility.

When Miss Miller comes down the stairs from Mountain's room and thus steps out of his life, she meets Maisch. An interesting thing happens here—for the first time the camera looks down on Maisch, because he is about to be found out for what he is—down, small, sick. This is definitely the way Grace Miller sees Maisch. Maisch gets what he deserves in her slap. Later he gets it again in the scorn in Mountain's eyes.

You must have noticed too that there were many mirrors used in the film: Mountain sees himself in the mirror after his knockout; mirrors are prominent in his room; mirrors corner the bar in the "Graveyard," reflecting a grim reality as Miss Miller and Mountain are pictured in that tender scene when they come as close as they can; and when Mountain goes to the theatre to see if he can get a job as an usher, Army, wishing to dress him up, rips a hankie pressing against the mirror. (Incidentally, what a wonderful visualization of a role, that of usher. It does not fit Mountain, but what role does?) Mountain needs many reflections around so he can see himself, but does he ever come to have clearer vision?

In the most tragic moment, when Mountain and Miss Miller realize that they cannot make it as lovers, he says "I don't sound so good. I sound like an immigrant off the boat." Later she says, "Mountain, why don't you see yourself as I see you?" "These are scars, they ain't medals," he answers. "For a while you had me believing things could be different." But it can't be any different. Still later, when he runs after her with her scarf, he says, "I was out of line. I belong with dirty towels and locker rooms." Here we have it, the finish, "the requiem for a heavyweight."

In the end, Mountain gives himself for a friend he finally knows is not worth it; he saves the dignity and life of a man who only toyed with Mountain's dignity and life. Preceded in the ring by the vaudeville midgets, Mountain, the noble savage, suffers even the ignominy of this degraded carnival and the loss of his proud boast that he "never took a dive." Mountain gives himself even for those he comes to see as his enemies. Granted that the film is not perfect, that the music at the end, the saga-ending of the western, is anything but good, that Rod Serling could have given Mountain better lines, and that there is a real touch of gangster-prize fighter melodrama, *Requiem for a Heavyweight* is still a vehicle for humanistic study.

If you were as impressed as I was with Tony Hodgkinson's description of a teacher as a Janus, one who reaches back in time in his own education before students who reach, as ours do, to the year 2000, you will realize that

Requiem for a Heavyweight

snippets here and there as we did and doing more talking about books and poems than actually reading them. And even today, I have come to see that the film belongs to tomorrow. Therefore, if a school administrator considers that using films in the classroom is taking time away from printed works that must be studied, I consider kindly that the administrator does not see himself as a Janus. If a principal were to tell me that films were superficial, peripheral, I would think, again kindly, that the principal's job is being principal, mine a teacher. If his day is yesterday, mine and my students' is tomorrow. And for tomorrow, there are some fires worth walking through.

Notes

1. "A Low Blow," *Newsweek* 60(October 22, 1962), p. 104. Copyright Newsweek, Inc., October 22, 1962. Reprinted by permission of Newsweek, Inc.
2. From *Death of a Salesman* by Arthur Miller. Copyright 1949 by Arthur Miller. Reprinted by permission of The Viking Press, Inc.

Eileen Wall is a teacher at West Side High School, Newark, New Jersey.

the teacher must sort out what he wants to give to his students, what it is they will need in their world. Long ago I gave up perpetuating many things that were taught to me in college, because I had come to see them as not worth passing on, and still later I stopped wasting my time teaching surveys of literature, since they came from a nationalism of the thirties that I could not accept and since it was at best pretentious to think that in one course we could survey two thousand years of writing, reading

Literature

Some people get very uptight about other people calling film "literature." Somehow, they must think that there is something sacred about those little squiggles that we put on paper to be decoded by others and that we call writing. But film fits every definition of literature that you can find except those that specify writing. There is no reason for believing, however, that film doesn't accomplish the same things. In the following articles, Richard M. Gollin describes film as "literature," and several other authors describe specific approaches: Frank Manchel discusses the genre approach, William MacPherson the thematic approach, and Michael Keisman the eclectic approach.

Film as Dramatic Literature

Richard M. Gollin

Whether as humanists, critics, scholars, or teachers, whether acting our usual professional roles or trying out others, when we bring film study into traditional courses in literature our colleagues regard us with genial condescension, as if we were harmlessly drunk. When we persist, their attitude grows more serious and they wonder if, like some old familiar bell making new noises, we have gone unsound or cracked. The view persists that movies belong in movie houses and late night television, films in art film houses, cinema in cinema societies, and none of these things in respectable college curricula.

Unless, of course, the film is not itself the subject of study. It is well acknowledged that films can serve subordinate purposes with great effectiveness. Audio-visual aids abound, so long as they remain sufficiently homely to be unobtrusive in themselves. Foreign films serve many purposes of foreign language study, so long as they provide sufficient dialogue to justify their viewing time. When filmmaking is itself the subject of study, ex-

Reprinted from *College English* 30:6 (March 1969) 424-429.

cellent films are screened and discussed, but only for the examples of their craft they provide; students in such courses examine camera angles, frames, images, and montages in the same way other students—often in the same creative arts department—examine chiseled surfaces, paint, plaster, angle-irons, and foam rubber. Occasionally a social historian will show a period film—an *Alexander the Great* or a *Tom Jones*—for its period props and backdrops, in effect borrowing a studio's researches into togas and sedan chairs in order to avoid the trouble of locating similar pictures. Occasionally an intellectual historian will show a film for its display of a culture's predicaments—*The Cabinet of Dr. Caligari* as a projection of helpless dread, and Leni Riefenstahl's *The Triumph of the Will* as helpless dread transcended into unity. But such use of films is as rare as historians with the sophistication to manage it.

Occasionally, as an adjunct to literature courses, an instructor will show students a movie version of a novel (a problem in genre translation rarely solved satisfactorily), for laughs or to sugarcoat the pill of the novel itself or to display the novel's greatness in contrast to the film's mediocrity. But this is a questionable practice. A film may provide running dramatizations of episodes in a novel, but usually it provides only vivid distraction from the novel's verbal surfaces, and sometimes it disables a reader's recreative imagination altogether. Though they share certain dramatic elements, usually emphasized by the film, novels and films require altogether different sensibilities. Novels are read by private individuals sunk deep into themselves responding to words according to their own pace and capacities for imaginative concentration, governed by narrative voices heard and overheard. A film is, on the other hand, performed on its audiences in a dark place where private and public consciousness merge into a single intensively shared visual and auditory experience, moving its viewers according to its own rhythms. Though modern readers' expectations, like the novels they read, are in large measure shaped by cinematic conventions, novels and films usually resemble each other only in plot outline or superficial recollection. And the best novels and films exist for themselves, not for each other.

Occasionally an instructor who knows or senses this much will show his students films made from stage plays, two genres enough related to avoid more flagrant violations of the genius of each. By convenience, Olivier's *Henry V* and *Hamlet* and the film versions of *A Streetcar Named Desire* and *Who's Afraid of Virginia Woolf* will no doubt play on in American high schools and universities, but chiefly by convenience, as stage plays preserved in cans ready to be served up on short notice. The best films are not photographed stage plays. Early filmed versions of stage plays were notoriously poor as films, attempting as they did to preserve the fixed proscenium frame and single audience perspective essential to most

Henry V

native places for escape than the relentless single set of the stage play escaped only in fantasy. In the film version Willie Loman's problems accordingly become more those of his personal compulsions, less those of the limited world he inhabits. The opening stage performance of *Henry V*, in Olivier's version, transmuted itself into a film as if liberating itself from archaic imitation into the thing itself. But this was of course factitious: what was liberated was a film of *Henry V* from a film of a stage performance of *Henry V*. The film nodded not too respectfully at the play's original medium and then got on with its proper business. Much of the originality and vitality of recent films comes from their having done the same, especially from liberating themselves from stage conceptions altogether and conceiving themselves entirely according to their own medium. They need to be studied as themselves, not as versions of something else.

Where can this occur? Where should it occur? One place is obvious and can detain us only briefly: it occurs in courses in the history and nature of the film, courses designed from inception to educate and enlarge the trained, perceptive, knowledgeable audiences that major films require, deserve, and have somehow anyhow managed to jerry-build for themselves with no help from the academy. Or nearly no help: students do move from concern with the imagistic configurations of a lyric poem, the shifting points of view of a novel, or the symbolic structure of a play to their equivalents in a film, carry-

naturalistic drama, with its deterministic assumptions, by substituting a static camera for a fixed theatergoer watching entrapped characters live out their limited destinies. Later versions of stage plays were more cinematic, built up from images varying closeness and camera angle; but their depth of dramatic space, absorbing the viewer's participating imagination into that space, created a different kind of drama despite itself. The open film city of *Death of a Salesman* offers many more altering their critical literacy off into the movie houses. But there they are often tasked beyond their ability to comprehend what they are seeing and feeling. A powerful and subtle articulation of themes and images often seems to them to be a powerful and subtle display of random images, finally baffling. Recently, in some institutions, film courses have come into existence designed to enlarge what has been the cult privilege of the few: reasonably intelligent understanding of profound films as works of art (whatever else they may also be to the sophisticated and illiterate alike). Films are now recapitulating in universities the same course traveled by another popular genre, the novel, which only a century ago seemed an entertainment beneath academic notice. They have achieved this much measure of respectability, but usually not in literature departments, whatever the respect professors of literature may hold for some films after hours.

This is more than a pity. It verges in fact on violation of professional responsibility, because films also belong in any traditional course in the nature of drama and in any traditional course in modern drama. For all their technological and conventional differences from stage dramas, films remain unquestionably a mode of dramatic literature, no more a mutation from the common stock of drama than was the masque from its several origins or renaissance drama from earlier pageant plays or drama itself from earlier religious rituals. We can properly refer to stage drama and screen drama as two major branches

Hamlet

from the same plant, but we cannot assert at this late date that stage drama is coextensive with drama itself. Too many films have been made during the past half century, of too excellent a quality, by too much dramatic genius, religiously attended by too many people. No course in drama can fairly represent its variety, and no course in the drama of this century can fairly represent its period and obsessive concerns, which does not include study of some of the major films of this century conceived and made as films.

This may seem controversial, but it is more merely a truism. It is sometimes argued that a film, like opera, employs many art forms, drama being but one, and that it therefore tends to be created by a committee rather than a dramatist. The only proper answer is, to the same extent, so does a stage drama experienced as intended— not read but performed. There is only one troublesome difference apart from the media themselves. A film exists in definitive production, preserved photographically in entirety, while a stage drama exists in optional production, varying slightly even with each performance, preserved in minimal essentials in book form as a script. And herein lies the chief problem for academics as they ponder this truism. To teach films properly we need their scripts as well as the films, and there are too few scripts available of films worth teaching.

With stage drama the problem is reversed: scripts abound while performances available to students are only occasional and fortuitous. And so we teach scripts. In fact, we are so accustomed to teaching drama from scripts that we tend to confuse the scripts with the dramas themselves. What was and remains a memorandum for actors, a frame of dialogue and suggestive gestures for dramatic production, we think of as the work itself.

Some reasons for this are trivial: we think so because it has always been thought so, or our teachers thought so; or we prefer anyhow to think of drama as a form of dialogue novel; or the confusion is convenient to classroom purposes, books being at hand when actors are not; or we believe the covers of our anthologies, which call their contents "dramas" rather than "scripts" or "reading versions." Some reasons are less trivial. Our chief literary theorists, from Aristotle through Northrop Frye, have held that literary works are structures of action and language made available through language. Aristotelian criticism could consider plot the "soul" of drama and spectacle a mere adjunct; the shape of an action could be contemplated in the mind disembodied even from character, and certainly from performance. For critical purposes based on these presuppositions (and be we structural, exegetical, archetypal, or cultural critics, we all share them to some degree), scripts are virtually sufficient.

Moreover, for many dramas written before this century, scripts *are* virtually sufficient. For Shakespeare as for Sophocles, language was the prime instrument of reason for exploring and revealing truth. Soliloquy and dialogue mattered, exhibiting in their turns and evasions nearly all that is essential to an understanding of the human condition, and invoking with power and exactitude nearly all that imagination can conjure. Even as recently as Ibsen, dialogue could be considered the chief means whereby people reveal themselves building, misaligning, and destroying their identities, communal relationships, and civilizations. A script contained the core of the drama. It is no wonder that our publications and conferences still treat drama as if it were to be read, not seen and heard.

Yet even as early as Chekhov, non sequiturs and silences signaled that language and action alike were beginning to seem futile in life and so in the dramatic image of life, a view now incarnate in much contemporary theater. Increasingly, tableau, gesture, innuendo, mime too subtle for stage directions, the orchestration of acting spaces, the modulation of temporal rhythms, and the implication of ritual have become the substance of drama. These are only hinted in scripts by Ionesco or Pinter, for example, and so go unnoticed by the casual reader though not by an audience. The cross-cut animosities beneath the polite banalities of Pinter's dialogue can be heard but not seen; and without them, his plays seem far more obscure than they are, and far less logical in their revelation. Again, the theatrical revolution initiated by Pirandello and carried on by such playwrights as Genêt, Albee, and Gelber (not to say such film directors as Fellini, Bergman, and Godard), that of making theater out of the theatrical situation itself and so displaying life as theatrical, implicates the audience in participatory acts of fantasy, voyeurism, role playing, and complicity with the action. The effects created by these conventions can be felt only by a reader with a highly experienced imagination, if at all; yet they are felt immediately by everyone attending a performance. It is

difficult to teach many modern plays from scripts, in some ways more difficult than teaching Shakespeare's plays from scripts. Yet, with varying degrees of success, we persevere. We must, since we have no choice. Meanwhile, we are shielded from the knowledge that we are doing something peculiar by the fact that it is done in the best of academic circles.

People frequently object to the teaching of films from scripts as if the same objections did not apply to the teaching of stage plays in written form; and it remains true that some films are as ill-represented in script form as some stage plays. But it would seem, at first, that this problem need not arise at all: films are accessible in definitive production (for moderate fees) for convenient screening. Perhaps not perfectly convenient screening, since student schedules vary and the rescreening of certain sequences for discussion is always awkward in the absence of reels edited for the purpose (there are none available). On further reflection, it would seem that there are stronger reasons still for the use of scripts in courses studying films. Drama, as a temporal and sequential art, requires absorbed existential attention from its audience, precluding many forms of reflection and analysis until afterward. Films, with their special capacity to induce in their audiences an intensive, concentrated, virtually hypnotic trance, and their enclosing of audiences into their own spatial domain (the audience perspective changing with each shifting camera angle), are even more difficult to analyze *in medias res*. Afterward, if the film is an intricate one, memory simply does not serve the needs of a reasonable critical intelligence. Even the best trained memories have difficulty recovering the sequence of self-revelatory reveries in Bergman's *Wild Strawberries,* though these finally work the main character's salvation, and how much *more* difficult the examination in retrospect of the complex interfolded fantasies making up Fellini's 8½.

Good minds pondering the absorption of transient lovers into permanent place names in *Hiroshima Mon Amour* and puzzled by the final dialogue of that film, may not notice that the final dialogue was prepared even during the opening sequences. Few people can piece out the levels of interjected, recollected, imagined, and created experience of *Last Year at Marienbad* even from several viewings of that film, and yet the film rewards such knowledge at every step of its rationally plotted course. We need scripts as well as films, so we can recall the film, locate its crucial scenes and statements, and find for our consciousness what our instincts only groped to comprehend in darkness. We need scripts of important films for the same reason we need scripts of important plays we have seen performed—for study and for more profound comprehension.

We have scripts in abundance for plays. We have even third-rate Tennessee Williams and second-rate Arthur Miller. We have Cocteau's *Infernal Machine* in several

Hiroshima Mon Amour

anthologies, but not his *Orpheus,* a finer dramatic work and a more difficult one. We have Beckett's stage deserts of existential eternity but not Antonioni's more harrowing and compassionate view of the same landscape. We have much trifling Giraudoux, because he wrote for the stage; but we have virtually no Truffaut, because he did not. We have Genêt on the human urge to enact melodramatic roles, but we have not had Godard on the same subject, and Godard is subtler in his use of the dramatic medium as a metaphor for the subject. Quite simply, we need scripts of films.

They are now finally beginning to appear. Bantam has provided two Fellini scripts, *La Dolce Vita* and *Juliet of the Spirits*, though not the more difficult if less sensational *8½*. Simon and Schuster has given us four Bergman scripts, sufficient to glimpse the evolution of Scandinavian drama since Strindberg, and has now launched a series of modern film scripts such as *Jules and Jim* and *Alphaville*, as well as classic film scripts such as *Grand Illusion, The Blue Angel,* and *Children of Paradise*. Having prospered with two Resnais films—*Hiroshima* and *Marienbad* —as well as some lesser, Grove Press has now entered the field in force with many more titles. Appleton-Century-Crofts is meanwhile assembling the first large anthology of film scripts, chiefly of British and American films of varying quality. Most of these scripts provide still photographs interposed frequently in the texts to convey crucial visual frames and statements complementing the dialogue, and most of the novelistic or descriptive bridges employed between sequences of dialogue are quite sufficient for critical classroom purposes. Like the old familiar scripts of stage drama these film scripts deserve and reward study. They are perhaps the only form of literature to which all of our students eagerly submit themselves, even in classrooms.

And classrooms are altogether appropriate places for such study. It is piteous to sit in an audience at a student film society presentation, attending a beautiful, moving, and profound film, only to hear helpless bewilderment expressed as the film ends and the audience leaves. It is piteous to read of drama described as a dying art form—judgments based on recent stage history—when in fact it has never been livelier. It is piteous to teach modern drama from Ionesco, Albee, Pinter, Genêt, Frisch, and Brecht and to know that a large and brilliant part of contemporary drama, sharing the same preoccupations and dramatic conventions, carrying the great argument about the human predicament still further, is accessible only with difficulty.

Yet there is much pleasure in realizing that ours can be a rare privilege, that of bringing under formal surveillance a new, major, fully developed, but still unacknowledged literary genre, of exploring its classics, of training the sensibilities appropriate to its understanding, and of anticipating its great works yet to come.

Richard M. Gollin is an Associate Professor of English at the University of Rochester, New York.

The Archetypal American

Frank Manchel

A study of the Western genre is essential to an understanding of the American movie industry. Perhaps it is also essential to an understanding of America.

Having for a long time been the stepchild of various narrow academic courses, the motion picture is dramatically emerging as the forerunner of the global classroom. For the aspiring instructor who is organizing his first movie program, the bewildering variety of films (documentary and war films, cartoons, musicals, newsreels, etc.) can be confusing. To embrace this complexity, he may find it fruitful to have his students examine films from a particular vantage point. This necessitates the teacher knowing something about the kinds of movies that have been produced in the short but hectic history of the motion picture.

Although film teachers will differ on specific movie classifications, there are few who do not incorporate into their discussions references either to kinds or types of

Reprinted from *Media and Methods* 4:8(April 1968) 36-38, 40, 48.

movies. Should the teacher pursue the matter in detail, his conclusion might be that tradition plays a major role in classifying a movie as a melodrama rather than a thriller, or as a mystery instead of a spy story. This precedent may stem from an unequal stress on different aspects of a film: story, technique, aim, theme, structure, etc. Whatever the case, it seems apparent that the teacher will sooner or later be drawn into discussing the genres of film.

The teacher who has decided to introduce his students to film genres will do well to familiarize himself with the various rationales for categorizing motion pictures. The two more practical guides are David Mallery's *The School and the Art of Motion Pictures*[1] and the Beograd Film Institute's *Film Genres: An Essay in Terminology and Determination of Film Genres*. Mallery classifies the movies according to types, treatments, and themes; his method is eclectic. More helpful perhaps to the serious student of film is the Beograd Institute's system, which has as its aim the fixing of a complete and inclusive series of terms for existing genres, defining these types, and suggesting a procedure for interlocking the various kinds. Their method is to divide motion pictures into two categories: (1) a division according to criteria of structure and technique, and (2) a division according to the criteria of aim and theme.

The Western Film

One of the most useful ways to explain the genre approach to film study is to look briefly at a particular genre that originated in this country and has been widely enjoyed by the American public: the Western film. This will afford us the opportunity of discussing methodology and suggesting materials—books, films, articles—that may prove helpful. It is not the purpose here to prescribe a particular genre to be studied in the schools, but only to relate how the study of genre might proceed.

In formulating goals, the instructor might consider defining his meaning of the Western film according to aim, treatment, structure, or technique. Thus, for example, when he attempts to classify a movie like *The Covered Wagon*, he will be able to distinguish between a documentary and a fiction film. Whatever definition he eventually uses, it should contain references not only to a pictorial recreation of the settling and stabilizing of the American frontier but also to a *filmic emphasis on action and adventure*.

Another step toward presenting a teaching unit on the Western film genre might be a brief examination of the books and articles on the subject. Unfortunately for those who can only read English, the one book available, George N. Fenin and William K. Everson's *The Western: From Silents to Cinerama*,[2] is too general to be of much significance. There is an unduly heavy emphasis on bare storytelling and stars; however, the authors do provide the reader with a cursory glance at the Western film's importance in the growth of the motion picture industry.

In particular, one can recognize the genre's contribution in such areas as narrative film development, the growth of the star system, the training of directors, the establishing of American film myths, the rise of large studios, and the close relationship between film production and film audiences. Another book, not necessarily on Western movies, but one which illustrates an unusual void, for example, in the conventions and characterizations of the genre, is Philip Durham and Everett L. Jones' *Adventures of the Negro Cowboys*.[3] To put it another way, after reading this book you might ask, "Why hasn't the Negro, who has played a major role in the history of the western United States, ever been explored in the genre?"

In the case of articles, the researcher is much more fortunate. A good jumping off point is Robert Warshow's classic review of the genre's major conventions and characterizations, "Movie Chronicle: The Westerner."[4] Another worthwhile historical study is Richard Whitehall's "The Heroes are Tired."[5] Here the reader is treated to an excellent survey of the trend away from the Warshow tradition and more in keeping with current tastes and times. Still another useful review of the genre can be gleaned from the French point of view in Alan Lovell's "The Western."[6] Mr. Lovell's purpose is to highlight the main arguments in favor of the Western film as the best example of American movies in general. And finally, for a good bibliography of articles prior to 1960, the reader should consult "Film Themes and Background Books: The Western," compiled by Charles Cain.[7]

Having filled in some needed background in the history of the genre, the teacher is prepared to turn his attention to specific films for use in the classroom. To this end, I would like to recommend six important films. They are chosen for two reasons. First, these movies are recognized by many experts for their significance, and second, they have been successful in the past with young people.

The Virginian (1929, 90 mins., b/w, Museum of Modern Art). *Credits*: Paramount Studios; directed by Victor Fleming; story by Wister and LaShelle; adaptation by Howard Esterbrook. *Cast:* Gary Cooper, the Virginian; Walter Huston, Trampas; Richard Arlen, Steve; Mary Brian, Molly Wood.

This is the film that Warshow designed as the "archetypal" Hollywood produced Western. Here we are given the image of the hero who is a relaxed, easy-going fella with a clean shave, white hat, fast horse, quick on the draw, loving a woman who doesn't understand his actions or his code of honor, and seeming to drift from place to place. Here are the conventions of the villain, dressed in black, with whom the hero must finally resolve the issue of right and wrong in a climactic gunfight. And here also are the ingredients for the depiction of women on the American frontier: the lady from the East and the dance-hall floozy. The former is rarely able to comprehend the frontier ethos because she only understands culture, chastity, and civilization. Thus, she is almost always portrayed as an immature female. The barroom woman, on the other hand, knows the westerner's basic needs, primitive though they may be. But, alas, she serves only for the night, and, in the end, the hero searches for a greater wisdom, although a colder winter, in the eastern sweetheart's way of life.

The Virginian

Shane (1953, 117 mins., color, Films Incorporated). *Credits*: Paramount Studios; directed by George Stevens; produced by George Stevens; based on the novel by Jack Schaefer; screenplay by A.B. Guthrie, Jr.; music by Victor Young; camerawork by Lloyd Griggs. *Cast*: Alan Ladd, Shane; Jean Arthur, Marion Starrett; Van Heflin, Joe Starrett; Brandon de Wilde, Joey Starrett; Jack Palance, Wilson; Ben Johnson, Chris; Elisha Cook, Jr., Torrey; Emile Meyers, Ryker.

Of all the Western movies I've seen taught in the last ten years in the public schools, none has been more favorably received than *Shane*. If this fact alone were not enough to bring the movie to the classroom, the many virtues of the production itself would justify its continual use: a masterful marriage of sound and sight, some excellent color photography, and several outstanding performances, especially those by Ladd and Palance. In addition, the movie includes an unusually honest representation of the conflict between the cattlemen who had settled the land and the homesteaders who were in search of a new way of life. But most of all, in the concept of the heroic gunfighter, Shane, who has killed too often and realizes that the day of the gunman is over, director Stevens presents us with one of the best characterizations in all of Western films. In teaching this motion picture, the instructor might find it useful to begin his unit by reading the following quotation from *Life* which describes the impact that the image of the western hero has created around the world:

> Australian aborigines sail their dugout canoes 70 miles across the treacherous Clarence Strait to see "Jinorty" (Gene Autry) on the mainland. When Rhodesians set out to get their women in lonely hearts columns, they publish pictures of themselves in cowboy outfits. In South Africa so many amateur gunslingers have accidentally shot themselves that fast draw clubs now restrict their members to wax bullets. Across Europe "cowboy clubs" have been popping up faster than crooked gamblers in Dodge City. The members outfit themselves like Billy the Kid or Sitting Bull and spend hours with their six-guns practicing the border shift and the road agent's spin.[8]

There are also a number of instructional aids which the teacher might find useful: Bosley Crowther, *The Great Films: Fifty Golden Years of Motion Pictures*;[9] "A Film Discussion Guide of *Shane*," Films Incorporated; Joanne Stang, "Hollywood Romantic: A Monograph on George Stevens";[10] Penelope Houston, "Shane and George Stevens";[11] Eugene Archer, "George Stevens and the American Dream";[12] Alan Stanbrook, "The Return of *Shane*";[13] and Douglas McVay, "George Stevens: His Work."[14]

The Ox-Bow Incident (1943, 90 mins., b/w, Films Incorporated). *Credits:* Twentieth Century-Fox Studios; directed by William A. Wellman; from the novel by Van Tilburg Clark; screenplay by Lamar Trotti; produced by Lamar Trotti; film editor, Allen McNeil. *Cast:* Henry Fonda, Gil Carter; Dana Andrews, Martin; Mary Beth Hughes, Rose Mapen; Anthony Quinn, Mexican; William Eythe, Gerald; Harry Morgan, Art Croft; Jane Darwell, Ma Grier.

For the teacher who wishes to compare two mediums—novels and films—this is probably the best Western movie to use. George Bluestone has given a definitive analysis of the story and treatment in *Novels into Film*.[15] In addition, the script of the movie is available in *The Best Film Plays of 1943-44*, edited by John Gassner and Dudley Nichols.[16] And if that were not enough, there are two helpful study guides for teaching the film: Encyclopaedia Britannica's *Dialogue with the World*[17] and Ernest Callenbach's *Our Modern Art: The Movies*.[18] With these films, the teacher should be able to show his students the problems in translating a book to the screen: e.g., making the implicit, explicit; being more attentive to the representation of the main characters; simplifying plot lines; omitting, condensing or adding in relating to the cinematic needs of the story; using sound for creative additions to the main plot; and being concerned with the audience's ability to assimilate material.

My Darling Clementine (1946, 65 mins., b/w, Museum of Modern Art, Brandon Films and Films Incorporated).

Credits: Twentieth Century-Fox Studios; directed by John Ford; story by Sam Hellman, adapted from a book by Stuart N. Lake; produced by Samuel Engle; screenplay by Samuel Engle and Winston Miller. *Cast:* Henry Fonda, Wyatt Earp; Linda Darnell, Chihuahua; Victor Mature, Doc Holliday; Walter Brennan, Pop Clanton; Tim Holt, Virgil Earp; Cathy Downs, Clementine; Ward Bond, Morgan Earp; John Ireland, Billy Clanton.

One of the most famous of all Western movies, *My Darling Clementine* retells for the "zillionth" time the legendary story of Wyatt Earp's sojourn in Tombstone, his trouble with the Clanton gang, and the notorious battle at the OK corral. The picture's fame rests as much with the pattern of John Ford movies as with its technical and filmic quality: set-ups, incidents, lighting, and characterization. But this movie also provides the teacher with an opportunity to discuss some of the misleading myths about the old West. For the youngster who conceives of the true frontier hero as someone who was clean-shaven, dressed in store-bought clothes, living with fine folks, and existing as a respected member of the community, the teacher can present a more critical interpretation. Class discussions might possibly center for part of the time on facts such as: (1) Billy the Kid was a crazy killer who either ambushed his twenty-one victims or "monkeyed" with their guns before he challenged them to battle. (2) Jesse James never gave a cent to the poor.

My Darling Clementine

(3) Bat Masterson was a slick operator who, when a fight broke out, hid behind the nearest piano. Incidentally, he literally made his own legend by buying a gun late in his life and carving twenty-two notches on it. And (4) Wyatt Earp was more interested in making money than in preserving justice. If you are interested in pursuing this approach further, I recommend reading an informative article in *Time,* "The Six-Gun Galahad."[19]

High Noon (1952, 85 mins., b/w, Brandon Films, Twyman, Cinema, Incorporated, Trans-World, Cinema Guild, The Film Center, Ideal). *Credits*: United Artists Studios; directed by Fred Zinnemann; produced by Stanley Kramer; story by John W. Cunningham; screenplay by Carl Forman; photography by Floyd Crosby; edited by Elmo Williams; music by Dimitri Tiomkin; ballad sung by Tex Ritter. *Cast*: Gary Cooper, Will Kane; Grace Kelly, Amy Kane; Katy Jurado, Helen Ramirez; Thomas Mitchell, Jonas Henderson; Lloyd Bridges, Harvey Pell; Otto Kruger, Percy Mettrick; Lon Chaney, Jr., Martin Howe; Harry Morgan, William Fuller.

Around the fundamental, deceptively simple structure of an impending gunfight between a marshal and a man he sent to jail, director Zinnemann has bridged over twenty years of Western film tradition. A basic reading in connection with this movie is, again, the Warshow article. In addition, the teacher might find useful two

High Noon

Cat Ballou

available study guides: A. W. Hodgkinson, "High Noon,"[20] and Frank Manchel and Dan Ort, *Study Guide for High Noon*, produced by Brandon Films.

Cat Ballou (1965, 96 mins., color, Columbia Cinematheque). *Credits:* Columbia Pictures; directed by Elliot Silverstein; produced by Harold Hecht; based on a novel by Roy Chanslor; screenplay by Walter Newman and Frank R. Pierson; music by DeVol; director of photography was Jack Marta. *Cast*: Jane Fonda, Cat Ballou; Lee Marvin, Shelleen-Strawn; Michael Callan, Clay Boone; Dwayne Hickman, Jed; Nat King Cole, Shouter; Stubby Kaye, Shouter; Tom Nardini, Jackson Two Bears; John Marley, Frankie Ballou.

Outside of the 1939 version of *Destry Rides Again* (Contemporary Films), *Cat Ballou* is the only good spoof of the Western fiction film. The movie's plot traces the familiar conventions of the genre, including the traditional revenge theme. Miss Catherine Ballou, the virginal, school-marm heroine, returns from her eastern finishing school. Back at her daddy's ranch, she sees her father heroically defending his property against the landgrubbing railroad men who are in cahoots with the evil business interests in Wolf City. To make matters worse, Sir Harry Percival, head of the eastern monied interests, has hired the villainous gunslinger Strawn, whose nose was bitten off in a fight. Our lady of propriety has no choice but to help her kinfolk. This results in her being transformed into a tough, two-fisted tomboy of the West. She forms a gang of her own: an amorous cattle rustler, his preacher-outlaw uncle, an amateur Indian broncobuster, and the villain's alcoholic, unemployed twin brother, Kid Shelleen. After Cat's father is killed in cold blood in broad daylight and the corrupt sheriff refuses to help, she leads her gang in a daring train robbery. After escaping from the posse, Cat's raiders take refuge in the outlaw's impregnable fortress, Hole-in-the-Wall. Much to the gang's horror, Strawn comes to demand that they return the money in twenty-four hours or face the consequences. Obviously, this necessitates a showdown between Kid Shelleen and Strawn. And there is also the necessity of Cat revenging her father's death. What happens is film history. Also, it's a nice way to end a unit on the Western film.

In conclusion, as one reflects on the various types of pictures represented, it is not hard to recognize that movies in treatment and emphasis respond to the influences of a mass audience. That means that endings are often contrived, characters too frequently stereotyped, and prevailing attitudes reinforced. Rarely do we find a film that represents an unpopular viewpoint or situation. Hopefully this brief unit will provide an impetus in helping students understand and appreciate a major genre in American film history. Such exposure will not only highlight some of the conventions and variations within the genre, but will also shed light on the limitations of the movie industry itself.

Notes

1. David Mallery, *The School and the Art of Motion Pictures* (Boston: National Association of Independent Schools, 1964).
2. George N. Fenin and William K. Everson, *The Western: From Silents to Cinerama* (New York: Bonanza Books, 1962).
3. Philip Durham and Everett L. Jones, *Adventures of the Negro Cowboys* (New York: Dodd, Mead and Company, 1965).
4. Robert Warshow, "Movie Chronicle: The Westerner," *The Immediate Experience* (New York: Anchor Books, 1964).
5. Richard Whitehall, "The Heroes are Tired," *Film Quarterly* 20(Winter 1966-1967).
6. Alan Lovell, "The Western," *Screen Education* 41(September-October 1967).
7. Charles Cain, "Film Themes and Background Books: The Western," *The Film Teachers Handbook* (London: British Film Institute, 1960).
8. "The Western Hero," *Life* 55(December 20, 1963), p. 104.
9. Bosley Crowther, *The Great Films: Fifty Golden Years of Motion Pictures* (New York: G.P. Putnam's Sons, 1967).
10. Joanne Stang, "Hollywood Romantic: A Monograph on George Stevens," *Films and Filming* 5(July 1959).
11. Penelope Houston, "Shane and George Stevens," *Sight and Sound* 23(October-December 1953), pp. 71-77.
12. Eugene Archer, "George Stevens and the American Dream," *Film Culture* 3(August 1957), pp. 3-4.
13. Alan Stanbrook, "The Return of Shane," *Screen Education* 26(September-October 1964).
14. Douglas McVay, "George Stevens: His Work, Part One," *Films and Filming* 22(April 1965); "Part Two" (May 1965).
15. George Bluestone, *Novels into Film* (Berkeley and Los Angeles: University of California Press, 1961).
16. John Gassner and Dudley Nichols, *The Best Film Plays of 1943-44* (New York: Crown Publishers, Inc., 1945).
17. *Dialogue with the World* (New York: Encyclopaedia Britannica Films, Inc., 1949).
18. Ernest Callenbach, *Our Modern Art: The Movies* (Chicago: Center for the Study of Liberal Education for Adults, 1955).
19. "The Six-Gun Galahad," *Time* 73(March 30, 1959), p. 52.
20. See note 7.

Frank Manchel is a Professor of Communication and Theatre at the University of Vermont.

For the Future: The Science Fiction Film in the Classroom

William MacPherson

All too often, the fantasy film is left untouched by educators. Very rarely is the "imaginative" film considered a serious contender for classroom use. Classic films such as *The Cabinet of Dr. Caligari* and *The Phantom of the Opera* are often shown and discussed as examples of the genre, but the large body of fantasy films is left virtually alone. Perhaps more emphasis should be placed on the fantasy film because this type of movie can be used to both motivate students and introduce literary techniques while at the same time being viewed and discussed as social comment. In particular, the science fiction film often mirrors the concerns of a society, reflects an attitude, and expresses a forecast of the "shape of things to come" in regard to the tone of a specific generation.

The science fiction film, or specifically the film that attempts to portray a future generation, can be used very effectively by the teacher to discuss either the concerns of a particular time or a general concern of man. In addition, this type of film can also be viewed as a direct form of social commentary and evaluated as such. To illustrate these points, I would like to look at four major science fiction films that are concerned with the state of the immediate future. Each one of the films comes from a different decade: *Metropolis,* 1926; *Shape of Things to Come,* 1936; *1984,* 1956; and *Alphaville,* 1965. Each reflects that age in its view of the future while expressing a similar theme–the dehumanization of man.

Fritz Lang's *Metropolis* (1926) was probably the first film to present a coherent picture of a future society. The story is set at an unspecified year close to the end of this century in a vast complex that is a maze of skyscrapers built upon a subterranean "city of the workers." These workers are slaves of the machines that control Metropolis and they exist in a robotized condition of poverty and servility. In their midst, one girl, Maria (Brigitte Helm), preaches love and understanding and tells them about the Tower of Babel and how it fell "because the toilers did not know of the dreams of the planners." The Master of Metropolis, John Fredersen (Alfred Abel), hears of Maria and is determined to suppress her, but his son (Gustav Froehlich) is captivated by Maria and follows her into the city of the workers. Fredersen is determined to stop the girl, and he orders his evil cohort Rotwang (Rudolf Klein-Rigge) to capture her and to make in her image a robot which will preach revolt among the workers. Rotwang is successful, and the robot, as Maria, incites the workers to revolt and destroy the machines. The undergound city is flooded, but the real Maria

Metropolis

escapes from Rotwang and saves the workers' children. The robot Maria is then unmasked, Rotwang is killed, and Fredersen realizes his mistakes when he sees the love between his son and Maria.

Theavon Harbou's Victorian plot clouds the real concerns of the film with its simplistic moralism, but one is still caught up in the power of the film as a harbinger of the theme that will crop up in later films—the dehumanization of man. Lang's visions of the robotlike workers toiling at their machines, the creation of the robot Maria and the faceless masses filing through the city streets stress the depreciation of human life and meaning. It is interesting to note that Lang claims to have gotten the idea for *Metropolis* upon first seeing Manhattan from the deck of his incoming ship. Considering this point, the film takes on added meaning as a comment on the human condition.

In another sense, Lang provides us with a reflection of German society during the 1920s. At this time Germany had reached economic stability and technology had regained its peak; and *Metropolis* expresses the concept of the power of machines. Underneath, however, there appears to be a real human distrust of technology—a leitmotif that will return again and again in later films. The uncontrolled sadism of the workers, when they burn the unmasked robot Maria at the stake, sums up their real feelings toward machines.

The next major science fiction film to appear was produced in England in 1936, when William Menzies directed *Shape of Things to Come* based on H. G. Wells's novel. Wells himself dismissed *Metropolis* as "quite the silliest film," but his screenplay for *Shape of Things to Come* is similar in tone and viewpoint to *Metropolis*, although the presentation is more logical.

In *Shape of Things to Come*, Menzies and Wells drew on two of the latter's stories, "The Sleeper Wakes" and "A Story of Days to Come," to produce a film colossal in scope, but somewhat ponderous in impact. The film takes the viewer from the 1930s through a terrible world war to an undetermined time in the future where man is living in small groups in ruined cities under feudallike "Bosses." Man exists in this state of semibarbarism until a visitor comes in an airplane and announces that the last remnants of civilized man have banded together in a city of scientists in order to save mankind. The visitor attempts to convince the Boss to give up his command of the tribe but is unsuccessful and is held captive. Then more airplanes come from the city and gas the tribe, thus destroying this blight on the emerging superstate.

Shape of Things to Come then takes us to the future super city. Massive transparent skyscrapers, moving sidewalks, fantastic vehicles, and people moving purposefully along suggest a tranquility that is not present. The scientists have prepared a rocket-cannon to shoot man to the stars, but their plans do not meet the approval of the dissenting group of artists, who feel that man must find his destiny on the earth. This final conflict comes to focus as the sculptor leader of the artists sends a band of men to destroy the rocket. The group arrives too late and the film ends as the rocket takes off, leading man and woman to their destiny in the stars.

The tone of *Shape of Things to Come* is quite similar to *Metropolis,* but with a significant difference. In *Metropolis,* humanity is led from destruction at the hands of the scientists, while Wells's film portrays the scientists leading man from destruction at the hands of the mob. In *Shape of Things to Come,* man is dehumanized by reversion to savagery through the rule of self-interested leaders. Wells rather dogmatically points out that science holds the key to man's survival.

This film seems to reflect the concern with the capacity of science to save or destroy which was evident in the late 1930s. Nazi Germany was on the rise, war was being forecast, and the spectre of destruction was hanging over Europe. Perhaps the most effective scenes of the film mirror this concern: Menzies shows the destructive power of vast war machines as they crush buildings and men alike. This disquietude was to prove well founded, since World War II began in 1939.

In 1956, Michael Anderson directed a cinematic version of George Orwell's novel, *1984.* In *1984* Anderson presents a future world that is cold, repressive, and inhuman. Set in Airstrip One (London), the film tells how one man, Winston Smith (Edmund O'Brian), attempts to break away from the restrictive, structured, socialistic government of 1984.

Smith works as a rewriter of historical records—he changes history to fit the present situation. This job causes Smith to dote on the past, the time when England did not suffer under a repressive government, and he longs to return to that situation. He is joined by a female rebel, Julia (Jan Sterling), who is drawn to Smith, and together they try to escape to their own private world away from the spies, the Inner Party, the Outer Party, and Big Brother.

Smith's real break with the world of 1984 occurs when he begins to feel that O'Connor (Michael Redgrave), an Inner Party official, is really a member of the underground organization which plans to overthrow the government. Smith trusts O'Connor and he and Julia join the organization. When Smith and Julia meet in an antique dealer's spare room in the Prole section of the city, they are surprised and captured by the Thought Police, and they realize that O'Connor had really been testing them and that the underground movement was nonexistent. They are brainwashed and forced to forget their love. The film ends with Smith's impassioned expression of love for Big Brother and the government.

It is significant to realize that there were virtually no films during the 1940s that attempted to forecast the future and that the tone of *1984* returns to the more pessimistic tone of *Metropolis* rather than to the optimism of

Shape of Things to Come. Perhaps the memory of the horrors of World War II, the Cold War, and the threat of Communist domination inhibited a natural desire to look into the future and determined the pessimistic outlook of *1984*. The fear of Communism is evident in the Stalin-like character of Big Brother and the structure of the socialistic government in *1984*. Echoes of *Metropolis* can be observed in Anderson's crowd scenes of the party members venerating Big Brother, which are reminiscent of Lang's shots of the machine as Moloch, feeding on rows of workers. The two future societies are also similar in their desire to eliminate emotion and to value logic.

1984 differs from *Metropolis* in that Winston Smith is primarily self-interested, while Maria is selfless. Smith's prime concern is not with his fellow men but with himself. He would rather improve his own condition than the lot of his fellows. Even his love for Julia is selfish. When confronted with the thing he fears most, Smith quickly gives in and betrays Julia. The Victorian morality of *Metropolis* is conquered–man is completely dehumanized.

Jean Luc Godard's *Alphaville* (1965) is similar in concept to the three films previously discussed if only for its pessimistic view of man's future. In this film, Godard presents a simple story line contained in a visual structure intended to alienate his audience. Negative, short, slurred dialogue, bright lights, and obscure references contend to confuse the viewer and force him to partici-

Alphaville

pate in the cinematic experience to a degree not usually expected.

Alphaville begins when Lemmy Caution (Eddie Constantine) arrives from the outerlands. Caution is a spy, sent to locate Professor Von Braun, exiled from the outerlands thirty years before, and to induce him to return. If Caution cannot persuade Von Braun to come back, he is to kill him.

Lemmy Caution finds Alphaville to be a city of robotlike humans, devoid of emotion, governed by logic and reason in the name of a gigantic computer, Alpha-60. The control by Alpha-60 has brought about a mass cult of logical behavior. Emotional conduct is punishable by ritual murder. As in *1984*, the language is controlled by the government through constant change in the meaning of words. A daily bible/dictionary is issued so that no mistakes are made.

Caution eventually finds Von Braun and kills him. He then destroys Alpha-60 by feeding it unclassifiable material (poetry) and escapes from the crumbling city with Von Braun's daughter (Anna Karina). The film ends on a happy note as Caution forces her to remember the meanings of such words as love, tenderness, and robin redbreast.

Godard's theme in *Alphaville* is similar to the other three films, but because of its proximity, it has more meaning for the contemporary viewer. In forcing the observer to participate, perhaps Godard is also commenting on the contemporary situation by forcing the viewer to realize his own dehumanization. Lang, Menzies, and Anderson were all concerned with this dehumanization, but only Godard has allowed for an active response to the situation. In *Metropolis, Shape of Things to Come, 1984*, and *Alphaville*, the human condition has suffered when the individual has not been allowed to participate in determining this condition. Perhaps the main thematic lesson contained in the four films is this concept of active participation.

Another theme common to the four films is distrust of machines. The robot workers and the great machines in *Metropolis*, the vast war engines in *Shape of Things to Come*, the telescreen and the torture devices in *1984*, and the great computer-god Alpha-60 in *Alphaville* all reflect this fear of the power of the machine. Again this subtheme relates to the main thematic lesson by showing that man becomes dehumanized when he loses control of his tools. It is interesting to note that only in Anderson's *1984* does man fail to regain control of his destiny, because the huge machine of state has become too powerful for man to overcome.

The four films are all basically concerned with the dehumanization of man, but the approach to this problem differs with each film, as a reflection of its age. The social comment contained in these films is easily evident and concrete, and it can be effectively pointed out and discussed in the classroom. From the educator's point of view, a stylistic analysis of science fiction films can also prove both interesting and informative. The interest level of the student for this type of film is high, and it follows that the science fiction film is meaningful to the student.

Many literary concepts can be taught and reinforced through the medium of the science fiction film. The idea of "conflict" can be stressed quite easily because it is often expressed in basic terms. The "good guy-bad guy" moralism of Winston Smith versus Big Brother and Lemmy

Caution versus Alpha-60 is conflict shown in direct form. The easily identifiable confrontations between the protagonist and antagonist can be used to illustrate the concepts of crisis and climax while discussing plot structure.

Symbolism can also be introduced with success through the science fiction film, if only for its rather obvious, heavy-handed use. In *1984*, the symbolic value of Smith's diary, the paperweight, and the rat can be easily shown. In *Metropolis*, the various symbolic manifestations of the "machine" can be used to add meaning to a discussion of symbolism.

In general, many literary conventions can be introduced through the science fiction film. Then, when a firm basis for literary/cinematic analytic techniques is established, the transition to the study of classic cinema and literature can be effectively attained. The science fiction film can be a useful tool when thoughtfully utilized by the instructor.

Stanley Kubrick's recent film, *2001*, can be used in the classroom as an example of a serious, contemporary science fiction film that lends itself to a classic analysis. This film could first be discussed in class for its own literary/cinematic merit and then could be analyzed from the viewpoint of basic techniques.

2001 was scripted by Arthur C. Clarke, and, while it is not evident at first glance, the film follows classic dramatic structure. The beginning of the film is set many years ago, and the story line develops when two bands of primitive man-apes squabble over the rights to a water hole. When the losing man-apes leave to lick their wounds and sleep, their rest is disturbed by the appearance of a huge, black, monolithlike structure. Clarke has introduced conflict in the first confrontation between man and the monolith.

The film then shows how the monolith has affected the man-apes with a burst of intellectual stimulus, when these primitive people quickly discover the use of bone weapons and defeat their rivals at the water hole. Clarke implies that primitive man has been helped along his evolutionary trail by the alien monolith.

The film then takes us to a moon base in the year 2001 for the next confrontation. Man has discovered another monolith buried under the moon's surface. As he investigates the structure it gives him another intellectual jolt that motivates him to seek another monolith in the vicinity of Jupiter. A giant space ship is constructed and sent on its way under the leadership of David Bowman (Keir Dullea). The ship is governed by a super computer named Hal who tries to wrest control from Bowman because he/it "feels" that man is too weak and fallible to be entrusted with this important mission. Bowman succeeds in stopping the computer, but only after it has killed all the other members of the crew.

Bowman finally reaches the monolith near Jupiter, and he is strangely transported to a hotel room on the planet's surface. Time sequence is distorted as Bowman lives

2001: A Space Odyssey

out his life alone in the hotel room. *2001* ends when the monolith reappears in the room with the dead Bowman and a human embryo is seen floating in the vastness of space.

In retrospect, *2001* seems to be concerned with man's evolutionary progress. Every time man is confronted with the alien monolith he suffers some form of intellectual stimulus that jolts him farther down the path of evolution. Bowman's battle with Hal implies that man has reached his peak at that stage of development and needs to evolve beyond the level of the homo sapiens. Man's final confrontation with the monolith is the climax of the film—the conflict is resolved and man (the embryo) appears to have transcended this stage of existence.

The major symbols in *2001* seem to support the theme of evolution or rebirth. From the spinning bone of the primitive to the space station, the concept of cycles or recurrent patterns is symbolically reinforced. In the space ship, the crew runs along a circular track and walks along circular catwalks. These recurrent cycles thematically suggest the main concern of *2001*—man's rebirth with the help of the monolith.

In addition to the theme of rebirth, *2001* can be viewed as social comment. The film suggests that rebirth is necessary because man has lost control of his situation. He fights with his machines and while he has conquered outer space, he has done so at the price of his humanity. The humans in *2001* appear vaguely machinelike and un-

emotional. Man has progressed, but he is dehumanized.

Kubrick's and Clarke's *2001* is open to many different interpretations from many different viewpoints, but it is significant that the film can be analyzed in many different ways. *2001*, *Metropolis*, *Shape of Things to Come*, *1984*, and *Alphaville* are serious science fiction films that deserve more recognition by educators. These films can be used either as social commentary or as introductory vehicles to the study of classic cinema and literature; as such they deserve consideration as serious contenders for classroom use.

William MacPherson is an Assistant Professor at Essex County College, Newark, New Jersey.

"Frankly, My Dear, I Don't Give a Damn"

Michael Keisman

In the thirties and forties, the adolescent's pulse would quicken each Saturday afternoon as he stood in line waiting to purchase a ticket to the movie matinee. The thrill of an escape into the marvelous world of the imagination tended to block out whatever was happening in Europe, in Asia, or even in our own national environment. These adolescents sat astonished by the screen version of Margaret Mitchell's phenomenal best seller, *Gone with the Wind*. The film took most of the Academy Awards in 1939 and provided us with hours of war, the burning of cities, and the loss of life from a very safe distance through an aura of buttered popcorn.

The war surrounded us. The mass media, basically the printed page and the voice of radio, kept adults abreast of world events. Adolescents continued in their peripheral relationship to the world as on the screen in the early forties Walt Disney offered *Pinocchio*. Loaded with sentimental appeal, it offered to us the lesson which perhaps typified our generation—perfection can be reached, not by going to a carnival, but by going to bed on time. How strange to recognize now that this wooden

Gone with the Wind

boy who exemplified the real way had only three fingers and a thumb.

America was in turmoil. Did we relate the horror depicted on the screen in *The Grapes of Wrath* (1940), *Of Mice and Men* (1940), and *Tobacco Road* (1941) to what was happening in reality? As American film classics of the early forties were being produced, what awareness was being conjured up in the youth of that generation? With this, the year before our loss of innocence, the

darkened theater still served as a temple to a false security.

As the reality of war became translated into the bombing of Pearl Harbor, American youth was permitted to know more about the subtleties of war as the mass media and its stars popularized the sale of war bonds and promoted patriotism. Attempts to orient youth to the wages and rages of war were done so in glossy, propaganda films such as *Bataan* (1942), *Guadalcanal Diary* (1942), and *Wake Island* (1942). These led a multitude of screen attempts at providing audiences with stereotypes of white, young, innocent American boys (ethnic types evenly distributed) opening crushed boxes of Mom's apple pie while sneaky, tree hidden, toothy, smiling Japanese soldiers, screaming "Bonzai," rushed in hoards over machine gun emplacements.

And here *we* are, grown educators, products of the silver screen orientation, deciding on the role of film in the curriculum of today. Shades of Margaret O'Brien!

With the advent of television—the tool education wants to tame—the visual demands change. Our students come to our classrooms with, perhaps, a finer sense of the auditory and the visual than we had. From a constant bombardment of sound and sight, the average student's ability to perceive more from film is much greater, because experimentation with film has been the bill of fare ever since he can remember. In addition, what was to us a Saturday afternoon treat with overtones of the occult

is to today's youth an established life style.

From the hour that the child is capable of sitting up, mother places him in front of the television set. Constantly viewing this baby sitter, how can he help but learn to see? Follow this emphasis on the visual through adolescence, and one can imagine the number of hours of visual and aural experience garnered by such a viewer and listener. How do we in education deal with human beings who possess this great raw material when we were motivated differently? The generation gap may be the written page versus the silver screen: the literature-centered approach ("Now that we have read *The Good Earth*, we shall see the movie.") versus the "now" orientation to film ("Let's make a film, not write.").

Perhaps the first step, and a very painful one, would be to admit to the premise that we are out-classed in this area. Secondly, how to consider whether or not we should approach an area such as film study if there truly exists this gap, because we, as teachers, may attempt to pull that old educational "gag"—"Since I've had more experience, I know what is good and what is bad." If one is willing to admit a knowledge gap in film study and yet desires to experiment, a wonderful experience may be in store. Consider this possibility. The teacher comes to the class with years of experience working and counseling students, with degrees from colleges, years of personal experiences, a smattering of middle-class values, and a sense that Greer Garson and Walter Pidgeon made a lovely couple. The Woodstock generation arrives in the classroom with great suspicions about you, a general and beautiful naivete, long hair and beads, an awareness of exactly what the Beatles are saying, and a curiosity about the real meaning of contemporary films rated *R* and *X*, along with a puzzlement as to why Mr. Valente sees anything immoral in them. Can you imagine the possibilities of learning if there could be a recognition of these offerings and a genuine melding of them to summon forth an experience which could bring together the beauty of traditional thought and the excitement of the new morality?

"The movie, by which we roll up the real world on a spool in order to unroll it as a magic carpet of fantasy, is a spectacular wedding of the mechanical technology and the new electric world." Marshall McLuhan's statement from *Understanding Media* appears most relevant at this time. Couple it with S.I. Hayakawa's statement that "in the age of television and the visual media image becomes more important than substance," and perhaps we are prepared to discover this "meeting" earlier proposed.

Accepting the gauntlet as thrown, how are films selected for study? What films succeed? Which fail? Since an amount of expense is involved, everyone concerned should be cautious. Remembering the fusion of ideas, perhaps the answers should come from a complication of problem ideas garnered from the members of the class

—one of which is the adult therein. The process of selecting problem areas can be very rewarding, since honesty in free discussion could result in the development of trust and respect for one another, in class. The temptation may be great on the part of the adult member to usurp the role of discussion leader, but, remembering that this is a sharing experience, he should assume a member role and demand his right to be heard as well. From this discussion should arise the selection of problem areas which are of concern to the group. These problem areas are generally a concern about the values within our society which appear to be inconsistent with the acts within our society.

One recent discussion group concluded in the selection of the following problem areas: (a) nonconformity, (b) the judgment of society, (c) the role of the black man in a white society, (d) adolescent/adult relationship, (e) coping with failure, and (f) religious faith in a changing world. What evolved was an educator's dream— a student-oriented thematic approach.

The task was to identify these problem areas in films so that there would exist a common experience to which all members of the group could relate. In addition to this, an attempt would be made to concern oneself with the various ways in which the camera was used to relate the visual experience. The adventure was to be a twofold one—the consideration of a common problem area through a new medium and the evaluation of how this problem area was related to the film.

The selection of the film itself was accomplished by splitting the original group into film review boards based on specific interest in individual areas of concern. The review boards read film catalogues, saw films when available, and sought advice from reviews, criticisms, and from specialists in the field. Each board returned to the group with four or five selections, providing a synopsis of the films available. In addition, the review board determined the relationship between the problem area and the films suggested on the basis of this presentation. One film was selected to correspond to each of the areas of concern which had been proposed earlier: nonconformity, *Morgan!*; judgment of society, *Sundays and Cybele*; role of black man in a white society, *Nothing but a Man*; adolescent/adult relationship, *Nobody Waved Goodbye*; coping with failure, *The Bicycle Thief*; and religious faith in a changing world, *Winter Light*.

V.I. Pudovkin, a famous Russian film maker of the mid 1900s, provided the basic aim of film. Perhaps it is most significant to this experiment: "The basic aim of cinema is to teach men to see all things new, to abandon the commonplace world in which they blindly live, and to discover at last the meaning and beauty of the universe." Accepting this premise, then, one is able to divorce himself from the world in which he "blindly lives" and see new answers evolve in a situation which he watches. Hopefully then, the members of the group, having expressed a desire to learn more about their concerns and problems, were going to receive fresh insights from observing them as they are portrayed on film and discussing them with other members of the group. In addition, the group would evaluate the sincerity of the problems portrayed by considering as best they could the attempts by the film makers to present the film honestly.

To accomplish this, the group felt a need for guidance, since their novice state as film critics and reviewers became most evident. Although the group adopted film handbooks, which were read and discussed, there existed a desire to coordinate ideas and suggestions prior to the group showing. A guide was to be completed in several sections, including a discussion of the background of the film and of its director. This section would deal with the film and its contribution to film in general, discussing any innovative or unusual effects, the film's cinemagraphic significance, and the director's technical role. Next was a consideration of those aspects of the film's content deserving special attention. Following this, an attempt was to be made to assess the success of the director and camera in presenting the problem area. This section would be comprised of suggestions made to direct the eye of the audience to see the use of camera techniques and evaluate them, yet drop the pseudocritical jargon of the pretender film buff. The by-product of this activity, it was hoped, would be the development of a more discerning filmgoer.

Next would be a group of questions to be considered by the viewer. These would serve as a leveler prior to any discussion. At the start of a discussion problems relative to content would be raised, and the questions would aid in providing the basics required for an understanding of the film content. A section then would be completed to serve as impetus to conversation or writing or merely informal lunchroom "rapping." Finally, a section would be provided to include the criticisms of professional reviewers and critics. These film study guides were used assiduously in some cases and completely abandoned in others. Nevertheless, the group felt that the development of the guide and its help caused the members of the group to participate without the authority of an educational disciplinarian.

For a film to correspond to the area of nonconformity, *Morgan!* was a unanimous choice. The major reason for the choice was the presentation of the nonconformist, Morgan, without prejudgment on the part of the film makers. Morgan's character, the committee insisted, was not portrayed in a light which could be construed as in need of sympathy. There existed neither a harangue about the need of compromise nor a final message that one need not. Because of its seemingly honest visual approach in general, and for its portrayal of the nonconformist in our contemporary society, *Morgan!* was accepted by the class for study.

Non-conformity—*Morgan!*

Background of the Film and Its Director

In the early 1950s, film innovation was felt in most European countries except England, which was still concerned with light-hearted films about coalmines, London slums and postwar friendships. A group financed by the British Film Institute's Experimental Film Fund sponsored some young film makers who, influenced by the Italian neorealists (*Bicycle Thief*) and the French "new wave" (*Sundays and Cybele*), were eager to try new cinematic techniques. They began with shorter films. Among the more prominent ones were two by Karel Reisz (*Momma Don't Allow*, 1955, and *We Are the Lambeth Boys*, 1958). These two films established Karel Reisz as an innovator in British film; with Tony Richardson, he established a new school of film in England—the school of British social-realist film.

In 1958, this new school of film reached its peak with the presentation of its first feature-length film, *Room at the Top*, which was freely adapted from a novel about a ruthless young clerk whose only aim in life is to intrigue his way to success. It was evident that the public was prepared to accept more outspoken films and heroes who were unsympathetic and ruthless.

Room at the Top, in spite of its acceptance, was essentially a theatrical film. The film which better expressed the new movement was Karel Reisz's *Saturday Night and*

Morgan!

Sunday Morning (1960), which presented a realistic rather than a theatricalized film of its subject. Reisz presented a film unconcerned with balance of characters, neat story line, or theatrics. The film dealt directly with one phase in the experience of a young man—money problems, sexual encounters, abortion. The film, when released, was recognized as the nearest to true social realism that the British feature film had yet reached. Reisz's success led to a number of films genuinely realistic or giving a passable imitation of realism. The best of these included *A Taste of Honey* (1961) and *The Loneliness of the Long Distance Runner* (1962), both directed by Tony Richardson; John Schlesinger's films *A Kind of Loving* (1962) and *Billy Liar* (1963); Sidney Furres' *The Leather Boys* (1963); and Karel Reisz's *Morgan!*

In his film *Morgan!* Reisz goes beyond the realism and enters a field now established as black comedy. Much of the film is undeniably funny in a quite black way. Reisz's instant cuts from reality to fantasy are not only a contemporary film technique, but also a peculiarly appropriate key to the central character, Morgan, who would naturally fantasize in sharp and visual images. So, accepting a new freedom, perhaps surrealism, Reisz sustains the free flowing tone of his film with cinematic stunt work for which the viewer should be prepared. He freezes the action, speeds it up, reveals the texture of Morgan's fancies by inserting film clips of Tarzan and King Kong roaring approval of Fay Wray. More contemporary films have adopted this surrealism, and Karel Reisz, in his film *Morgan!*, may well have been the innovator.

Characters

Morgan Delt .... David Warner
Leonie (his former wife) .... Vanessa Redgrave
Mum (Mrs. Delt) .... Irene Handl

Credits

Direction .... Karel Reisz
Photography .... Larry Puer
Screen Writing .... David Mercer
Film editing .... Karel Reisz

The Story

The film *Morgan!* is probably impossible to synopsize. The story line is erratic and difficult to follow, since the film makers involved consider film a visual art rather than a literary one. At any rate, Karel Reisz's film *Morgan!* was originally shown under the title *Morgan—A Suitable Case for Treatment*. Perhaps the appendage title is more appropriate.

Before an explanation of the plot, mention should be made of two themes which appear to run through the film. The first is an animal theme. People remind Morgan of animals which the viewers then see. In keeping with

this, his mother's boyfriend is a wrestler named Wally the Gorilla; Morgan keeps a lifesize stuffed gorilla in his attic; he "crashes" his ex-wife's wedding party in a gorilla suit; and he has King Kong fantasies. The second theme is a social one—a Communist theme. His cockney mother is a loyal party member, as was his deceased dad. Karl Marx is a hero. Mum is full of slogans, and Morgan uses the hammer and sickle as a source of jokes.

The screenplay is about a young London painter, Morgan Delt, who is convinced that the vegetarian communism of the gorilla is a better way of life than the one of his own species. Morgan comes by these views legitimately—his mother and his late father were Hyde Park Marxists. The problem here arises from the fact that Morgan has married (perhaps shrewdly so) a girl from the upper classes.

As the film opens, Morgan has returned home from Greece to learn that his wife has sneaked a divorce and is marrying a sleek art dealer who is very upper class— hardly anthropoid. Morgan is outraged, both as husband and dependent, and he determines to upset the divorce before it becomes final. In his attempts he tries terrorism and charm but finally abducts his former wife to a remote Welsh lake. Throughout all this, Leonie, the wife, finds herself being strangely aroused by Morgan's buffoonery, and there ensues the reaffirmation of their troth. Until now, the film has moved at a comic pace. Morgan suddenly realizes the danger he is in and says, "I'm frightened." The film viewer will be aware of a sudden change in tone. The man has melted and only the juvenile remains. The film is no longer comedy or fantasy; it is perhaps pathology—black comedy.

The day of Leonie's second marriage arrives, and Morgan dons an old gorilla suit. The fantasy turns to nightmare, the eccentricity becomes insanity. The film is nine-tenths fantasy and one-tenth sadness. Visually, the audience witnesses the degeneration of Morgan. At the end of the film, Leonie, now married to the respectable art dealer, visits Morgan at a mental hospital. She is pregnant with Morgan's child.

Study Guide

I. *The Camera and the Eye*

   A. Characterization
      1. The director of *Morgan!*, Karel Reisz, is concerned with providing visual characterization. Discuss the specific visual techniques which were used to establish the following characterizations: Morgan, Leonie, Mother Delt, Wally, Leonie's Mother, and Leonie's future husband.
      2. Contrast (visually) Morgan and Leonie's future husband, and Mother Delt and Leonie's Mother.
   B. The story line of the film is interrupted by

film clips of other films obviously not of the same era. The director has used these so that the viewer sees as Morgan sees in his fantasy.

1. How well did the director accomplish the transition from his film to the film clip? Was it smooth? Did it interrupt the film for you?
2. How successful was the technique of inserting these film clips to depict Morgan's fantasy? Give examples.
3. At the end of the film, Morgan's fantasy is no longer depicted in film clips. In what visual ways is Morgan's fantasy depicted? Why didn't the director choose film clips here?

C. Other films, such as Richard Lester's Beatle films, have used techniques (film clipping, speeding up, slowing down) exhibited in this film. Compare these films with *Morgan!*

D. Reisz specializes in the "visual surprise." He attempts to keep his audience off-balance. Consider how the following visual surprises accomplished this: bizarre automobiles; devastated living rooms; bomb planting; a comic policeman; house renovation; a grave site (Karl Marx); a bedroom window shade that flies up to disclose a house painter; and a floral hammer and sickle.

II. *Content*

A. How does Morgan differ from Leonie? From Leonie's intended husband?
B. What about Morgan is most eccentric?
C. Why is Morgan so monkey-oriented?
D. If Morgan is such an oddball, why do we find him appealing?
E. How does Morgan react to the divorce? What does he do? Does this seem right? Why?
F. How does Leonie react at first to being abducted? Does she have second thoughts?
G. What does Morgan mean when, out in the country, he says "I'm frightened"?
H. How does Morgan choose to break up the wedding? Why does he choose this way?
I. Think carefully about the final fantasy of Morgan. What happens to him in this fantasy? Who is in the fantasy? What does each character do to Morgan?
J. Why may we say that this last fantasy is unlike any other in the film?
K. How does Morgan react to Leonie's visit to the hospital? How does he react to becoming a father? Is he happy where he is?
L. The final joke, the floral hammer and sickle,

must hold some significance. What is it?

M. *Morgan!* has been called a very funny comedy. Did you find this film funny?

III. *Suggestions for Writing and Conversation*

A. *Morgan!* is a film which tends to make a bleak and sobering comment on our times and on the empty, frustrating lives of people who have acquired more freedom than they know how to handle. Discuss the validity or lack of validity of this statement.

B. Morgan believes that Leonie really wants to break loose from the life she will have to lead with her new husband when he says of her—"She married me to achieve insecurity." Is Morgan correct in his belief? Why? (Remember Leonie's comment to her fiancé—"You'll have to fight him, and the winner will drag me off and have me.")

C. The film appears to have two elements connected. The first element is concern with animals; the second element is concern with Communism. How is each of these themes used in the film?

D. Morgan's relationships with women are puzzling. He is surrounded by a left-wing mother, a right-wing mother-in-law, and a middle-of-the-road wife who doesn't know which way to turn. How does each influence Morgan?

E. Morgan appears to be two different personalities. In his world of fantasy, he is brutal and primitive. To the real world he is a perpetual adolescent. Which is the real Morgan? Why does he appear split?

F. Morgan, from a background of Marxist philosophy, marries Leonie, a girl from the extreme right wing. Doesn't this appear strange even for Morgan?

G. The anti-hero is one who, although he is involved negatively with other characters in the film, is irresistible. We tend to forgive him to the point where we wish him success. How does Morgan become an anti-hero?

H. A review of this film in *The Nation* (April 25, 1966) said of it ". . . the flick has been called 'howlingly funny,' '. . . a wildly wacky British comedy.' It is cast in a farcical mold, but it is fundamentally black, black, black. A film so full of despair that, in order to remain sane in Morgan's mad world, one must laugh." Discuss this comment.

I. "Karel Reisz used the character of Morgan to sum up the situation of today's youth untrammeled by any code of living within organized society." Discuss this statement, which was

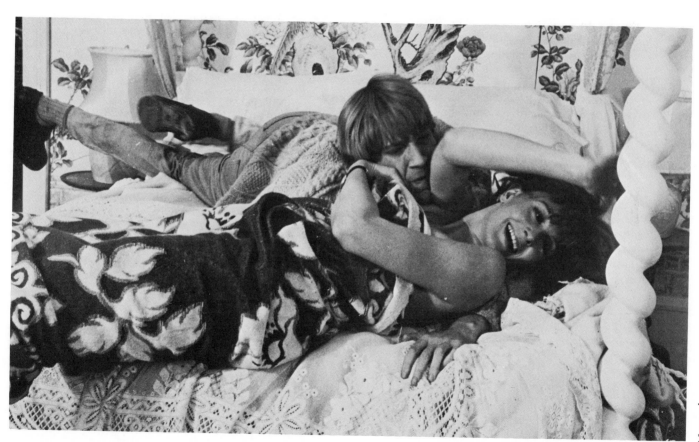

Morgan!

made in *Saturday Review* (April 16, 1966), in light of demands made by today's youth for freedom of choice and rights of decision in today's society.

J. Characters in literature have created their own fantasy life to avoid the realities of the world as Morgan did. Consider this as it occurred in the following works: *Fahrenheit 451; The Scarlet Letter; Death of a Salesman; Macbeth; Diary of a Young Girl; Old Man and the Sea; Silas Marner; Catcher in the Rye;* and *Return of the Native.*

IV. *What the Critics Said* (These may be used as writing or discussion subjects from the aspect of supporting or denying a specific critical comment. Supporting evidence for the students' comments must be supplied from the film.)

"Our hero survives his grotesque, self-induced pratfalls and self-dug pitfalls, and the price he pays, though desperately high, is made to seem worth paying." *New Yorker*, April 9, 1966

"Safe pseudo-seriousness, I think. *Morgan!* offers us the attitudes of revolt without ever posing a genuine threat to our conventional comforts or wisdom." *Life*, April 15, 1966

"Mr. Reisz, clever editor, cuts from reality to fantasy and back again with adroitness. Nevertheless, the animal fantasies become tiresome, their symbolic value far too vague, until one suspects that pictorial effect is being sought rather than meaning." *Saturday Review*, April 16, 1966

"Where is the frolic in having watched the antics and fantasies of a man who ends up in the asylum where he ought to have begun. Or are the film makers saying that madness is the only sanity possible in the world?" *The New Republic*, April 30, 1966

"Black comedy is horrible and appalling when you come to understand it. *Morgan!* is black comedy. The audience may be appalled but it is obliged to thank you for it. And finally a Morgan who is imaginative enough to throw in his lot with the gorillas and canny enough to make his associates join him in his apish Eden, makes a contemporary point that is not insanity. A lunatic Morgan makes no point at all." *The Nation*, April 25, 1966

Film study is threatening, Miss Dove, only if you permit it to be. The film today is everyone's medium, and everyone reserves the right to judge for himself. Educationally, we finally discover an area in which there exists no definite right or wrong to grade, where hand raising is a detriment, and where talking out-of-turn means interested involvement. All that may be left to say was said by Carl Sandburg: "Anything that brings you to tears by way of drama does something to the deepest roots of personality. All movies good or bad are educational."

Michael Keisman is a teacher at Columbia High School, Maplewood, New Jersey.

Composition

Composition makes everyone think of setting pen to paper but, one asks, why not camera to film? The process of composing a film is not unlike writing a paper. The technical stuff is not described because that's easy, just as it is easy to write a series of spelling words on a paper. The cameras are almost entirely automatic. The problem is, as Dean Swift said, putting "proper words in proper places." The articles which follow tell how to teach students to put proper film shots in proper places.

Freaking Around with Film

Rodney E. Sheratsky

Turning them on, opening their minds, showing them how groovy it is; or, bringing it all down.

Film, we have been assured by four writers under thirty, is "the art that matters."[1] And, for uncomfortable proof, those of us over thirty need only to join those who line up in front of Manhattan's art theatres which show *Easy Rider, Midnight Cowboy, Downhill Racer,* and *The Graduate.* In more ways than one, waiting in line has become fashionable diversion; the fashion editor of the *New York Times* recently wrote an article which described currently prescribed ritual attire (bells, baubles, beads, minis, maxis, and midis) for going to the cinema.

During the fashion conscious 1960s, educators, desperate "to turn their students on," succumbed to the latest fads in innovations by announcing "relevant" and individualized curricula. For a generation of students who learn more by watching television, film is supposed

This is a revised and expanded version of an article which originally appeared in *Media & Methods* 7:3(November 1970) 40-42, 54.

to be the most "meaningful" medium. Note, for example, that 979 individuals are education members of the American Film Institute;[2] presumably there are more than 1000 teachers in the nation's schools who are "using" film. How intelligently or skillfully they are using film is another matter; if someone wishes to study how films are being "used" as teaching "tools," he should possess two essential credentials: skepticism and cynicism. More than 73 members listed in the directory have advised the American Film Institute that their institutions are sponsoring filmmaking activities.

Why do students want to make films? Stefan Kanfer, film critic of *Time*, has reported some of the reasons: "Everybody's making a movie . . .,"[3] ". . . [it is] a form of artistic expression . . .,"[4] ". . . film is the most vital modern art form."[5] Where will all this burst of creativity lead? "In the long run . . . the contemporary enthusiasm for student films is likely to turn out a far greater number of enlightened appreciators than new creators. That in itself could be a boon to movies; whether cinema grows as an art form depends largely upon whether film-educated audiences demand better things of it."[6]

Fortunately, Mr. Kanfer's article acknowledges that, because of the limitations of certain equipment and the talents of some students, not all films are excellent, imaginative, or worthy of an audience. If one doubts the notion that film "is the medium of youth"—and it is a notion that could be challenged—he should ask students why teenagers should *not* make films. After studying film production for four months, two high school seniors expressed it this way:

> Too many students want to major in filmmaking after their initial exposure to the medium. Although these students' first films might be excellent, only a handful of people in the world will ever become renowned for their films. Filmmaking is a terribly expensive interest; as such, it is a fine diversion for the rich.[7]

> Isn't it more important for students to become involved with techniques and ideas which are absolutely essential? Frankly, making films is not essential. The majority of students could spend their time much more profitably reading about the history of man and thinking about what he has done to cause the horrible dilemmas we face. The "film freaks" I know are "freaks" because they know nothing about the history of ideas; all they know is the method necessary to achieve certain effects with the cameras.[8]

Who can reject either statement, particularly the last, in which one student has implied why so many student films are failures? Without respect for the tradition of ideas, a film maker can think only of technique.

But, no matter how many argue against teaching students to make films, some are still going to insist that students have a right to "use" *their* medium to foster their "creative expression," even if they have nothing worth expressing. There are at least eleven types of students who should not make films. The types, by the way, were compiled by high school seniors who completed the first half of a two semester course in film production. Who should not study filmmaking? Students who . . .

1. are not willing to admit their films do not have even adequate photography and lighting
2. habitually announce projects they are not intellectually capable of fulfilling
3. cannot work alone ("Much of what is good in a student's film is the result of working alone, during those periods in a project when the work is tedious," cautioned one senior.)
4. insist that a good film can be made only after a committee of seven, eight, or more, designs and approves every phase of the project
5. are irresponsible, lazy, and undisciplined
6. do not respect the equipment (cameras, editor-viewers, lights, and exposure meters) and budgets they have been permitted to use
7. want to make films because they cannot read or write
8. think they have become "expert" film makers just because they have learned the elementary techniques of filmmaking
9. cannot realize that their films are hopelessly inept, boring, and banal
10. want to make films because filmmaking is "in"
11. do not have an appreciation of and a feeling for life.[9]

There is a very practical reason to discourage students from making films. The reason was suggested by a poet, working on a screenplay for Warner Brothers:

The question remains: how many will get a chance? A person can become a great poet in the privacy of his home, accumulate twenty or thirty years' worth of manuscripts and bitterness, and, perhaps, finally have his day. A film maker without the machinery for making films can accumulate only twenty or thirty years of bitterness. It is a conceit of the successful that talent will out. However, as there are always so many incompetents among the successful, it seems clear that there are no doubt many gifted people among the failures. "You have to sell yourself," says Steven Gaines. "In the end, it's luck, says Jeff Young."[10]

The writer, of course, referred to those who hope to work in the film industry. What about those who want to work independently? Or those who insist on making their films their way, the Establishment be damned? Or those independents, members of the American underground, whose work has the look of home movies rather than *real* movies? According to Jonas Mekas, the "mid-

wife" to underground film makers, home movies are important:

> We *are* making home movies. What we are doing comes from the deeper needs of man's soul. Man has wasted himself outside himself; man has disappeared in his projections. We want to bring him down, into his small room, to bring him home. We want to remind him that there is such a thing as home, where he can be, once in a while, alone and be with himself and his soul—that's the meaning of the home movie, the private vision of our movies. We want to surround the earth with our home movies. Our movies are like extensions of our own pulse, of our heartbeat, of our eyes, our fingertips; they are so personal, so unambitious in their movement, in their use of light, their imagery.[11]

Although Mekas defends home movies with the Messianic fervor of one who embraces celestial objects, he has a practical point: if one's Super Eight films look like home movies, it need not be the fault of a narcissistic home-movie maker. Super Eight equipment, which most students use for financial reasons, is geared for the home-movie market. If a student manages to make a technically commendable film, he does so in spite of Super Eight film stock, which has such inferior emulsion that it is extremely difficult to splice and edit.

There are still other practical questions to answer before a high school encourages students to make films. Who will teach filmmaking? The English teacher who has never made a film? The art teacher who has been trained in the visual arts? Graduate students of film schools? (Because professional film makers do not have the time to teach on a regular daily or weekly basis, graduate students could be trained to teach high school students. This is a suggestion the American Film Institute could explore. If those who have no training in film decide they are capable of teaching filmmaking, a fad of the sixties will pass into oblivion during the seventies.)

Is there, then, no reason to teach high school students to make films? Yes, there is, but it does not pertain to any of the dramatic, fashionable, grandiose reasons cited and questioned previously. Indeed, the reasons for teaching filmmaking are so basic, they might seem blatantly obvious. Still, it might refresh teachers to analyze the obvious before they announce the grandiose. Two prominent people of the twentieth century—a film maker and a mathematician—can help us.

At the summary session of the 1969 Robert Flaherty Film Seminar, Mrs. Frances Flaherty, a woman dedicated to preserving her husband's memory and passing on to a younger generation the heritage of her husband's art, reminded seventy-five film makers, teachers, librarians, and students of Pudovkin's charge, "The basic aim of cinema is to teach people to see all things new."[12] Later, she quoted the French philosopher De Chardin: "To see more is to become more. Deeper seeing is closer union . . . to see or to perish in man's condition."[13]

In the remarkable study film for *Louisiana Story*, Mrs. Flaherty reminisces, "Bob always used to say that the camera is a seeing machine. And the job of the director is to help the viewer discover and explore for himself." Robert Flaherty's idea is striking. Yet, the documentarian's point raises some complex questions. If the camera is a seeing machine, whose sight is more crucial—the operator's or the viewer's? If it is the camera's operator who is seeing, then how can we be certain that his seeing machine will work if he does not have Flaherty's confidence in an audience astute and willing enough to want to discover and explore? If the camera is a seeing machine, should the photographer and director record every reality they feel the audience should see? And what about the camera and the functions we have expected art to fulfill—namely, to communicate ideas and emotions. To organize life into meaningful patterns. To make order out of chaos. To reveal universal truths through the self-imposed individuality of the artist. What becomes the function of the seeing machine when one renounces these traditional beliefs about art's functions? Suppose one accepts, instead, composer John Cage's argument that art is meaningful only when it is born of chance and indeterminacy? Cage believes the artist must work to make discoveries in his daily life. Only chance will open to us possibilities we could never realize if we accepted only another person's notions of life and art.[14]

But what about students and the seeing machine? In too many high schools in this country, a deplorable condition exists. Most students in our country's high schools will be graduated without ever having been taught how to see. Rightfully, we train our students to read, write, think, listen, and speak. Although our fashionable schools encourage students to use reading machines, tape recorders, and slide, overhead, and movie projectors, too many neglect to cultivate their students' visual perception. By the time they have graduated from high school, too many students are visually illiterate. Many of our students look, yet do not see. Work with high school seniors who have just begun film projects and you will understand why the old saying, "They have eyes, yet see not," is a cliché. It's a cliché because it's true for so many people in so many places. Unless students have been made aware of the process of visual perception, how can they help their audiences to see the phenomena they have arranged to have projected on the screen?

We have seen how today's magazines report the development of high school filmmaking activities throughout the country. Some educators claim that when students have convincingly demonstrated throughout their high school years that the book and pens they have been using are purposeless, a camera might help unsatisfied students to develop images of themselves that will increase their self-respect. Or, to state it another way, because film is supposed to "turn kids on," it is instant nirvana. This justification for filmmaking should be questioned by all who deplore the use of any art form as a device to "save" people. This practice of using film to "save" children is as debasing as sending a shy adolescent afraid of sex to the town whore. With all of the other acts of educational prostitution too many teachers commit—supposedly in the best interests of their students—must film be treated as yet another vehicle for sordid motives? The only contemporary film maker of any prominence who was saved from adult delinquency was Francois Truffaut. He was passed through his period of juvenile delinquency not by a social worker who shoved a camera into his hands, but by his innate, brilliant intelligence and a foster father who was a genius, the French film critic, André Bazin. Before he made his first short films and first feature length work, *The 400 Blows*, Truffaut had studied thousands of films and written many pieces of film criticism. Rodger Larson, Jr., with his students in New York City's ghettoes, would be the first to admit that his students do not make films for therapy. They make films because they are so committed to the art that they are willing to work ten hours for each minute of film that is eventually projected on the screen. The students, whose films project unbelievably vital reactions to life, are fiercely dedicated. They want their films screened not because they reflect products of people whose lives have been saved by film. They want their films screened because they are valid, important works which have become so because of the talent, intelligence, and stamina necessary for their creation.

Others believe that the camera provides us with a machine that can cultivate, sharpen, and deepen our powers of seeing. When students have cultivated these powers, then they can help to fulfill the Flaherty ideal: helping viewers discover and explore. In addition to helping students learn how to see, a filmmaking program can help students to make patterns. The intelligent making of patterns depends upon one's intelligent manipulation of materials to express the patterns. Twenty-nine years ago, one of the world's most honored mathematicians, G. H. Hardy, expressed concern about patterns—artistic and poetic as well as mathematic. One passage from his book, *A Mathematician's Apology*, expresses the importance of patterns and is relevant to students who make films:

> A mathematician, like a painter or a poet, is a maker of patterns. If his patterns are more permanent than theirs, it is because they are made with *ideas*. A painter makes patterns with shapes and colours, a poet with words. A painter may embody an "idea" but the idea is usually commonplace and unimportant. In poetry, ideas count for a good deal more; but as [A.E.] Housman insisted, the importance of ideas in poetry is habitually exaggerated: "I cannot satisfy myself that there are any such things as poetical ideas. . . . Poetry is not the thing said but a way of saying it."

Not all the water in the rough rude sea
Can wash the balm from an anointed king.

Could lines be better, and could ideas be at once more trite and more false? The poverty of the ideas seems hardly to affect the beauty of the verbal pattern. A mathematician, on the other hand, has no material to work with but ideas, and so his patterns are likely to last longer, since ideas wear less with time than with words.

The mathematician's patterns, like the painter's or the poet's must be *beautiful;* the ideas, like the colours or the words, must fit together in a harmonious way. Beauty is the first test: there is no permanent place in the world for ugly mathematics. And here I deal with a misconception which is still widespread (though probably much less so now than it was twenty years ago), what [Alfred North] Whitehead has called the "literary superstition" that love of an aesthetic appreciation of mathematics is a "monomania confined to a very few eccentrics in each generation."

It would be difficult now to find an educated man quite insensitive to the aesthetic appeal of mathematics. It may be very hard to *define* mathematical beauty, but that is just as true as beauty of any kind—we do not know quite what we mean by a beautiful poem, but that does not prevent us from recognizing one when we read it. Even Professor Hogbein, who is out to minimize at all costs the importance of the aesthetic development in mathematics, does not venture to deny its reality. "There are, to be sure, in-dividuals for whom mathematics exercises a coldly impersonal attraction. . . . The aesthetic appeal of mathematics may be very real for the chosen few." But they are "few," he suggests, and they feel "coldly" (and are really rather ridiculous people, who live in silly little university towns sheltered from the fresh breezes of the wide open spaces). . . . The best of mathematics is *serious* as well as beautiful—"important" if you like, but the word is very ambiguous, and "serious" expresses what I mean better. . . . A mathematical idea is "significant" if it can be connected in a natural and illuminating way with a larger complex of other mathematical ideas.[15]

What about the patterns in student-made films? What assignments can students be given which will help them to cultivate visual awareness and make patterns which connect with ideas and points in the film?

After they have been taught and shown why it is important to care for and clean their cameras, as well as projectors and other pieces of equipment, students might shoot the following assignments. The assignments are basic; they are also necessary if students are going to approach their work with care, thought, and discipline. Each assignment is for one roll of film.

1. Select an area with definite boundaries (a room, a house, a street, a field). With images and lighting, capture the atmosphere of that space.

Emphasize good lighting, sharp focus, and meaningful framing. Keep the camera stationary. Use a tripod. Do not pan, tilt, or zoom.

2. Return to the area used for the first assignment. In addition to shooting for the same specifications, use such camera movements as the pan, tilt, or zoom.

3. Shoot a person leaving for and arriving at his destination. Stress continuity and character motivation so the audience understands how and why the individual travels from point to point.

4. Edit the exercise in continuity.

5. Shoot two persons conversing. Do not rely on recorded sound, obvious signals, or titles. Rely, instead, on significant gestures, so the audience understands the topic of the conversation.

6. Edit the conversation exercise.

7. Shoot a one minute commercial. Rely on striking images, sounds, and lighting to "sell" the product.

8. Select a composer whose last name begins with *B* (Bach, Beatles, Beethoven, Bernstein, Brubeck, etc.). Choreograph and edit the movement of the images to the music of the composer.

During the remaining weeks of the course, students

may work on "longer" projects (about ten to twenty minutes). After students have selected the ideas for their films, they may submit treatments, scripts, or storyboards before they shoot. (Incidentally, the technical crew should have no more than a director, cameraman, and editor. If too many students are assigned to a project, those who are not actively involved will lose interest.) Ask students to screen their unedited rushes so others may comment on the quality of the shooting and the possibilities for final editing.

Instant success and recognition cannot be promised to anyone who makes films; indeed, the teacher who promises and expects instant rewards contributes to one of the said failings of the under-twenty-five generation. Instant success as a substitute for hard work can destroy the person who made the work and offend those who are subjected to it. George Martin, the Beatles' music advisor, has commented that the Liverpool phenomena like ". . . everything to be like instant coffee. They want instant recording, instant film, instant everything." Ending her review of two recent books about the Beatles, Joan Peyser bitterly remarked, "How true of them—and of their time."[16]

Robert Flaherty did not use his seeing machine for instant purposes. During a thirty-year career as a film maker, Flaherty made only four feature length films. Today, *Nanook of the North, Moana, Man of Aran,* and *Louisiana Story* still seem in advance of their day.

A man committed to the ideal that a film maker must help the audience to discover phenomena, he knew one does not learn how to see instantly. One learns how to see after much careful and thoughtful work with his camera. The goals of a filmmaking program—to help students see and to encourage them to make meaningful patterns—are modest. And yet, properly realized, these are goals one can spend a lifetime trying to fulfill.

Introducing students to an awareness of the essentials required for seeing may well be the only realistic, honest, and sensible reason for encouraging students to make films. On the high school level, all one can—and should—do is introduce students to an awareness of the essentials required for seeing. A high school filmmaking program should not become a professional filmmaking school. Why? Most public schools cannot compete with the facilities many college and university film departments offer their students. If a high school teacher encourages his students to think they are film makers on the basis of one course in filmmaking, he's as dishonest as his colleague who tells a child, "My! Only someone with your rare talent could have made this work of art," when the work of "art" was thoughtlessly conceived and artlessly completed. During the sixties we have witnessed the damage done by such dishonest, though well-intentioned, teachers who were more concerned with protecting the child's ego than with cultivating his intellect and artistic talent. Film critic Pauline Kael has questioned the

results: "Did anyone guess or foresee what narcissistic confidence this generation would develop in its banal 'creativity'? Now we're surrounded, inundated by artists. And a staggering number of them wish to be or already call themselves 'film makers.' "[17]

Notes

1. "The Art That Matters—A Look at Today's Film Scene by the Under-Thirties," *Saturday Review*, December 27, 1969, p. 7.
2. The American Film Institute, *Education Membership Directory 69*, "Introduction."
3. Stefan Kanfer, "The Student Movie-Makers," *Film 68/69* (New York: Simon & Schuster, Inc., 1969), p. 247.
4. Ibid., p. 248.
5. Loc. cit.
6. Ibid., p. 252.
7. A survey, "Why High School Students Should Not Study Film Making," conducted at the Center for Film Production, Northern Valley Regional High School at Demarest, New Jersey.
8. Ibid.
9. Ibid.
10. R. J. Monaco, "You're Only As Young As They Think You Are," *Saturday Review*, December 27, 1969, p. 17.
11. Jonas Mekas, "Where Are We—The Underground," *The New American Cinema: A Critical Anthology*, ed. Gregory Battcock (New York: E.P. Dutton & Co., Inc., 1967), p. 20.
12. Robert Flaherty Film Seminar, August 26-September 2, 1969, The Hotchkiss School, Lakeville, Connecticut. Remarks made September 2, 1969.
13. Ibid.
14. John Cage, "45' For A Speaker," *Silence* (Cambridge, Massachusetts: The M.I.T. Press, 1967), pp. 146-193.
15. Godfrey H. Hardy, *A Mathematician's Apology* (London: Cambridge University Press, 1967), pp. 84-89.
16. Joan Peyser, "The Boys From Liverpool," Review of *The Beatles: The Authorized Biography* by Hunter Davis and *The Beatles: The Real Story* by Julius Fast, *New York Times Book Review*, September 27, 1968, pp. 7, 54.
17. Pauline Kael, "Movie Brutalists," in *Kiss Kiss Bang Bang* (Boston: Little, Brown and Company, 1968), p. 17.

Rod Sheratsky is director of the Center for Film Production at Northern Valley (New Jersey) Regional High School.

Shaking the World with an 8mm Camera

Elenore Lester

One day last spring on the prairie campus of Creighton University, a Catholic institution in Omaha, suave, custom-tailored Otto Preminger—maestro of such high-powered movie epics as *Exodus* and *Hurry Sundown*—and explosive, rumpled Stan Brakhage—poet of the 8mm camera and creator of the underground opus, *Dog Star Man*—were co-starred in an academic spectacular that drew standing-room-only crowds. Establishment Man and Underground Man, who turned out to be as cozy together as Batman and Robin, talked film and filmmaking from the way in to the far out before the sea of students.

A few days later Preminger did a single at Yale several hours after Brakhage had hit the campus on his way from his show at Dartmouth. Also at Yale on that day were animation artist Robert Breer, who had come to address a class in the graphic arts department, and underground film maker Gregory Markopoulos, who had come to show his film, *Himself as Herself*. While Markopoulos was run-

Reprinted from the *New York Times* Magazine (November 26, 1967), 44-60.

ning his work for nearly two hundred students in one auditorium and Preminger was chatting with a group in a faculty lounge, a number of students were viewing Godard's film *Masculine-Feminine* in another building. In dormitories and campus hangouts other groups were talking about the dozen or so student-made films shown by the campus film society the night before, and several students were busy with films-in-progress. And at the drama school, a group of young playwrights was getting ready to go down to Bimini to make a film about Adam Clayton Powell.

Neither Creighton nor Yale has a film department and Yale was not having a film festival. It was just another Wednesday on campus, an ordinary day for a generation of students steaming toward an art revolution that appears to be stamping the twentieth century as the age of film just as the Elizabethan era was the age of drama and the nineteenth century was the age of the novel.

Courses in film production, film appreciation and related areas have nearly doubled in one hundred of the nation's largest colleges and universities in the past ten years; it is possible that as many as twenty-five hundred film courses are now being taught in all American colleges and universities. Most schools have neither the equipment nor the teachers to cope with the number of students who want to make or study films. Students are turned away whenever a new film course opens.

An additional clue to the new enthusiasm is the growth

of film societies, which in the past five or six years have become the most popular innovation on campus since the introduction of coeducation. The number of these non-profit organizations for viewing old and new films has been doubling each year until now a quarter of a million students are involved.

But most indicative of all, this new age has produced a new crop of creative young people who see an almost magical potential in making films themselves. These embryonic artists speak of their film mission in tones of revelatory rapture. They see the camera as uniquely the instrument of their generation, still rich with unexplored possibilities. "Do you realize how you can rock the world with an 8mm camera?" asks Gordon Ball, a recent graduate of Davidson College in North Carolina, who gave up writing for filmmaking. "Words are so limited and the film is still so unexplored as an art form." And Ann Gilbert, a New York University student, explaining her "commitment" to films, says intensely: "It is the one art that everyone can relate to, regardless of his cultural or educational background. It *reveals* people to themselves in a very powerful way."

To an older generation, reared in the happy innocent days when films were called movies and seeing them was a delightfully lowbrow amusement or a fairly harmless vice, it is all very strange—both the academic interest in films and the passionate idealism about making them. Today's young people who sling a camera over their shoulders and bicycle off to a vacant lot in the Bronx to make a film based on some highly personal view of things seem an odd new breed. Indeed they are.

First of all, the present college generation is the first to be born into Marshall McLuhan's "electronic age," with the television screen a member of the family and books a rather peripheral influence. Young film makers like Martin Scorcese, whose comic short *Murray* has been seen in local movie houses, report that their visual orientation was so strong that they started thinking in filmic terms as early as age seven or eight. "I used to have the television screen in front of me, and at the same time I was drawing those comic strip figures that move from frame to frame," says Scorcese.

Second, this group reached adolescence during the period of the flourishing of the "art" movie house and the influx of foreign films. Some see this as a more important factor than television. "These kids aren't the ones who have had their eyes glued to the television set," claims Robert Saudek, an NBC-TV producer who heads NYU's new graduate institute of film and television which opened in fall 1967. "They may be reacting against television. When they start dating they go to the art houses and see how people can use the film medium to express themselves and they want to do the same. Bergman, Godard, Truffaut, Fellini, the independent American film makers are to them what Hemingway and Fitzgerald were to earlier generations."

The final and perhaps most crucial factor in producing the filmmaking explosion is the development of the camera as an inexpensive, easy-to-use piece of equipment. "I've had a camera since I was eight," says John Palmer, who at twenty-one is cameraman on a low-budget film backed by an independent producer. "I got hold of a movie camera when I was fourteen. I've never wanted to do anything but work on films." And Kirk T. Smallman, a film instructor at Pratt Institute, finds that "the person moved and intrigued by films no longer thinks he has no hope of doing any real filmmaking himself—all he needs is an 8mm or 16mm camera and his filmic imagination, which is something that can be developed." Today a young experimenter can make a creditable short film with a borrowed or rented camera for between thirty and three hundred dollars.

Some of these experimenters are enrolled in film schools and special departments, but many come out of places like the psychology department or may even be dropouts. The thinking of a good many students is expressed by Edward Landler, a Yale sophomore: "I've been obsessed with films since I was thirteen or fourteen, but I feel that I should first get a good general education. You can pick up technique as you work. I've already made a few short films and I've learned a lot from them." He smiled mischievously. "I get rid of some of my frustration by writing my physics papers on 'Space, Time, and the Cinema,' giving examples on the use of time from Eisenstein's *Potemkin*." A dropout said: "The film is a rebel art. I found I couldn't study it at an Establishment institution. Film schools are trade schools for people who want to get into television or make documentaries for big corporations."

But there appears to be a generational solidarity of vision joining the long-haired hippie who wants to film "what I feel inside" and the buttoned-down conservative who is solemn about craftsmanship and structure. Both tend to view the camera as a probing instrument revealing private truths and public lies. Both tend to mistrust the traditional moral order and social disorder and to be contemptuous of hypocrisy and bombast. When a student manages to produce a substantial film, these ideas come across with the extraordinary impact inherent in the medium.

Some of the award-winning films in the student festival held at Lincoln Center last fall illustrate the drift of the young film makers' thinking. *Riff '65*, a documentary by Eric Camiel of NYU, followed in beautifully composed images the frustrated life of a Harlem boy until the day he exploded and smashed up a schoolroom. *The Season*, by Donald MacDonald of UCLA, offered a scathing, yet funny and sad documentation of the crassness of the American Christmas celebration. *Match Girl*, by Andrew Mayer of Boston University, was a narrative about an alienated young girl who wanders numbly into a swinging cocktail party before taking a suicidal dose

of pills. The films were technically professional, though not daring, and interesting enough to keep an audience of twenty-seven hundred, including a high percentage of the over-thirty age group, seated and applauding until the end.

The best student films are so good that in fact they tend to find their way to a broader public. Many a master's thesis film grows into a product worthy of general interest. Merle Worth, whose short, *The Kite,* ran for a year at the Little Carnegie, started the film as a class project at Columbia. Jerry Cott, whose *Hey, Little One,* a *cinéma vérité* report on the teenyboppers of Macdougal Street, was shown at last winter's festival of New York films sponsored by the Parks Department, made the film at NYU's summer workshop.

Student films have been selected for the Museum of Modern Art's film library by curator Willard van Dyke, and some films have been chosen for one or another of the nation's thirty-odd rental agencies or for student festivals.

Student movie making runs the gamut from fad to fanaticism. There are plenty of students who do it because it's the in thing and cameras have a way of attracting swinging chicks. Others do it out of the same impulse for fun and self-expression with which they might involve themselves in a play, a musical instrument, painting, sculpture or poetry writing. Many students are discovering that making a film is an excellent way of "writing" a sociology or science paper.

A number of the creative students have moved into films after experiencing frustration with what they consider to be more atrophied art forms. "I started in the theater—acting," reports Michael Johnson of the School of Visual Arts. "Then it began to look to me like the theater was dying, nothing really being said. But I felt I had heard things said in films—Godard, Truffaut, Bergman, Kubrick in *Dr. Strangelove,* Renoir in *La Grande Illusion.* I felt that if I had anything to say, it would have to be in this form." Mark Sadan, who was an art student,

describes the sense of illumination he experienced when he suddenly realized he was trying to put real motion into his drawings: "The wash of the waves, the gentle rocking of the boat, the flight of the birds overhead, and the sort of blending together of all these things was what I was trying for. Suddenly I saw it—I had to make films." He has already made five shorts and is now doing graduate work in films.

But the making of films is no easy matter. Even for those who make a fetish of the Godard-influenced rough, improvised look, projects inevitably get more expensive as they become more ambitious. "You think you'll put in another fifty or a hundred dollars, and before you know it you're up in the four-figure bracket," said one hard-bitten student.

Nicholas Macdonald, who graduated from Harvard this year and is a veteran of five short black-and-white 16mm films, says: "One thing about filmmaking is that it is *not* fun. The pressures are just too great."

Macdonald describes himself as an anti-experimentalist. "The kind of movie I am interested in making is dramatic and carefully constructed or documentary and carefully constructed." Three years ago Macdonald bought a 16mm camera with his earnings from a summer job and resolved to make a gangster parody (the most popular form, incidentally, for fledgling film makers). "I was seriously interested in filmmaking and I wanted to see what I could do," he says. "I wrote a very detailed script and got together a group of about twenty-five friends to work as actors and actresses. Mark Woodcock, the main actor, was also lighting man. We shot the whole thing in different people's rooms. The job was far more painstaking than we expected it to be. The first time we worked we kept blowing fuses and spent about six hours filming some shots that finally took one minute on the screen.

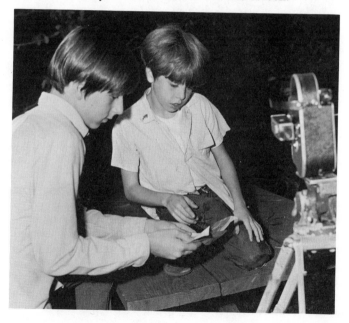

"We couldn't wait to get the first prints back from the lab. That was really exciting—seeing that it actually came out. It was a movie! I worked on it every weekend for a couple of months. I bought a viewer and splicer—that came to about fifty dollars—and did the editing in my room. By the time I finished, *The Big Dream* came to a little over two hundred dollars for a forty-five minute film. It's black and white and has a tape of theme music that one of my friends wrote especially for it. I showed it at school and people seemed to like it. Of course, it was particularly funny if you knew the actors—they were all under twenty and were trying to look very tough."

When he looks back on his first effort today, Macdonald winces a little: "It's sophomoric, acutely adolescent." But he can smile indulgently about the whole thing. "A first film is purely for learning; it doesn't matter how crude it is. You can make it with the worst of cameras and make every possible mistake and you still get a great deal out of it."

Macdonald went on to make two silent comedies: "Making silent movies has one overwhelming advantage besides cheapness. It forces you to think in visual terms." Then he made a thirty-five minute documentary about Spanish Civil War veterans living in the south of France. This film is now used as a fund-raising movie for the Spanish Refugee Aid.

Finally, with Mark Woodcock, he did a training film in the technique of interviewing for the Massachusetts

Institute of Technology political science department. This commissioned film was made with synchronized sound and required rented equipment. "We made it for nine thousand dollars—very cheap for the kind of thing it is," says Macdonald. "Now I'm going to try my hand at the poetic use of the camera—I'm going to do a five-minute movie which will be a purely visual and abstract description of a war. It's like making a first movie all over again."

For most young film makers their first film represents as much a trial of character as of talent. Each summer some fifty students are put to the supreme test at the NYU Film Workshop, under the direction of Haig P. Manoojian. They are divided more or less arbitrarily into groups of six or seven, and each group is required to create a script, select its own director, cameraman, unit manager, editor, sound director and assistants, and produce a short film (about ten minutes long) in six weeks.

One day recently, just before the start of the shooting of *Animus*, a seven-and-a-half minute mood piece, one tense, excited group sat in a studio in the university's film department and hotly debated the details of their shooting script. They had already considered and rejected the idea of doing an anti-Vietnam film and decided to do one that was anti-war by virtue of being pro-life—therefore, it would be about an artist. Each of the six members of the group wrote a script and one written by Warren Pearson was accepted. The artist was a painter.

Cynthia Lynes, warming up for her work as editor, wanted to know what was the point of having the artist run down a corridor trying doors that wouldn't open and finally seeing some dim "authority figures," representing critics, examine his work. "That door-trying business, that's trite!" she cried. "Besides, you don't need it."

The others disagreed and the debate raged. But they finally came to feel that they could do without the door trying or "authority figures."

Cynthia had further challenges. "You have three shots from the bed to the window—what do you need all that junk for?"

"It's the little things that count," said Bob Breakstone, the director.

Soon there were shouts of "Who's being hostile?" "Define your terms!" "So what are we arguing about?"

Then there was the matter of the nude love-making scene with its shots of "body parts." Wanda Grendys, an editor and the sound director, cried out in dismay: "Body parts! That sounds like a delicatessen!"

Jerry Rothenberg, the unit manager, and Peter Morrow, the cameraman, looked at her sternly. "You've surely seen *Woman in the Dunes* and Godard's *A Married Woman* and Resnais' *La Guerre Est Finie*," said Jerry. Wanda looked crushed.

The day the shooting began the group still hadn't found an actor, so they took "background shots" of children playing in a playground. The next day they found

Scott Mulhern, a student at the American Musical and Dramatic Academy, whose face and bearing seemed to the group to reflect sufficient sensitivity to make him plausible as an artist. Scott, with the wind of a twenty-year-old and the quiet determination of a beginning actor, obligingly ran up and down fire-escape steps between two NYU buildings for hours on end, while director, cameramen, and writer tried to get just the right degree of frenzy in his flight.

Finding an actress proved to be a big problem. Few young acting students went for the nude love-making scene. Finally a member of the group brought in a girl friend. ("It was quite an experience," Scott reported afterward. "I wouldn't have believed a scene like that could be done in such a clinical way. But with a cameraman, an assistant cameraman and a director hanging over you . . . well. . . .")

After two weeks of working long hours every day, Scott, who saw no end to what had been sold to him as a few days of unpaid labor, was getting restive. The group decided that it was time for a change of regime and that Warren should take over as director since he had written the script and supposedly knew what he wanted.

Things then moved a little more smoothly for everyone—except Cynthia and Wanda in the editing room. "Total chaos!" cried Cynthia after poring over the first prints. "Nothing hangs together." Warren then ordered more shots to create better continuity.

After two more grim weeks in the editing room, Cynthia was willing to concede that the film "had some kind of structure—but the structure had to be put in afterward." Jerry didn't see things that way: "The structure was there all the time; it just had to be brought out."

The final version of the film showed a young man running down a fire escape in an alleyway as if trying to escape. He suddenly stops, peers into a window, and sees a lovely young girl playing the sitar. Then he sees himself playing the sitar. Then he sees himself and the young woman nude, making love. The young man peering in the window seems anxious, disturbed. Suddenly he is walking, looking very solitary, in a desolate street. He goes to a playground filled with abstract, oddly suggestive shapes. He watches the children play and then turns sadly away. We again see his face peering through a window.

The members of the group felt that the emotional message had come through and were gratified when an outsider said that the film gave her a sense of "quiet uneasiness." However, it was apparent that various members of the group had somewhat different concepts of what the emotional content was—some seeing the film as a man's flight from himself, some seeing it as his search for wholeness. The fact that the man was supposed to be an artist turned out to have no relevance and shots establishing his vocation had been eliminated.

"The great thing was seeing it out there—a finished creation," said Warren. "That, and doing the actual work. We all learned a lot."

And many others like this NYU crew are learning a lot, on campuses all across the country. Because of difficulties with money and equipment, the medium is still the province of the most venturesome, creative, "with it" or affluent students, but there are many who fill that bill and many more to come when the tidal wave of youth hits the campuses in the 1970s. Along with those flocking into the courses, pushing into the art houses, and forming the campus film societies, they promise that a new, more sophisticated, mass audience will eventually come into its own. We can only pray that on the day the cinema officially enters the world of belles-lettres, the plebeian joy of moviegoing will not be lost.

Elenore Lester writes frequently about the avant-garde and is now working on a book on the current scene in the arts.

Student Film Makers
The 1970 Kodak Teenage Movie Awards

Page 114/Fifteen-year-old Eric Goldberg, Cherry Hill, New Jersey, won second prize ($100) with his three-minute animated film, *Up, Up, and Away,* starring his original cartoon character, Norman Noodnick.

Page 117/Rob Mortarotti, Orinda, California, a nineteen-year-old cinema student at San Francisco State College, was awarded first prize ($150) in the sixteen category for his film, *The Tenth Life of a Laboratory Tom,* the tale of a cat cadaver that persists in coming back to life.

Page 118/Robert Weltman, 17, Willowdale, Ontario, Canada, was awarded third prize ($50) in the sixteen category for his 16mm color animation film, *Eden.*

Page 119/*Almost,* a film by Joseph Goldman, 16, Yorktown Heights, New York, won second prize ($100). It tells the story of a city slum child who, through his imagination, discovers the wonders of nature.

Page 120/Dale Ramsey, 19, Newport News, Virginia, tied for second prize ($100) in the senior category with an animated cartoon extravaganza, *Operation Grocery Store,* the story of a little dog that turns a grocery store into a shambles.

Page 121/Seventeen-year-old Torv Carlsen, Stockton, California, tied for second prize ($100) in the senior category with an amusing comedy, *Guess Who's Coming to Lunch,* starring a housefly that is looking over a neighborhood for the most interesting lunch.

Page 122/Guy Brown, 18, Paramus, New Jersey, won the grand $1000 scholarship award and first prize ($150) in the senior category for his twenty-eight-minute, 8mm color film, *Where We Seldom Wander.* Described by judges as "an 8mm masterpiece," the film is in a contemporary mood and has ecological implications.

Film and the Ghetto

Cliff Frazier

In the summer of 1968, George Stevens, Jr., Sidney Poitier, and Father John Culkin, all members of the executive committee of the American Film Institute, determined that there was a need to relate to film workshops springing up in disadvantaged communities throughout the country. Since the American Film Institute had primarily focused its attention on the professional film maker, it was unprepared to deal with these minority film groups or individuals who had little experience and/or were using film as a means of personal or sociological expression.

Numerous requests for support had come from the various groups—"repair my equipment . . . give me some equipment . . . I need money for raw stock and processing . . . we need money so that the community which has never had an opportunity to express itself via this medium has an opportunity to do so." It was decided to establish an organization which would relate directly to the needs of these various groups. So the Community Film Workshop Council was born. In July 1968 I was asked to come on as executive director. Since that time

we have dealt with approximately sixty groups throughout the country.

You know, when you have a new project in motion, you must define your objectives as the activity is getting geared up, but frequently those plans change as you realize that the needs of the groups must influence your action. Should you come in dictating that the rules and regulations are specifically this or that and will continue to be this way, that the situation is unalterable, then you're making a big mistake. You have to remember that you're dealing with human beings who must articulate themselves, in many instances, on their own terms.

It also became apparent that greater emphasis should be given to film groups rather than individual film makers. It is preferable to aid a workshop in St. Louis that actively involves twenty young people rather than one in Detroit which involves only one or two. This priority must be given when money is so scarce.

In January 1969 we developed a proposal and approached the Office of Economic Opportunity for funding. The concept was this: give significant support to eight film workshops around the country and in Puerto Rico, enabling them to use film as a means of communication and allowing them, hopefully, to develop meaningful inter-relationships among the many different races and economic groups in these communities. We determined that one area would be Hartford, Connecticut, where there's a significantly large black, Puerto Rican, and white population. The blacks and Puerto Ricans were, to some extent, at odds with each other, and both were at odds with the white community. There was the earlier Hartford Film Project which involved using professional film makers in an effort to film the profile or the personality of the community, but this kind of film activity, although exciting, remains superficial. You can't bring in the professional, who has his own ideas about what life styles and situations are all about, because he will probably be unable to relate to the community, and he will communicate that inability on film. Community films must come from the people of the community. This is the essence of what we hope to be about—the people of the community reflecting what and who they are in their own terms with their own developed technical abilities.

There's also a workshop in Tulare County, California. Now this area was in the heart of the grape pickers' strike. Here we have Chicanos, whites, and a small black population. The intent there, again, was to use film to communicate needs, desires and, hopefully, future directions. We have a film instructor who is able to relate to all of the groups in this area. Within the next three months we anticipate receiving several films which will honestly depict life styles and situations in Tulare County.

We are not exclusively black, Chicano, or Puerto Rican—we also have a workshop in Appalachia dealing primarily with rural whites. As many of you know, the Appalachian region is constantly depicted on television. Some of the documentaries, because of certain limitations, have been less than accurate in their portrayal of the residents. In some of the films approximately five or ten minutes will be accurate, the rest, facade.

This inaccuracy is understandable when we examine some of the reasons. Imagine that you live in Appalachia and a stranger with a camera comes into your community or even your home. You know that outsiders think lowly of you because you are mountain people. You put on your face; you give him what he thinks he wants. He leaves believing he has captured an accurate view of the community. Later, we see it on television. This has been the situation in the past.

Imagine now several of the community people walking around with cameras in their hands. Many people who have been exploited—and *realize* that they were exploited—will still be uptight even when they see one of their own with a camera in his hand. But it will be less of a reaction than he will have in front of a stranger.

Too often a backwardness has been reflected. We've seen how the Hatfields and the McCoys go through their ridiculous feuds. L'il Abner and Daisy Mae are typical of the image we have of the Appalachian region. We must find out who the real people are. That applies to the black man, the Indian, and the Puerto Rican. All Puerto Ricans don't carry knives and get drunk. All black families do not have too many babies, and all black fathers do not leave home. We must begin to discard these unfair stereotypes, which have existed entirely too long. The only way to begin to deal with them is to reflect what people really are through this medium which has so hypnotized the country. Seeing it on television is equal to a sacred affirmation. A family sits in front of television hour after hour, and images become fixed in their minds. There must be no doubt about the authenticity. There must be other outlooks, other images, other tunes. Hopefully the growth and development of these various film talents around the country will begin to communicate some of these truths.

A fourth workshop is in Puerto Rico. It is a workshop run by a young lady who fancies herself a very heavy revolutionary and an older director who is with the film department at the University of Puerto Rico. Although he wants to see change, he's a little more conservative in that he wants to bring about change through the Establishment. So we have an interesting combination. There are also workshops in San Francisco, Los Angeles, Harlem, and Washington, D.C.

Yesterday and the day before we had a conference, with five of the workshops represented, and it was really successful. There were many disagreements, but there were also constructive suggestions. One young man was quite vocal about the Puerto Rican's role. "There's such a heavy concentration on what the blacks say and mean. What about the Puerto Rican? How are you going to communicate with him? What are you doing in films that is going to be relevant to what the Puerto Rican is about, and how are you trying to bring him in? If there's a workshop in Harlem, are you making any efforts to reach out to that Puerto Rican cat who might be two or three blocks away?" The assistant director from Hartford responded, "Look, Man. We have tried our damnedest to get some Puerto Ricans, but we can't. The cats won't join." Our Puerto Rican director replied, "They would if you had a Puerto Rican film maker as one of the directors."

Now we will attempt to find a film maker who can relate directly to the Puerto Rican community. Again, the problem is the absence of the ingredient that is always evident in inner-city programs—money. It is the major problem with which we must deal.

So there are eight existing workshops that are receiving support, raw stock, equipment, processing, and technical expertise. They have some sound equipment, moviolas, and many feet of raw stock.

After several months of settling down and winning the support of the communities, the project is beginning to gain some momentum. Now, many communities want to make films. They are beginning to realize the importance of using this means of communication. We hope what will come out of these situations will be of importance, not just to the individual communities, but to the country in toto, perhaps the world, because ignorance is what's destroying it. And we see a time when we will either live together or we will die together.

I'm impatient. I've been patient too long and have answered to far too many unfair questions and situations. I'm uptight. We're all tense. How can we begin to honestly relate to each other and hopefully bring about a real understanding, a real communication? A year from now, five years from now, I might have a gun in my hand. A year from now I might kill someone. I don't think I will, but we don't know the exact direction things are headed. We have got to begin to understand who the other cat is to understand his anger. I know to some extent what has shaped the attitudes and reactions of the whites that I've known. It's part of environment; it's part of the desire to be a man, to stand tall, to have a sense of self-worth. I can understand that we are very far apart, and if we don't get a little closer, something horrible is going to happen, because it's happening now. Film can be that medium through which we can begin to bridge some of the gaps which exist.

Summertree

That brings us then to another area of the OEO project. It is our television careers program, which was designed to train television newscameramen and place them on stations throughout the country. We recently completed the first cycle, involving nine trainees. They have now been placed at various stations. Last month we received a letter from one of our graduates. It is quite touching and I would like to share part of it with you. It reads:

> Tonight is very special to me, having talked to you earlier about being unable to find quarters here in Miami and wandering about Saturday night and part of Sunday morning—feeling rather anxious about the rushes (news film) that I shot this morning and worried about whether I was in focus—and then I saw the film and it was crystal clear.

The Learning Tree

> They put it on the 6 pm news. I felt so proud that I wished you were here. I wished everyone at CFWC (and believe me everyone) were here. . . . I feel so damn good, let me repeat "Thanks" because without CFWC and the American Film Institute, I probably wouldn't be doing anything. The program helped me, for I feel that I can stand beside anybody. Brothers, believe me, it's beautiful.

It was signed "Joe." This letter makes all the sweating, frustration, and pain worthwhile. It indicates that he has found a sense of self-worth, and *that* discovery is breathtaking.

There was also a Puerto Rican brother who is working in Louisville, Kentucky. He was born on the Lower East Side of New York City and had never been out of New York. He is now working as a newscameraman. The owner or manager of the station has indicated that he is their best news photographer. In this we have a statement of the quality of the program.

Soon we will begin another cycle. It will involve sixteen trainees. We will have Appalachian, black, Puerto Rican, Oriental, and Chicano students going through this same training and getting the same placement on stations around the country. That, to some extent, is what has happened to the OEO project.

Again, the only way these projects can be continued is by acquiring additional funds. Foundations have been indifferent to films. They have given money to drama, dance, and other art forms, but rarely do they give it to films, particularly films in the hands of the community. This has also been true of government. There has been indifference to the use of this tool.

Speaking of money and foundations, we were recently funded by the Ford Foundation to do a survey on employment opportunities which exist for minorities in the television and motion picture industries and to get some kind of barometer on opportunities which will open within the next ten years. Afterwards we will arrange a gathering with executives in both industries, plus government officials and advertising and union executives, for the purpose of setting up a meaningful training and placement program for minorities. It is our desire to deal with the industry in toto. With all segments of industry represented, you avoid one using the other as a cop out. Too often the producers have used the excuse that the unions opposed nonunion technicians working on the films and that since the union has less than ten percent nonwhites, the minorities are not hired. The unions, in the meantime, cited unemployment, fewer productions, technical qualifications, and a long waiting list. So, you have two groups saying opposite things, and nothing is being done. We hope to bring all the groups involved into some real interchange and have them relate to the existing situation. We already have a program in motion with one cameramen's local. We have about eight cameramen who are being trained. That's not enough, and

they know it's not enough. Changes must come. We will continue working hard to effect these changes. As you will notice, we're not only working with the workshops. We're also relating to many film activities as they involve the poor and minorities. If something meaningful is going to happen, it will happen to all of us. It will include the white and the black communities.

Since we can't stay indefinitely, it is hoped that all of the workshops we have assisted through the OEO will become self-supporting. The funding will soon run out. When it does, I would like to think that the workshops will have demonstrated to the community and to the different businesses in the area that they're capable of producing quality work. Therefore, they should be contracted, hired, or in some way utilized, perhaps to make local commercials, films for the school systems, films made as a means of personal expression, or film products for the black studies programs which are being developed in universities and colleges around the country. The only ones who can really make many of these films will be people who know the subjects well. They must be people with experience. They must be black and Puerto Rican film makers. So what will begin to happen? You will see a force growing more and more and more. This force will be important to this country. I hope the force will be encouraged. I hope you will begin to know it. I hope you will not be frightened by it.

We've also started an apprenticeship program on feature films. We have placed approximately fifty minority apprentices on films in this country, Puerto Rico, and Nigeria. It began on Harry Belafonte's film, *Angel Levine,* and was subsequently adopted by productions involving Sidney Poitier, Ossie Davis, Godfrey Cambridge, Norman Jewison, Elaine May, Stanley Kramer, and Walter Matthau. Recently, Ossie Davis was joined by three black apprentices in Lagos, Nigeria. He will be filming the play, *Kongi's Harvest,* by Wole Soyinka. That, I would like to think, will be a move toward expanding the program beyond the United States, toward the growth and development of it throughout the world.

We're now dealing with the Institute of International Education. We're trying to develop an exchange program, bringing foreign film students here to work on American films and sending Americans abroad to work in Africa, Latin America, Asia, and, hopefully, in Europe. These are the areas that my emphasis is sharply focused on, and the programs I have discussed are examples of some of the projects we're about.

There is no doubt about the necessity of these programs. There have been some films which have come out of the white community that were made by sincere people who wanted to really do something that was relevant. And there are some that have been complete or partial mistakes. I saw a film recently, *A Very Special Day,* that was charming but for two scenes. The film deals with a very young white child who is lost at Coney Island. She is befriended by a cute, intelligent, white youngster, and together they blossom into lovely flowers. But the two scenes that involved black kids put me up-tight. There is a shot of the two white youngsters passing a bridge, and as you look up you glimpse a group of grinning, dancing black youngsters. The second shot is the same type of scene. Why can't we see a black youngster walking along the beach looking as intelligent and as attractive as the young white kids. Better to have left them out of the film altogether. That kind of slanted addition causes, on my part, a negative feeling about the film.

Now the white community might dig it because it does tell about a little child who is lost and befriended by another child and together they make a discovery. They discover each other. He becomes a young adult, and he is charming, dashing, and mature. But when it deals with blacks, my sensitivities tell me there should be more significant representation. We need more sensitive and heartfelt treatment of blacks within the film content.

Since we're on a theme of misrepresentation and sensitivities, let me tell you of a feature film I saw on television. Cornel Wilde appeared in a film that had an African theme. Here is this guy in the jungles of Africa. All the whites are killed but him. Here he is running, and now he's hiding, and now he's pulling tricks that surpass even Tarzan. He is able to outfox the gorillas, the lions, the snakes, and especially the Africans. There is one scene in which he is being chased by seven Africans who are approximately forty feet away. But Cornel Wilde has enough time to gather some dry grass, take his flint-stones, make a fire, light five arrows, and shoot them into the sky, encircling the Africans in a wall of fire. There's a gigantic blaze and they frantically try to escape the inferno. This type of film is diminishing to the image of the intelligence of Africans. It also reflects on me because of my African heritage. The horror of this is that Wilde has the distinct reputation of being a liberal. He was trying to make a social statement; a statement on the universality of man. Many might regard this film as representing that statement.

There is another scene in which Wilde finds and befriends a black youngster who is hiding from a marauding band of Arabs (they have just razed the boy's village). Two situations develop enabling them to assist each other. They walk on, hand in hand, showing that two people can meet and have contact. But the interesting thing is the level of contact. Here's a child relating to an adult. The question is, where is the man-to-man relationship? Where is the respect and dignity which should be found between two equal adult individuals having contact? That becomes very important. The white character in the film would surely have soft or tender feet. Yet, like the African, he is able to run over rocks with his bare feet. He's able to run through knife-cutting

The Naked Prey

blades of grass and not have any physical reaction or injury.

Tarzan is equally bad. He can whip the entire continent. All he has to do is let out a loud penetrating call: the lions shudder in fear, the elephants respond to him, and the Africans are petrified of this single human being, who happens to be white.

When I was a child, I sat in the theatre rooting for this man to defeat the black brothers. In essence I was rooting for him because I'd reached a point where my self-hate of my blackness caused me to escape whichever way I could. It was an embarrassment to be a black in white America. Fortunately, the growth of black pride will erase much of this weakness, which caused many brothers to apologize for their color. The day of apologizing for race or color must never return.

Student Film Makers

Page 126/Trainee Joseph Maynard works in the background while editing instructor Herb Aust gives some personalized editing assistance to trainee Mary Vaultz.

Page 127/TV Careers trainees on shooting assignment in Herald Square (left to right: Mary Vaultz, Val Cruz, Jimmy Rueda, Ngaio Killingsworth, and Phillip Ghee).

Cliff Frazier is the Director of the Community Film Workshop Council of the American Film Institute.

Into the Curriculum

The problem, of course, is fitting film study into an already crowded curriculum. And, of course, it is expensive. What are some of the ways that film study has been integrated into the curriculum? The first article deals with a highly structured curriculum; the others deal with several other methods of organization.

Film as Language: Its Introduction into a High School Curriculum

G. Howard Poteet

Film study is a part of many high school English programs, but it seldom seems to be developed sequentially and cumulatively. We tried the following: *Shane*, along with the study of the novel, for ninth graders; *Julius Caesar*, to run concurrently with the study of the play, for tenth graders; *The Red Badge of Courage*, along with the study of the novel, for eleventh graders; and *Children Adrift* and *The Red Balloon* for twelfth graders. All but *Children Adrift* and *The Red Balloon* are available in paperback.

To develop a meaningful sequence as suggested by the spiral curriculum of Jerome Bruner, we attempted to concentrate on more advanced concepts each year. We used as our objectives an understanding of those characteristics of film described by Sheridan and others in *The Motion Picture and the Teaching of English*.[1] Ninth graders study the language of film and its tremendous power to transmit information. Tenth graders analyze

Reprinted from *English Journal* 67:8 (November 1968) 1182-1186.

film technique in illuminating the study of the literature of print. Eleventh graders focus on filmic methods of producing irony, metaphor, and symbolism. Twelfth graders emphasize structure and style in the film. None of these approaches is intended to be mutually exclusive.

We organized the teaching of the film around key questions on film technique by using cross media analysis. Students learned what Raymond Spottiswoode has defined as the grammar of the film, e.g., close-ups, long shots, and montage, through discussion and a special presentation of a student made, twenty-minute 8mm film. The film linked together examples of various camera shots. An accompanying tape recording explained how the shots were made and how they could be used to obtain a particular effect.

Freshmen and sophomores read printed versions before, juniors read a printed version afterwards, and the seniors, of course, read none. Thus, for all students but the seniors, preparation consisted of two parts, preparation in the techniques of the film and preparation in reading the written work.

This is not to say that to rationalize the inclusion of film study in the English curriculum we have to connect it in some way to print media. However, insights into one art form or medium are often obtained by using the viewpoint of another art form or medium. We frequently use the film to give perspective to the novel, e.g., to show Joyce's techniques in the distortion of time or Heming-way's arrangement of short scenes—why not the reverse?

In the beginning stages of film study, the use of print media as well as nonprint media may give the student some concrete basis for critical judgment. It would be fine to be able to discuss the film in only filmic terms but this seems impossible if students lack the critical tools to use in making decisions about films. The hardiest advocate of the "new criticism" would scarcely recommend that an individual should attempt a close reading of a text without some background in literary techniques. So, too, a close reading of a film requires an understanding of the language of film. It is the job of the teacher to structure this knowledge in some way. If the English teacher views film as literature, then a good basis for a beginning judgment of film may be established through analytic techniques borrowed from the study of print literature. It may be that by this means the student can find out what happens when the products of print media change qualitatively when converted into nonprint media. Some understanding of why this change is inevitable may help the student understand the validity of the film's claim to autonomy as a form of communication.

The primary problem in viewing film is in obtaining the film. Commercial films are available in several ways: renting a film and projecting it in the classroom or auditorium, waiting for it to appear on television, or arranging for a professional showing in a theater. There are problems with each method.

The third alternative, projection of the selected film in a commercial theater, was our choice during the first year of our program. We reserved the theater, and only students were admitted during the school day. In most cases, a new print was available and was always projected by professionals under optimum viewing conditions. Lighting and sound were at their best; interruptions were nonexistent.

However, renting buses for transportation to and from the theater and paying for the professional projection proved to be too expensive; the total cost was four to five times the rental price of the film. We found, too, that too much time was wasted going to and from the theater.

Because of these and other problems, all future showings in our film program will be held in school. The acquisition of more sophisticated projection equipment and better scheduling arrangements may permit us to show films in our auditorium during the school day at no cost to students.

As part of the viewing activity, students were encouraged to look at film from one or more viewpoints: pictorial, musical, literary. Students could note pictorial composition and judge whether or not the language of film had been used effectively. The music could be analyzed to see if it added to or detracted from the picture. Students could, if they were interested primarily in the verbal part of the picture, note the effectiveness of the dialogue. If students wished, they could view the film by concentrating on all of these areas or none of them. No comments were made by instructors during the showing of the film at the theater.

After viewing the film, students discussed it in class; the teacher tried to act as a moderator rather than as an authority. Students compared key scenes in the film with key scenes in the book. They also discussed the theme of the film and whether or not it differed from the theme of the book. The way that characterization was achieved in film language was contrasted with the way that it was developed by the author in the print version. The instructors pointed out that the film shows us many things simultaneously; print builds meaning sequentially and cumulatively. Criticism, it was also pointed out, should not be based on whether or not the film was true to the novel. Instead, the classes compared the two to see how and why they differed. The emphasis was on the differences in how the media were used. Then students attempted to criticize the film.

Freshmen analyzed the language of film and how it is used by George Stevens in the film *Shane* to transmit vital information about Shane. Students studied the techniques of film such as the close-up, the montage, and the pan shot to see what these things contributed aesthetically to the film. The way that the film transmits ideas about Shane and his background that differed from the book were discussed by students. Some time was also spent on the ways in which the dialogue had been

Shane

how the distribution of the film in a wide screen process (new and popular at the time) destroyed some of the film's beauty (since it had been photographed in a standard process and the new process cut off the top and bottom of the picture). Students were interested in attempting to answer such questions as how both the scenery and Alan Ladd's impassive face contributed in different ways to the mythlike quality of the picture.

Joseph Mankiewicz's film, *Julius Caesar*, is a beautiful performance of the play. Sophomores analyzing this film studied the technique of film in illuminating the study of literature. Students discussed how Shakespeare's work had been changed to fit the medium of film.

The play is not the film, as students learned. Films use a shot-to-shot sequence and a scene-to-scene structure rather than that of the drama: act-scene. The theater's reliance on speech and the film's reliance on movement seem to be an essential difference that students must take into account. Students needed to be able to answer such questions as: have scenes been rearranged, omitted, or added? The way that the film presents the central conflict and whether or not it is different from the way that it is presented in print is of prime importance. Students attempted to see if symbolism had been communicated visually and, if so, how.

Other interests were whether or not the cast was well chosen: e.g., was Marlon Brando well suited to the role of Marc Antony? Is the play easily adaptable to the

changed, omitted, or its ideas presented visually. The stress was on both how and why this was done.

Contrasts were made between the novel and the film *Shane*. Students pointed out that scenes such as the visit of the farm implement salesman and Marion's burning of the pie were omitted from the film. Students discussed why Shane was clothed differently in the film from the way he was described as being clothed in the book. Our study of the history of the film proved useful in discussing

Julius Caesar

screen? As John Howard Lawson has pointed out in *Film: The Creative Process*,[2] the visual movement does not necessarily enhance the play but may have an opposite effect. Also, students needed to understand whether such devices as the close-up added or detracted from the film.

John Huston's film of Crane's *The Red Badge of Courage* was viewed, as David Mallery has suggested, before reading the novel and then discussed in terms of the imagery involved. Juniors examined the methods of producing irony, metaphor, and symbolism in the film. They discussed the irony of the soldier's cowardice and the difference in the ways that this is presented in the film and in the book. They attempted to identify metaphor in the film, for example, in the scene after the first skirmish when the private looks up and sees the sun shimmering through the trees. Students discussed the use of the same shot near the end of the film. Symbolism in the book was noted and its effectiveness contrasted. Lillian Ross's book, *Picture*,[3] proved to be a useful source in discussing why the film differed from the book.

Seniors studied the structure and style of two films, *Children Adrift (Les Enfants Des Courants D'Air)* and the better-known *The Red Balloon*. In *Children Adrift* unique camera work and natural acting get off to a slow start but finally develop into a poignant study of a boy in a Parisian slum as his best friend, an old man, dies of a heart attack. This is contrasted with the fantasy

The Red Badge of Courage

of a boy and a balloon in *The Red Balloon*. In this film a gang of boys puncture the red balloon (which has apparent magical properties) after a chase through Montmartre; other balloons "revolt" and carry the boy high into the air over Paris.

Seniors discussed the structure of both films as to whether or not the scenes were arranged in some order for a purpose and whether scenes should have been omitted or added. An interesting discussion developed around whether or not the action in both films developed

by a series of accidents. Students were interested in whether the outcome of *Children Adrift* was based entirely on the environment of the young boy or in part on his character. Since the two films were similar in many ways, students could compare the structure and contrast the style. If the use of black and white adds to the moody style of *Children Adrift*, students were asked, in what ways does color contribute to *The Red Balloon*?

In developing our program we looked at other attempts to design a film program; some were organized and some were not. Programs that were organized usually used chronology or genre as the basis for organization. The program that we are developing is concerned with the way that the medium works. In each case the film that we have chosen is illustrative, not definitive.

We have thus selected what we believe to be films which indicate a hierarchical order of ascending difficulty in comparing one art form to another: narrative novel to film, play to film, symbolic novel to film, film to film. The films selected are illustrative of what film can do as a communication medium, for they serve as various dialects of the language of film. One might say that the film makers relied primarily on the visual in *Shane*, the verbal in *Julius Caesar*, both the verbal and the visual in *The Red Badge of Courage*, and the purely visual in both *Children Adrift* and *The Red Balloon*. Just as we read one book and relate others to it because it serves as a center in our thinking, so can one relate other films to these.

In preparation for film study, paperback books such as George Bluestone's *Novels into Film*,[4] Rudolf Arnheim's *Film as Art*,[5] and Lewis Jacob's *Introduction to the Art of the Movies*[6] were ordered. Teacher's paperback reference works included Daniel Talbot's *Film: An Anthology*,[7] Marion Sheridan and others, *The Motion Picture and the Teaching of English*,[8] David Mallery's *The School and the Art of Motion Pictures*,[9] Neil Postman's *Television and the Teaching of English*,[10] Ralph Stephenson and J. R. Debrix's *The Cinema as Art*,[11] and Marshall McLuhan's *Understanding Media*.[12]

Our approach thus far has been that of comparative communication. Provisions are being made for students to make their own 8mm films. Students will plan and write the script and shoot and edit a film on subjects of their choice. A section in the library reserved for the use of a Technicolor 8mm projector will permit students to view and evaluate their own films as well as the films of others. Thus, they will gain an understanding of the creative process involved in making films.

Future plans also include the study of more films which can be discussed in filmic terms only and not compared with other media. Examples are *How to Make a Ewe Turn* (Brandon), *The Interview* (Brandon), *The Tender Game* (Story-Board), *Very Nice, Very Nice* (Contemporary), and *Reflections #11* (Radim). These films, which range in length from five to seven minutes, will be shown one a day during a week-long film festival.

Students will spend the rest of the period discussing them.

Film will constitute a great part of the literary experience of our students. We believe a carefully structured program will help these students develop criteria to evaluate film.

Notes

1. Marion C. Sheridan, et al., *The Motion Picture and the Teaching of English* (New York: Appleton-Century-Crofts for NCTE, 1965).
2. John Howard Lawson, *Film: The Creative Process* (New York: Hill & Wang, Inc., 1967), p. 188.
3. Lillian Ross, *Picture* (New York: Holt, Rinehart & Winston, Inc., 1952).
4. George Bluestone, *Novels into Film* (Berkeley and Los Angeles: University of California Press, 1957).
5. Rudolf Arnheim, *Film as Art* (Berkeley and Los Angeles: University of California Press, 1957).
6. Lewis Jacob, *Introduction to the Art of the Movies* (New York: The Noonday Press, 1960).
7. Daniel Talbot, *Film: An Anthology* (Berkeley and Los Angeles: University of California Press, 1959).
8. See note 1.
9. David Mallery, *The School and the Art of Motion Pictures* (Boston: National Association of Independent Schools, 1964).
10. Neil Postman, *Television and the Teaching of English* (New York: Appleton-Century-Crofts, 1961).
11. Ralph Stephenson and J.R. Debrix, *The Cinema as Art* (Baltimore: Penguin Books, Inc., 1967).
12. Marshall McLuhan, *Understanding Media* (New York: McGraw-Hill, Inc., 1964).

Film: The Personal Experience

Leonard Maltin

When I was eight years old, my parents took me to see a film called *The Golden Age of Comedy*. I was fascinated with this excellent compilation of great scenes from silent films starring Ben Turpin, Will Rogers, Laurel and Hardy, Billy Bevan, and many others. It was this film that planted the seed in my mind and got me interested in films of the past.

In the next few years I scoured the local library and borrowed every book I could find on movies; *King of Comedy,* Mack Sennett's anecdotal, entertaining autobiography, was one of the first volumes I read. Through this book and others, and through the silent-film compendiums that followed *The Golden Age of Comedy*, I became immersed in the world of the 1920s in Hollywood. Buster Keaton's *My Wonderful World of Slapstick* and John McCabe's *Mr. Laurel and Mr. Hardy* helped create in me a great love for the men who made these films, as well as for the films themselves.

I started saving my money to buy 8mm prints of these films with Charlie Chaplin, Laurel and Hardy, Harold Lloyd, Buster Keaton, and my other favorites. When I

Cecil B. DeMille, D. W. Griffith, and Mack Sennett

was old enough, I journeyed into New York to attend screenings at the Museum of Modern Art. During this time, in the early 1960s I knew what it was to be a non-conformist—not the kind of person who keeps track of every fad and calls himself one, but a loner in the true sense of the word. Virtually no one shared my interest in old movies, although I was able to "convert" several friends and whet their appetites with the films I ran on my 8mm machine. Together we started attending the various revivals in New York, not only at the Museum but at the New Yorker Theater, which for years was the mecca of all dedicated film buffs in the city.

In high school I was the resident weirdo because of my interest in old movies. I started a film club which had ten or fifteen loyal members; for three years we gathered on Friday afternoons to screen whatever we could get our hands on. Perennial advertising campaigns yielded no results, and we finally gave up, deciding that we would be content to enjoy the films ourselves and not worry about the rest of the student body. We ran *Metropolis, The Phantom of the Opera, The Mark of Zorro, The Thirty-Nine Steps, To Be or Not to Be, Foreign Correspondent,* and many other films—and we had a ball.

"Time passes," as a silent-movie title might say. It is now the 1970s, and things are very different from the situation not so many years ago. I am no longer a nonconformist; in fact, I find myself riding on the crest of a gigantic wave. Film is everything now, and old movies are, to use a terrible expression, "in." The Museum of Modern Art screenings, which used to be half-filled, are now overflowing. The handful of film books I read as a youngster are now eclipsed by literally hundreds which have come out in the past few years. Many people are discovering that old movies can be big business, as in the case of film rental companies, which used to charge five to ten dollars for their vintage feature films. Now the going price is as high as two hundred dollars.

Film is thriving in high schools and on college campuses around the country, and the cults devoted to W. C. Fields, Humphrey Bogart, the Marx Brothers, and Busby Berkeley are flourishing. Students walk around with copies of *Films and Filming* under their arms and provide an enthusiastic audience for films which a few years ago wouldn't have attracted more than a handful of people.

What distresses me is that I don't see the love or the sincerity that I felt when I first discovered these films. A large majority of the student film buffs today are convinced that film was only discovered a year ago and that any film from the twenties, thirties, or forties is an antique to be laughed at, occasionally enjoyed, but never taken seriously. Those who do appreciate these films dissect them so coldly that the question of whether or not they enjoy the movies never occurs to them.

Naturally, as a child I judged a movie very simply: did I like it or not? Growing older and learning more, I have come to appreciate the intricacies of filmmaking and have reached the point where I am aware of the director, the actors, the writer, and the countless other technicians who make each film I view. I screen every movie with a critical eye, emphasizing certain aspects in my mind, depending upon my reason for seeing the film.

But above all, I still enjoy movies. And if I ever stop enjoying them, it will be time to stop watching them. Many young film buffs are deluded by the mass of film criticism that is printed every week in this country and around the world; in their haste to accept film as art, they often forget that movies have always been made, and continue to be made, to entertain an audience. This concept sounds old-fashioned and outmoded today, but it is as true as ever. There are those who will argue that the film has come of age, and people no longer want to see films that merely "entertain"—they want to see a great director at work, putting an important theme into filmic terms, saying something relevant about our modern society. When MGM released *Zabriskie Point*, relying solely on the name of director Michelangelo Antonioni to attract audiences, alarmingly few went to see the movie. Recent box-office hits, on the other hand, have included *Diamonds Are Forever, The French Connection*, and *Summer of '42.*

This is not to say that the words "popular" and "good" are synonymous—by no stretch of the imagination. But in order to appreciate the films of the past, one must always keep in mind that the directors who made them always had one idea foremost in their minds—to entertain. One can make a relevant statement while entertaining (see the great Warner Brothers films of the 1930s which made stinging social comment—films like *Five Star Final, I Am a Fugitive from a Chain Gang, Massacre*, etc.—or any of scores of films from *Intolerance* to *The Ox-Bow Incident*), one can use dazzling film technique while entertaining (*Citizen Kane* comes to mind immediately), in fact, one can do anything with film and still fulfill that prime obligation. It is absurd to sit through some contemporary films which make no attempt to be coherent but, because they are flashy or filled with symbolism, attract widespread praise.

Michelangelo Antonioni was at his best with *Blow-Up* because, unlike his incomprehensible Italian efforts, he was utilizing all the technique and thematic know-how at his command *while telling a story*. The result was a film that succeeded on many levels, appealing to a more diverse audience than any of his previous films. Luis Buñuel took a fascinating premise and created a brilliant and engaging film called *The Milky Way*—engaging because while it was making abundant use of allegory and the most complicated and baffling symbols, it was also a witty and often hilarious film.

This may seem a long, roundabout, and strange way of getting into a discussion of teaching and appreciating films of the past, but if the reader is with me so far, I hope I can continue to hold his interest as I introduce an era and a style of filmmaking which may be unfamiliar: the silent movie.

One of the great injustices of all time is the fate of the silent film. Despite such excellent books as *Classics of the Silent Screen* and *The Parade's Gone By*, the majority of the American public (including, annoyingly enough, most modern Hollywood film makers) is under the impression that the silent film was a rickety, unreal, and generally mindless form of entertainment with little to recommend it to any sophisticated or intelligent audience.

The fact of the matter is that the silent film at its peak was more creative, more dazzling, more sophisticated, more universal, more innovative, *and* more entertaining than the sound film. In teaching as well as learning about silent films, it is imperative to expose the falsehoods which have grown over the years regarding this medium:

1. Silent films did not move jerkily, nor was the action faster than normal lifelike movements. People have this impression because silent film speed was sixteen to eighteen frames per second, while sound is twenty-four. Most silent films shown during the past forty years have been run at sound speed, creating the idea that silent films looked that way originally. (I should add that it is useless to bring up this argument if the teacher is then going to show a silent film at sound speed—most projectors have a silent-film adjustment which enables one to show such films properly.)

2. Silent films were not flickery, scratchy, or devoid of contrast. This again is an impression people have gotten because of *modern* projection of silent films. Celluloid is a very delicate material, and over the years many silent films have been subjected to brutal treatment by careless projectionists and neglectful film studios. Thus, many prints which survive today look abominable. The fact is that when originally shown, silent films were as sharp, clear, and natural looking as today's film. Original prints are shown at the Museum of Modern Art (and many are in their circulating library), and many 8mm and 16mm prints made from original negatives bear out this claim.

3. Silent films were not "corny." Some of them look that way today, but many more do not. The ones that do seem "corny" appear that way because of actors and directors who were unable to express themselves subtly, resorting to stagey techniques or unchecked exaggeration. One must also remember that the actors had to rely entirely on movement and facial expression to make a point, so naturally there was greater emphasis on this than was necessary in talking pictures.

4. Silent films are seldom shown today as they were when they first were released. First, no theatre showed silent films without sound. The smallest theaters had a pianist, and the major ones employed a full orchestra which played musical scores often composed especially for the film being shown. Secondly, most silent films were shot with various tints, not just for special effects (dark

blue for night scenes, amber for desert or Western scenes, red for fire scenes) but for an overall pleasing effect. Showing a third-generation copy of a silent film in black and white, without any musical accompaniment (as most classes do), one cannot hope to recapture the original audience response to a film.

The most important point one must make to students who have never seen silent films is that they must try to put themselves into the context of the time. Films date just as fashions and language do, and if an audience is going to rock with laughter every time someone says "Swell!" or "Give me a nickel for a phone call," or when the leading lady enters wearing a gawdy outfit that looks odd today, there can never be any appreciation of silent films. Students looking at films in our sexually liberated era will find many silent films naive in this respect as well.

If a class is going to adopt a "show me" attitude toward silent films, as most classes do, the worst thing an instructor can do is show a film that supports the popularized ideas about silent films. Many silent classics cannot be seen unless the audience is already accustomed to silents and will know how to appreciate one. It is important to win over a hostile, or neutral, class with the first film, in order for them to develop an interest in and a serious appreciation of the medium. Most courses examine film chronologically, which is an excellent idea, but I would add one suggestion: make the first film an example of silent film at its *best*, to give the class an idea of what

Sunrise

the medium could do. With this under their belt, they will be more willing to view more primitive or dated works with a basic faith and understanding of silent movies. A Chaplin or Keaton comedy—as funny today as ever—would make a good opener, as would one of the great silents from the final years of the era—the stunning *Sunrise*, the electrifying *The Last Command*, or any number of other slick, polished films from the late 1920s. Or, instead, one could show David L. Wolper's excellent television documentary (available on 16mm) *Hollywood: The Golden Years*, a respectful, enjoyable, and accurate overview of the silent era which ought to make anyone want to see more.

It is difficult to say how one can impose an appreciation of the silent film upon a student—just as there are those who will never know what good music is and those who have no interest at all in art. But in dealing with film, the one popular medium to which we are all exposed, enabling the student to make his own discoveries will probably produce the most rewarding results. Encouraging students to find the outstanding points in each film they see is one way to carry this out; the ideal way, of course, would be to have the students see silent films on their own, without the automatic stigma of a film being an "assignment."

Most of all, reading lists, especially for the novice, should include books that portray the silent film and film makers as something *alive*, not as waxwork. Biographies of people who worked in that era, like the aforementioned *King of Comedy*, Rudi Blesh's *Keaton*, Theodore Huff's *Charlie Chaplin*, Mary Pickford's *Sunshine and Shadow*, and Bosley Crowther's *Hollywood Rajah*, are excellent, vivid reading. Richard Griffith and Arthur Mayer's *The Movies*, Joe Franklin's *Classics of the Silent Screen*, and Kevin Brownlow's *The Parade's Gone By* capture the essence of the silent film, in all of its aspects, perfectly.

My point, very simply, is that the silent film was a marvelous medium. Its pioneers and creators were fascinating men, and the work they did was truly unique. It seems a crime that many courses being taught today on silent film treat it so coldly, so dully, that students are quickly turned off.

One problem is that a survey course on silent film offers no continuity. One of the most fascinating ways to examine the silents is to take one person and follow his career over a span of twenty years. Chaplin offers a convenient example. Many people would like to remember this artist as having had the Midas touch—that every film he made was a masterpiece—but that is far from the truth. It is rewarding to watch Chaplin grow and develop as a comic artist, both in front of and behind the camera, and, fortunately, most of his films are easily accessible, so that such an experiment is feasible.

You could start with his first film, *Making a Living*, although it might be wiser to pick his second effort, the first one to utilize the tramp character, *Kid Auto Races at Venice.* The character was an on-the-spot invention, his costume supposedly thrown together at the last minute by Chaplin when his boss, Mack Sennett, told him to dress funny for a new one-reel comedy. *Kid Auto Races at Venice* is not an exceptionally funny film, but it does show the original conception of the tramp. Already Charlie is skidding on one foot as he runs along and is poking fun at authority—here in the form of a newsreel cameraman. Later Sennett films like *Laughing Gas* show the character a bit more developed, already taking on the universal qualities he was to capitalize upon in later years. But throughout the many one- and two-reel films made for Mack Sennett in 1914, one sees a penchant for the easy laugh and a preponderance of vulgarity—a lot of unfunny gags like throwing bricks and kicking an adversary in the stomach. In later Sennett films one can observe Chaplin's first attempts as a director; largely undistinguished, they nevertheless show his almost immediate grasp of the camera as used by fulltime directors at Keystone during that era.

In 1915 Chaplin left Sennett to join Essanay studio. The two years at Essanay have accurately been called his transitional period, for it is in these films that one sees a gradual moving away from the vulgarity and anything-for-a-laugh foundation of the Sennett films, and an equally gradual shift into the more lovable, more profound Tramp of the later Chaplin endeavors. *A Night at the Show* is one of Chaplin's funniest Essanay films, with

a particularly interesting ancestry: it is, in essence, the music-hall act which brought him to America from his native England. The film abounds with the most basic slapstick gags, but it also shows a more knowledgeable method of setting up these gags for the maximum response. There is also the poking fun at the rich and snobbish sophisticates who attend the show where the film takes place. These upper crust types were to remain Chaplin's favorite comic targets for many years.

Finally, in 1916 and 1917, Chaplin reached maturity as a film maker and as a comic when he moved to Mutual Studios and made his "golden dozen" two-reelers for them. *Easy Street, The Immigrant, The Vagabond, The Cure, The Rink, The Pawnshop, Behind the Screen, One A.M., The Adventurer, The Floorwalker, The Count,* and *The Fireman* show Chaplin at the height of his powers—combining the rudiments of slapstick comedy with the genteel nature of the Tramp, a flair for telling a story with the mastery of the sight gag, and a deft knowledge of how to combine comedy and pathos in just the right quantities.

Unfortunately, not many of Chaplin's later comedies—mostly feature films—are generally available, except on theatrical reissue, but if it is possible to screen such films as *Shoulder Arms, The Gold Rush, The Circus, City Lights,* and *Modern Times,* the student can easily see the full bloom of Chaplin as a film artist, not only providing brilliant material on-screen (which he did in his Mutual comedies of 1916 and 1917) but presenting them in a creative way. If an examination of his career can end with *City Lights,* the student will have traced Charlie Chaplin's development from the crudest beginnings to what is probably his masterpiece, one of the most beautiful movies ever made.

Similar programs can be arranged for such men as Douglas Fairbanks, following his evolution from comedian to all-American boy to swashbuckler par excellence; D. W. Griffith, following his career from his earliest one-reel vignettes to his classic *Birth of a Nation* and on through great films like *Broken Blossoms,* and following his unfortunate and sad decline; or any number of other actors and directors who worked during this era.

Another problem in film teaching is the insistence of most people upon relying on the doctrines of the "classic" films and "great" film makers invented years ago. Most of the so-called classics are deserving of that designation, but, on the other side of the coin, there are many fine silent films which rival these films in quality—some which surpass them—but these films are traditionally ignored by film instructors who refuse to let each film stand on its own merit. Many of the standard film history books which have given us the standard rules of thumb concerning film classics were written decades ago, before there was an opportunity to examine the full body of films of the past. Today, hardly a month goes by that a major film archive or film society does not discover a "lost" film of the past that, when re-viewed, shows up many of its contemporaries. For years John Ford's *The Iron Horse* (1924) has been regarded as one of the all-time great films, with historians offering no apology for the hopelessly trite and banal storyline, only praising its directorial values. Not long ago an original print was discovered of another silent Ford film, *Three Bad Men* (1926), which has long been unavailable for reevaluation. That it is an outstanding film and a fine piece of Americana is indisputable.

Three Bad Men

But additionally, in the opinion of many historians who have seen the newly found film, it is far superior to *The Iron Horse* in almost all respects—an opinion with which this writer concurs.

One need not point to such an esoteric example to prove this point, nor must one confine this theory to the silent film. The number of great American films of the thirties and forties which have little or no status among film instructors and historians is amazing. How many times can one see *All Quiet on the Western Front* and *Citizen Kane*? Both are superb, unforgettable films, but many people would have the novice believe that virtually all films produced in Hollywood during the sound era have been bland and uncreative efforts, with just a handful of exceptions. I would like to offer a few examples of neglected films which deserve recognition of the highest order:

1. *Hallelujah I'm a Bum* (1932), directed by Lewis Milestone. A truly offbeat, experimental kind of musical with Al Jolson, Madge Evans, Frank Morgan, and Harry Langdon all at their most ingratiating, with most of the characters speaking in metrical rhyme. The songs by Rodgers and Hart are lovely, and the overall mood that the film creates is strangely haunting—it is not soon forgotten. Practically all of Milestone's films are first-rate and full of unusual camera devices and direction, but this film manages to do more with the depression-style musical than any other film of the era. It is also a notable

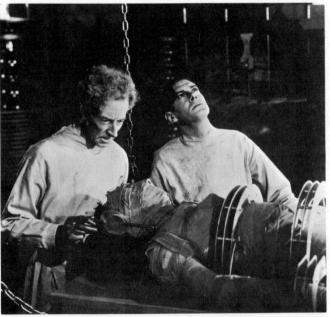

The Bride of Frankenstein

film for Al Jolson, who is more subdued and infinitely more effective than he is in his more famous films (reportedly the entertainer was dissatisfied with this film, precisely because he *was* kept in check by the director), and for Harry Langdon, the great silent-film comedian who never gained his footing in talkies.

2. *The Bride of Frankenstein* (1935), directed by James Whale. Whale was a witty, versatile, and flamboyant director whose work in horror films has always earned him the respect of fans of that genre, but little praise otherwise. All of his films show great fluidity with the camera, and truly imaginative and bizarre visual concepts—even his relatively minor B-pictures, like *Wives under Suspicion* (1938), a remake of Whale's own *The Kiss before the Mirror*. In any event, *Bride of Frankenstein* is one of the most accessible of his films, and one of the most beautiful. His ability to handle suspense, terror, lyricism (in the sequence with the blind man), and even black humor with equal finesse is supremely evident throughout this film. The use of mammoth indoor sets is in itself unique, and the *way* these are filmed is beyond compare. The climatic sequence where the Bride is created is one of the most unforgettable segments of film ever made in Hollywood—and a masterpiece of editing and camera placement. In short, the film is superior in every department and remains today not only a model of filmmaking but a vastly entertaining movie.

3. *His Girl Friday* (1940), directed by Howard Hawks. Here is another example of the compleat Hollywood movie which succeeds on every level: as an actor's vehicle, as a hilarious comedy, as melodrama, and as a director's film. This remake of Ben Hecht and Charles MacArthur's *The Front Page* stars Cary Grant as the conniving editor, Rosalind Russell as his star reporter,

and Ralph Bellamy as the man who is going to marry Russell and take her away from the newspaper business. In addition to these three stars, however, *His Girl Friday* has one of the finest casts of character actors ever assembled for one film. They are individually superb, but more than that, they work together as a group with remarkable results: Gene Lockhart, as a bumbling sheriff;

Mr. Deeds Goes to Town

John Qualen, as a meek little man about to be hanged; Clarence Kolb, as the blustery mayor out to give the whole city a snow job; Alma Kruger, as Bellamy's domineering mother; Billy Gilbert, as thick-witted Joe Pettibone, who unwittingly exposes the mayor and sheriff as frauds; Abner Biberman, as Cary Grant's crony who carries out his dirty work; and the hard-boiled reporters (Roscoe Karns, Porter Hall, Regis Toomey, Ernest Truex, and Cliff Edwards). The dialogue comes fast and furious, with actors talking over each other's lines in spots and conversations running so fast that one is liable to miss something if he doesn't listen carefully. One aspect of the film that is often ignored is its uncanny ability to shift from frantic comedy to stark melodrama and back again. The transitions are completely smooth, there is no awkwardness, and both muses are played for full effect. The opening shot of Qualen's isolated jail cell when Rosalind Russell goes to interview him is vivid and dramatic, yet it is treated almost as a throwaway by Director Hawks. In every respect *His Girl Friday* succeeds and earns its rightful place among American classics.

4. *Foreign Correspondent* (1940), directed by Alfred Hitchcock. Although brushed aside by almost everyone, including Hitchcock himself, *Foreign Correspondent* stands as one of the director's masterpieces. Its memorable sequences are too numerous to detail, but among more expensive, flashier Hollywood efforts like *Suspicion* and *Spellbound,* this film stands out as being a beautifully visual film without becoming self-conscious about it. In addition, it also has one of the finest scripts Hitchcock ever filmed—written by, among others, James Hilton and Robert Benchley. Benchley also appears in the film, adding his distinctive wit to several scenes and helping to maintain the light-hearted attitude that makes this film so enjoyable. The cast is outstanding (Joel McCrea, Laraine Day, George Sanders, Herbert Marshall, Edmund Gwenn, Eduardo Ciannelli, etc.) and last, but certainly not least, the film has the unique touch of William Cameron Menzies, the great art director, production designer, and sometimes-director, who conceived some of *Foreign Correspondent's* most striking scenes.

A complete list of personal nominees for widespread recognition could fill this book. But the idea is that every film instructor should be as broad-minded as possible, not just accepting others' ideas of what is good and what is not, but deciding for himself and letting his class participate in evaluating every film they see. With a mature class it would be worthwhile to screen a film that is unfamiliar to both the teacher and the students and together formulate a critical reaction to the picture.

Career examinations can be held in the sound era as well as the silent period. A class can learn a great deal from tracing a career from the silent era *through* the talkie period. A good example would be Ernst Lubitsch, the famous German director noted for his sparkling sense of humor, impeccable taste, and the indefinable "Lubitsch touch." One can begin by viewing *Passion (Madame Dubarry)*, one of his earliest German film successes, made in 1919, with Emil Jannings and Pola Negri. It is unusual for a silent, particularly a German silent set in historical times, to be so light and tightly paced—but that was what set Lubitsch apart from his colleagues. Then one can view one of his Hollywood silent films—*The Marriage Circle* or *Lady Windemere's Fan*—and see how he brought his subtle hand to high comedy in this country. (In his excellent book, *The Lubitsch Touch*, Herman G. Weinberg explains the effect Lubitsch had on other Hollywood directors after scoring such a success in America.) Next one can view the director's first talkie, *The Love Parade* (1929) with Maurice Chevalier and Jeanette MacDonald, which not only is further affirmation of the Lubitsch touch, but a testament to his complete knowledge of film— few other early talkies move so smoothly, completely unburdened by the new and cumbersome addition of sound. A final tribute to the talent of this director can be seen in *The Man I Killed (Broken Lullaby)*, his only drama, made in 1932. A box office failure when it was first released, it remains a stirring, emotional film today, a powerful indictment of war with a very contemporary ring to it. It shows how the Lubitsch touch was not just limited to frothy comedies and lighthearted musicals and proves (if such proof is still necessary) what a genuinely great director Ernst Lubitsch was.

The same process can be used with an actor—Gary Cooper, for example. Cooper drifted into films with no previous acting experience and was hired mainly because of his good looks. But in following his career one sees how completely Cooper was able to learn his craft through constant experience. The Museum of Modern Art's notes on *The Virginian* (1929) include this evaluation: "Gary Cooper's first all-talkie, the picture reveals that intimate accord with the camera and microphone which made him one of the few really great screen actors." It is possible to follow Cooper from *The Virginian* through *Design for Living*, where he tackled sophisticated comedy for the first time; *Mr. Deeds Goes to Town*, where he firmly nailed down the all-American, virile but basically backward personality he was to project for so many years; *Sergeant York*, his Academy Award-winning role; and *For Whom the Bell Tolls*, one of his finest screen portrayals in a beautifully filmed adaptation of the Hemingway novel. In the 1950s Cooper starred in such diverse pictures as *The Hanging Tree*, an intelligent and starkly dramatic Western, and *Love in the Afternoon*, in which Cooper proved that age has little to do with genuine charm and, to use a more modern term, charisma.

The world of film is so rich, so bountiful, that it seems a shame to confine study of the subject to a preordained handful of films and film makers. By opening the doors to a wider, freer examination of film's past, the student can learn everything there is to know about the medium—but what is more, to my mind, he can learn to love it as I have.

Leonard Maltin is the Editor-Publisher of "Film Fan Monthly."

Film Aesthetics in the Curriculum

Katherine McKee, S.S.N.D.

Woodrow Wilson is quoted as saying that the University should make "young gentlemen as unlike their fathers as possible." Yesterday's advice is today's reality; whether it is happening by direction or indirection is another inquiry.

All living organisms change. All people and institutions must consciously and conscientiously pursue change or face obsolescence. Today every large organization "diversifies," i.e., it invests a portion of its budget in research and development. In effect, this means pursuing change. What about the academic curriculum which excludes film study? Such a curriculum is *approaching* obsolescence.

When one asks why, he receives many answers. Here are a few. Since young people raised with ever present portable radio and television can concentrate on multiple sights and sounds, they are seeking, without the use of conventional plot or text, the aesthetics of a new language and inquiring into the nature of man. About this

Reprinted from *Today's Speech* 18:3(Summer 1970), 18-22.

new phenomenon Anthony Schillaci observes that "the young are digging the strong humanism of the current film renaissance and allowing its currents to carry them to a level deeper than that reached by previous generations; one might almost say that young people are going to the film maker's work for values that they have looked for in vain from the social, political, or religious establishments."[1] Henry Mueller voices the belief of many educators "that the film is as capable of producing as wide a variety of works as is the printing press."[2] At the Aspen Film Conference, William Arrowsmith began his contribution with the idea that film study "will challenge and eventually claim the place and prestige accorded to literature and the arts in the traditional curriculum."[3] These views converge in Vincent Lanier's statement that "the primary art form used by art education in 1978 will be film where the primary purpose of much of this study and production will be to deal visually, dramatically, and artistically with social problems."[4]

Such procedures require a film aesthetic. For each film type "we need a separate aesthetic, as we do for the various products of the press."[5] It is film aesthetics that is my immediate concern here. This subject is not new in the curriculum. As early as October 1965, Professor Hugh Gray from the University of California reported on his film aesthetics course at the Dartmouth Conference on Film Study in Higher Education. About the sensitivity of the whole area of film aesthetics in the curriculum he acknowledged: "In this area one must walk cautiously, humbly, experimentally, expecting for the moment no more than tentative conclusions. On the other hand one must be buoyed up with the 'feeling,' the 'sense,' the hunch, if you like, that there is indeed something there."[6]

Among the many reasons for the uncertain position of film aesthetics in the curriculum are the lowly origin and background of film and dearth of critical writing about the educational uses of film. Since film is only now developing a sense of its historical growth, aestheticians can lay hold of only a small body of critical writing on film technique and art. Film is an extremely young art form and its theory remains largely unformulated; there is scant critical tradition. Forrest Williams of the University of Colorado at Boulder considers "that the American tradition of film criticism is irresponsible because most film critics show no interest in distinguishing between film as art and film as entertainment or information. There are a number of French and Italian writings which show a keen sense for the importance of film as an artistic medium; many of these are generally unknown in the United States. I think that the appearance in English of some or all of the following [and then he lists thirteen French and eight Italian untranslated works on film aesthetics] might well raise the level of film culture in this country. Film culture doesn't only come from seeing more and better films; it also comes from sensitive discourse about cinema."[7]

Borrowing Professor Williams' terminology of "sensitive discourse," I like to think that "sensitive discourse" is the vehicle through which the students become aware of the formal elements which comprise film aesthetics. This "sensitive discourse" will necessarily consider "reality" and "structure," the "what" and the "how" which every speech teacher knows are the primary stuff in communication. However, the serious problem for the aesthetician of film is the composite nature of the art form. Film takes on the nature of sculpture when it deals with three-dimensional plastic figures; of painting when it captures visible forms; the rhythm in its editing makes film a cousin of music; its articulated story line is prose and its contemplation of images is poetry; the drama of man's encounter with man injects an element of the theatre. Susanne Langer in *Feeling and Form* calls this synthetic quality of film its "omnivorous" characteristic.[8] It assumes other arts into itself and transforms them into something different. It is much the same process as music fusing with poetry to produce song, something quite new and quite different from either of its direct ancestors. If film contains elements of all these arts, and yet is something different from all of them, then the aesthetician must use a distinct and new form of criticism; the language of painting, photography, ballet, or the novel cannot be used to discuss film without serious distortion. The new existent, with its many ancestors,

should then be the object of a new aesthetic investigation.

In the absence of a satisfactory formal book of film aesthetics,[9] the teacher may choose to organize the course into the two already mentioned components: *reality* and *structure*. Reality, in the broad sense, is the study of man *and* of the enhancement or destruction of his "humanity." A film aesthetician would discount or disqualify those directors who give things priority rather than the people as the loci of values and sources of power. For such film makers, man is naked without his artifacts. Things stand for different values, they are potent, they are what is destroyed, and they are the indispensable tools for repelling the alien invaders. Films, at this naive level, temper the sense of otherness and of alienness with the grossly familiar. Such films violate the criterion of *reality* for film aesthetics.

For the presentation of reality, the film maker has to filter the chaos of sensation and propose an abstracted meaning. He selects bits and pieces of reality and by fusing them into a new form says something new and significant. Structure, then, is not only regrettably inevitable for a filmic reproduction of reality, but it is to be embraced and used as the only possible means of unveiling humanity. With structure, there is art and reality; without it, chaos.

Artistic descriptions of reality are cast in molds that derive not so much from the subject matter itself as from the properties of the medium. Even the most elementary processes of vision do not produce mechanical recordings of the outer world but organize the sensory raw material creatively according to principles of simplicity, regularity, and balance, which govern the receptor mechanisms. The film director requires a special kind of eye, a special kind of feeling about the relationship between things and things, events and events, and an intuitive as well as empirical knowledge of how to make the camera catch what his eye sees and his imagination creates.

It must be noted again that while the film exceeds all other media in verisimilitude, its reality is nevertheless a mode. The film maker uses the surfaces of life itself—literal photographic images and accurately reproduced sounds. But the arrangement of these images and sounds is totally controlled. Each moment, each detail is carefully coordinated into the structure of the whole—just like the details in a painting or poem. By artfully controlling his images, the film maker presents an unbroken realistic surface; he preserves the appearance of reality.

But film in its finished state is more than a series of photographs; what results from the arrangement is an edited montage, a series of shots and sequences with a rhythm of its own and a diffusion in time. From all possible shots and from all possible combinations of montage, the film maker abstracts the one inevitable form to give expression to his vision.

In the light of our definition of film aesthetics, an important part of the course is the analysis of films with particular reference to: (1) the techniques and methods that produce the "aesthetic effect" (this would include the "spatial art" of painting, the "temporal art" of music, the "dramatic art" of the theater); and (2) style as it is exemplified in the works of various outstanding directors. There are almost as many styles as there are film directors, so I will elucidate this phase as I suggest possible units of study for the course. These units of study necessarily

The Seventh Seal

will not be complete nor can they be given an explanation here other than a short qualifying description.

Fortified by a grant from the American Film Institute, I conducted a film aesthetics course with the following units of study:

1. *Swedish Ingmar Bergman's Filmmaking.* Film has developed into an art where the personality of the individual artist puts its stamp on the work. The film has learned to write. As an artist in film Bergman interprets and transfers his private dreams and imagining to the screen. As an artist he is firmly anchored in a Swedish and European tradition in which Strindberg, Kafka, and Proust were pioneers. He has succeeded in convincing not only a cultured, intellectual world, but also masses of people who perhaps know nothing of the spiritual background of his work.

2. *Italian Directors beyond Neorealism.* Fellini wanted his camera to look at "any kind of reality: not just social reality, but also spiritual reality, metaphysical reality, anything man has inside him."

Like his hero in *La Dolce Vita* and 8½, Fellini is unable to make a commitment in so sick a world as he finds around him. This has become the theme of his work, and it typifies the position of the whole avant-garde movement of our time. To those who would question so unresolved a position, it could be said that a lack of commitment to a way of life or to a social context or to a definite philosophy is not a lack of commitment of oneself.

Not concerned with a film of exterior surfaces but with interior realism, Antonioni's *L'Avventura* depicts an emptiness at the heart of modern society. In 1960 he was less concerned with accurately recording the surface social realities than were others in the original neorealism tradition. Since 1960 Antonioni has continued to re-create in filmatic terms the metaphors of human anonymity and impermanence in a changing world.

3. *French "New Wave": Francois Truffaut, Jean Luc Godard, Alain Resnais.* Nicknamed the "new wave" of French moviemaking, the films of Francois Truffaut, Jean Luc Godard, and Alain Resnais display a youthful and imaginative approach to the problems of young persons afloat in a world not of their making and totally unacceptable to them. In an attempt to find meaning for their lives, these young people drift from experience to experience often giving way to emotional and physical excesses. While these directors lack a sense of direction in thematic development, still their concern for the problems of human communication gives their films a vitality and urgency often lacking in the productions of more traditional film makers.

These young men are responsible for the development of the "auteur," the all-around film creator who, whatever the source of his materials and whatever collaborators he may take to help him realize his intentions, is essentially responsible himself for the whole film from initial conception to end product. Truffaut and Godard are examples of the complete film creator while Resnais is an interesting example of the pure *mettaur en scene* who seeks to collaborate with a series of notable writers on absolutely equal terms.

4. *Japanese Films of Ozu, Mizoguchi, Kurosawa.* Although one experiences the tremendous impact that Western civilization, especially a democratic form of government, has had upon the Japanese since World War II, it is the brilliant and varied filmmaking techniques (combined with stories which have several layers of meaning) that makes Japanese film so pleasing aesthetically. Moreover, it isn't the strong sense of movement, the rhythm, the editing and other virtuosity in the Japanese film which is so artistically satisfying, but rather the superior kinds of energy, vitality, and expressiveness which are incarnated in its style. Because the film style projects the complex movement of intelligence, grace, and sensuousness, these major film artists of Japan transcend the categories of propaganda or even reportage. One thing worth noting is that the pace and rhythm of many Japanese films are more leisurely and contemplative than those of American films.

5. *England's "Angry Young Men."* With her "angry young men" movement, England too has broken traditional thematic patterns. Writers like John Osborne, Alan Sillitoe, Shelagh Delaney and Stan Barstow have been translated by directors Tony Richardson, Karel Reisz, and John Schlesinger into strong cinema propaganda on behalf of a new generation of Englishmen. *Look Back in Anger* (1959), *The Entertainer* (1960), *Saturday Night and Sunday Morning* (1961), *A Taste of Honey* (1962), *A Kind of Loving* (1962), and *The Loneliness of the Long Distance Runner* (1962) display the younger generation's attitude toward the Establishment. Lindsay Anderson's *This Sporting Life* (1962) indicates a possible new trend in the "angry" approach, in that he seems to be as interested in how he presents something as in what he is presenting.

6. *Science Fiction.* Science fiction films are not necessarily about science. They are about disaster, which is one of the oldest subjects of art. The science fiction film is concerned with the aesthetics of destruction, with the peculiar beauties to be found in wreaking havoc, making a mess. It is in the imagery of destruction that the core of good science fiction film lies. Visually there is little difference between mass havoc as represented in the old horror and monster films and what we find in the science fiction films. A kind of satisfaction which these films supply is extreme moral simplification—a morally acceptable fantasy where one can give outlet to cruel or at least amoral feelings. These films invite a dispassionate, aesthetic view of destruction and violence—a technological view.

7. *Different Treatments of Same Subject: Race Relations.* Race relations (or lack of them) is an outstanding

example of an area in which films can provide understanding and emotional impact to a degree unobtainable in any other medium. Not until very recently did films on the Negro, integration and civil rights begin to live up to this potential. Nicholas Webster's *A Walk in My Shoes*, made for ABC-TV, is a fine film profile of the Negro community in the United States. William Jersey's *A Time for Burning* recorded in *cinéma vérité* style a white Lutheran minister's attempt to establish a visiting program with Negro Lutheran churches in Omaha, Nebraska. Shortly after this film, *Troublemakers* appeared again in *cinéma vérité* style. The fourth major film on the Negro was *Lay My Burden Down* by Jack Willis for NET Television.

Although these productions differ markedly in tone, pacing, cadence, and techniques, their directors had in common the ability to discover and capture on film individuals who through gesture, expression, and speech reveal something universal about the human condition.

8. *Different Treatments of Same Subject: War.* One of the most pressing problems facing the contemporary world is war. A teacher can explore this problem with students in a challenging way calculated to evoke thoughtful, critical response through the use of contemporary film. He can combat the subtle way in which war is often glorified on television. Unrealistic combat series on television contain much of the challenge and excitement of war but little of the sickness, suffering, and death. Some films question war as a solution to human

Ballad of a Soldier

problems, making strong comments through allegory and example. There are many film treatments: experimental and conventional, animated and traditionally photographed, documentary and feature. The question of individual responsibility arises in considering war as a social inevitability or an avoidable evil. When war is perceived as a choice, peace becomes an alternative.

9. *Experimental Films both American and Foreign.* These films exhibit intensified introspection: concern with exploration of the individual as a universe. There is

more emphasis on inner conflict than between classified confrontation of individual antagonists. At a time when technological and power structures challenge individualism, the individuals' minds and souls have become of prime interest. Technology has outraced self-discovery. Some exhibit experiment for its own sake; they regard it as a value instead of a means to value. The films show a release of different forms of consciousness as well as reaction on several levels against pressures of our culture. At the same time the films demonstrate both more spiritual and physical involvement; their makers believe that their conscious and deep images are reuniting man himself. The films project genuine experience and direct visions.

Works of American independent film makers include some by Stan Brakhage, Robert Breer, Bruce Conner, Bruce Baille, Kenneth Anger, Robert Nelson, and Edward Ames. Some foreign experimental films to explore are those by Chris Marker, Richard Lester, Valerian Borowczyk, Guido Bettiol, Yoji Kuri, Tadeusz Wilkoz, and Wolfgang Urchs.

10. *Young Hero on the Screen: American and Foreign.* Certain general questions are bound to arise: why do we have heroes, what function do they serve, are they "models," "ideal types," people with whom we "identify"? What is the common social experience, the "structure of feeling" which gives rise, at a particular point in time, to the introverted young rebel, the "hero without a

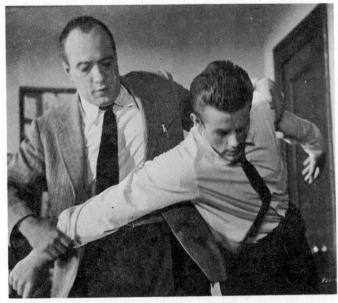

Rebel Without a Cause

cause": Brando, in that telling sequence from *On the Waterfront,* the rituals of the teenage dream in James Dean's *Rebel Without a Cause,* and then the startling appearance, out of a totally different background and in a wholly alien setting, of that Dean-like hero in Wadja's film *Ashes and Diamonds?* Within this broad social connection, the contrast between the heroes—indeed the whole mood and style and feeling—in Wadja's two films about young Poles, *Ashes and Diamonds* and *A Generation,* forces the students to relate the social interest to the artistic experience, and forces the connections between their general interests and the kind of truth and insight which they experience from attending closely to the screen. Worthwhile is the exploration of youth-oriented films such as *The Graduate, Wild in the Streets, Easy Rider,* and *Petulia* for their criticism of the age-old pattern of an adult generation resting on its hard-won creature comforts and fudging on its own moral standards (sex, materialism, drink, racism).

Let me close by saying that I think the mission of the teacher of film aesthetics goes far beyond mere artistic analysis. Because film has a potential for stating our cultural problems, complexities, anxieties, and powers naturally and comprehensively, it seems a natural adjunct —an adjunct to a curriculum-in-process—with which to supplement much that is now taught in literature, philosophy, psychology, and speech. Since film manifests man's continuous psychosocial evolution, film aesthetics in the curriculum should be a legitimate academic concern of educators.

Notes

1. Anthony Schillaci, 'Film as Environment," *Saturday Review* (December 28, 1968), p. 11.
2. Henry Mueller, "Film as Art," *The Journal of Aesthetic Education* 3(January 1969), p. 72.
3. William Arrowsmith, "Film as Educator," *The Journal of Aesthetic Education* 3(July 1969), p. 75.
4. Vincent Lanier, "Parameters of Change," *Arts and Activities* 62(September 1968) p. 28.
5. Henry Mueller, op. cit., p. 72.
6. David C. Stewart (ed.), *Film Study in Higher Education* (Washington, D.C.: American Council on Education, 1966), p. 69.
7. Forrest Williams, "Report from Boulder," *American Film Institute Newsletter* 2(April 1970), p. 4.
8. Quoted in Richard Dyer MacCann, *Film: A Montage of Theories* (New York: E.P. Dutton & Co., Inc., 1966), p. 199.
9. Some teachers of film study consider Ralph Stephenson and J. R. Debrix's *The Cinema as Art* (Baltimore: Penguin Books, 1969) an excellent book for a film aesthetics course.

Sister Katherine McKee, SSND, is affiliated with Notre Dame College, St. Louis, Missouri.

Using Films in Teaching English Composition

Adele H. Stern

Film is its own reason for being. It is an art form as much a part of our daily lives as literature, architecture, painting, or sculpture. But, because we are exposed to film in a set of circumstances which exclude distractions —a darkened room—it involves our senses completely. We are focused on a screen . . . and we feel, we hear, we see in an all-encompassing tangle of emotions and senses which no other art form demands. Just because film is so demanding of us—whether it be the "hotter" version of the local cinema or the "cooler" version of the television screen, it provides a powerful motivational device for the teaching of written composition.

All of the forms of writing—exposition, literary criticism, narration, dialogue, description, even poetry—can be found in parallels in film and provide stimulation for a composition program. We can say to students just about what we say about books, "What does the film say?" "How is it said?" "Did you like it?" And, most important of all, "Why did you like it?" "Or dislike it?" And they can answer in their writing.

Reprinted from *English Journal* 57:5(May 1968) 646-648.

If students learn to look at films, they can criticize validly—react to the characters, understand a metaphor, enjoy or resist a plot, appreciate a theme. The result will be not a book report, but a film review. The review contains references to scenery, character, plot, and action, as well as to theme. It comments on the director's techniques and may make reference to other films by the same director or other films of the same nature.

I suppose every high school teacher of English, at one time or another, has discussed with a class the theme of a popular movie. Many teachers in recent years have been able to bring into the classroom, through rental, such stimulating films as *A Raisin in the Sun*, *David and Lisa*, *The 400 Blows*, and *The Red Badge of Courage*. Any one of these, and an infinite number of others, can provide challenging discussion ideas which immediately, or eventually, lead to written composition.

Sometimes students want to talk about a film before they write about it. Sometimes the impact is so dramatic, so personal, that students want time to think about what they have seen, to muse on the values they have seen expressed, and with no prior discussion may wish to express their personal reactions on paper. If the film is exciting and dramatic, if the student has been personally touched by it, it will give him something he needs to say. And the composition will reveal the feelings and emotions of the writer. This is a far cry from the teacher's imposition of a topic, "Discuss the nature of good

A Raisin in the Sun

and evil in *Billy Budd*." Students will find their own theses, and they will use the film, much as they have used the book in the past, to support their contentions.

After having seen *Nobody Waved Goodbye* (the sensitive portrayal of a Canadian teenager who rebels against the comfortable middle-class society in which he lives, growing farther and farther away from his be-

Nobody Waved Goodbye

Vietnam, and teenage rebellion—all this, without the teacher's having to propose a list of teacher-made topics.

Because the screen has the power to involve the viewer so completely, students write about what they have seen more effectively than they might write about what they have read in print. No longer is it necessary to say, "This doesn't make sense," when students are trying to write what they think we want them to write. Books are our palaces; films are their pads. Students are far less self-conscious with the movie—more direct, more honest.

Such films as *The Ox-Bow Incident, The Hangman, The House,* and *The Critic,* make comments on the social structure of society, on man in relation to man, on the nature of man. Books do this, too, of course, but if we show a film, we are sure the student has seen the film (How sure are we that he has read the book?), and we can count on a reaction. We have a common reference point. We can write and then compare impressions. Because we are concerned in viewing a film with time and space and the use of both, because we have overcome the impediment of literary vocabulary, we give the students (endowed and deprived) a mutual experience on which they can comment. In their own words, then, they can discuss on paper the impact of the film, its effectiveness, its message (if it has one), its validity.

In teaching composition, we are concerned with the aspects of form and content. We have, in the past, discussed the styles of writers in relation to the content of

wildered, well-meaning, but not understanding parents, until he breaks himself off entirely from respectability, from the teenage girl friend whom he leaves pregnant, and cuts once and for all time the ties to any constructive future), students have chosen to write their opinions on such varied subjects as middle-class morality, the generation gap, the values of contemporary society, the war in a book or an essay. Film provides us with another medium in which to observe the merging of form and content. A film maker, like a writer, develops a particular style. He uses the camera and the actors to convey the image and idea. He edits the film and structures the entire work to create the impression he wishes to convey. Careful looking at and educated talking about the film —the director's use of scenery and shots, the transitions, the expression and movement of the actors, the position and use of the camera—will create an awareness in the students of how the artist uses his tools, of the choices he makes to create an effect.

It is relatively simple, then, to transfer from the film to the student's own writing the use of the specific word, the placement of a phrase, the structure of an essay.

A short film such as *Glass*, which compares the artistic production of the glass blowers with the commercial manufacture of factory glass, presents a series of choices to determine what the director is saying about individual artistic endeavor as compared with factory line production. From this, it is a short step to the teaching of comparison and contrast in writing.

Levels of fantasy, dream, and reality are exposed in *No Reason to Stay*, which is about a school dropout, a film which also develops a character by choices of examples. An incident in a history class, an experience with a girl in a car, the talk with a guidance counselor, the visit to his mother's office, an impulsive dash to the

The Pawnbroker

principal's office—all of these are used to build the frustration of the boy who is looking for a reason to stay in school but cannot find one. Isn't this exactly what we tell our students in teaching them to write a character sketch? "Show the person in action. Don't tell about him. Let your reader see him react to an experience."

The House, another short film, and *The Pawnbroker*, a long one, make use of the flashback in the narration. Students should look carefully at the points at which the transitions are made, so in their own writing they can insert the flashback where it most validly belongs.

We teach students that every writer assumes a "speaking voice," and we attempt to discover that "voice" in a book. The film director assumes a "voice" as well, and the choices of detail are determined by the nature of that voice. In *The House*, a series of flashbacks shows the experiences of an old house which is about to be demolished. The point of view is that of the house; it is the house that has experienced all of the incidents which determined the development of the life of the family that inhabited it. Only those things which the house could "know" could be shown on the screen. The student's own writing must adhere consistently to the "speaking voice" of the piece. And the film has given him an object lesson.

In a book, a student can *see* dialect. Only if he reads it aloud can he *hear* it. An interesting exercise is to have a student see and hear a film such as *Huckleberry Finn* or *Hud* or *On the Waterfront* and then write down some of the dialogue as he has heard it. Thus, he develops an awareness of the nature of dialect—which syllables are emphasized or deleted or inflected. Writers of dialect pieces have often said that they spoke the dialogue aloud before they wrote it down. Film does this for our students.

While the satirical tone might be difficult to pick up in a novel, even a poorly language-oriented student can easily distinguish satire in a film. For one thing, the

Hud

music frequently gives it away. Animated cartoons, *The Critic, The Adventures of an *, The Hand, Unicorn in the Garden,* are satires on things many people take seriously: abstract art, invasion of privacy, the secret life. "What do you see that makes you know the film maker is being critical?" "Again, what details in your own theme imply satire?"

And, now, poetry. We use the word *image.* This is the heart of the poem. It implies a use of the senses, mainly of sight and sound. The screen offers us a plethora of images which we can use to form metaphor. *The Leaf* and *Very Nice, Very Nice,* two short films very different from each other, offer a contrast in tone and in feeling and suggest many possibilities for the teaching of metaphor. The film, being a very personal thing, presenting one image after another, can evoke an emotional response which might lead to a young poet's muse . . . that is, if the teacher is willing to offer the film and let the muse do its work.

Film has enormous possibilities for the teacher of written composition. All he has to do is look and give his students a chance to look and he will see writing skills visually delineated and an infinite number of topics which are relevant to the student's own experience.

Films in Teaching Composition
Suggested Films for Stimulating Written Composition

Distributor	Film Titles
Audio Film Center 34 MacQuesten Parkway So. Mount Vernon, N.Y. 10550	*A Raisin in the Sun* (128 minutes) *On the Waterfront* (108 minutes) *A Unicorn in the Garden* (10 minutes) *The Pawnbroker* (114 minutes)
Brandon Films, Inc. 221 West 57th Street New York, N.Y. 10019	*The Critic* (5 minutes)
Contemporary Films 330 West 42nd Street New York, N.Y. 10036	*Hangman* (12 minutes) *The House* (32 minutes) *Adventures of an ** (10 minutes) *The Hand* (19 minutes) *Last Leaf* (20 minutes) *Very Nice, Very Nice* (7 minutes) *The String Bean* (17 minutes)
Continental Film Productions 2330 Rossville Boulevard Chattanooga, Tenn. 37408	*David and Lisa* (90 minutes)

Encyclopaedia Britannica
   Films
425 North Michigan Avenue
Chicago, Ill. 60611

No Reason To Stay
   (28 minutes)

Films, Inc.
1144 Wilmette Avenue
Wilmette, Illinois 60091

The Red Badge of Courage
   (69 minutes)
The Ox-Bow Incident
   (75 minutes)
Glass (11 minutes)
Hud (112 minutes)

Janus Films, Inc.
267 West 25th Street
New York, N.Y. 10001

The 400 Blows
   (98 minutes)

National Film Board
   of Canada
680 Fifth Avenue
New York, N.Y. 10019

Nobody Waved Goodbye
   (80 minutes)

United World Films, Inc.
221 Park Avenue
New York, N.Y. 10003

Huckleberry Finn
   (71 minutes)

Adele H. Stern is the Chairman of the English Department at Montclair High School, Montclair, New Jersey.

...And Beyond

And what lies ahead? Will the use of films in the classroom turn out to be nothing more than a fad and disappear once again? Will we reach the stage where we show *Easy Rider* and perhaps even *I Am Curious (Yellow)* in the classroom? Will libraries become movie theatres? Will the reel replace the book? Ronald E. Sutton suggests what might be seen if one only had a crystal ball in good working order....

Film Study: The Seventies and Beyond

Ronald E. Sutton

There are three basic needs that face film study as the seventies open before us. They are *definition, teacher training,* and *materials.*

In the area of definition, there exists a need for educators to say quite simply what they mean by film study. This and related terms are covering quite a lot of ground today. Clearly and concisely, we need to say what we aim for when we teach under the general banner of film study. Why are we doing it? With whom are we doing it? What is it exactly that we *are* doing? We need to be as descriptive as possible so that others can learn from our experience.

Film is being used by educators in schools in a variety of different ways. It will continue to be employed as an instructional tool, viewed simply as an audio-visual aid supplementing other media of communication such as lectures, readings, or demonstrations. It will undoubtedly continue to be used by some to motivate the unmotivated to read and write. And as a motivation for the language arts, films of substance and impact have an important role to play.

Some teachers will take this one step further in the modern language arts or communications curriculum. In addition to having the student learn reading and writing, and listening and speaking, they will also help the student to understand or "read" visual images and learn how to respond by creating visual images. I suppose the concept of "visual literacy" comes in here, though it is a term that causes one increasing discomfort as to its exact meaning. My colleague, Jim Kitses, gave quite a simple, if obvious, definition of the term in a speech at a National Conference on Film Study held in early April 1970 at the University of Cincinnati. He said that visual literacy in the context of film study is "an acquaintanceship with the people who make film, their films, and a way of talking about them. . . . The real problem about being visually literate has nothing to do with sense ratios, has nothing to do with editing and camera angles, and so on. It *has* got to do with knowing how to talk about a film." Film in this approach will get its due as an artistic form, but the literary link will be present in greater or lesser degree depending upon the teacher and his training.

Film study will also take place as a study of our times, past and present. In social science or humanities or inter-disciplinary electives, artistic statements will be discussed as comments on and expressions of the nature and destiny of man.

Film will also be examined as one facet of the media presently shaping our environment. The approach here will be on the medium as well as the message, and the experience will seem incomplete if students are prevented from exploring their environments with cameras in hand.

Rarely in secondary school, but with increasing frequency at the junior college and college level, film will be taught fully and completely as an art form. Supported by extensive but carefully chosen screenings, the body of material that is film will be examined by students. They will grapple with film history, film aesthetics, and film criticism. These students will join their teachers in creating a critical body of writing and research that will support the development of film as a discipline of study in its own right.

In spite of a few prophetic warnings, I see little danger that this general process of definition and clarification will destroy the power and delight that has drawn so many of us to the study and teaching of film. If we approach our task in the proper spirit of dialogue, we should provide checks upon one another. Let's also hope that we can learn from the past experiences that proved fatal to other disciplines attempting to develop an institutional study of a lively art.

A second major area of need is that of leadership education or teacher training. It is of interest to note a statement that serves to open a book published in 1935. The author has just admonished teachers that their concern in film study should be the same as with any other form of the drama, "a concern with the subject content that is presented and with the manner in which this content is expressed."[1] The author then adds a few pages later that:

> The English or dramatics teacher says, "I know so little about motion picture appreciation." You need not be unduly worried about this, however, for only a few people have much information upon the subject. The available literature is so limited that one can soon become an authority.[2]

This rather cavalier attitude toward professional training reveals that perhaps there was more than the force of World War II that caused the demise of film study in the thirties.

Few would dispute the fact that there is an immense need for well-trained teachers to handle the ever increasing number of courses in screen education. Indeed, many observers feel that more educational institutions would mount courses in film education if only qualified personnel existed to teach them.

The problem related to teacher training in screen education breaks into two parts, inservice and preservice. For those at work in the field there is the need for inservice training opportunities. Conferences, workshops, institutes, seminars, summer schools, and extension courses must be developed in enough quantity and quality to provide necessary training for the educator already at work. This training will increasingly call for commitment and involvement on the part of institutions of higher education. Courses that carry proper accreditation and graduate credit will attract more participants and strengthen the discipline as a whole. At the same time, the nature of film and media should provide some excellent opportunities for experimentation with new modes of teacher training. We are hopeful that some guidelines in this area may emerge from the work the American Film Institute is supporting in the field.

So much for the inservice side of things. One eventually wants to get out of the stopgap atmosphere of inservice training by developing proper educational experiences for teachers at the preservice level. It is imperative that we target our thinking in the seventies toward those colleges and universities providing the bulk of preservice training for the educators of our country's children and youth. If one can get to these headwaters with proper training experiences, the crisis in leadership should pass. Given the teacher training apparatus as it exists, this may be easier said than done.

To illustrate, who is going to convince the trainers of teachers that *they* need further training? Who would train them if they should decide they need such experiences? It seems a vicious circle—lack of leadership fosters lack of leadership.

However, lest the picture appear too bleak, one should not overlook the significant role film/media education can play in equipping the prospective teacher to deal with the students of the twenty-first century. Film/media education is interwoven with a number of necessary educational innovations. The nature of the curriculum, the role of the teacher and student, the relationship of the school to the community, the organization of planned experiences within the curriculum (their duration and scope), the question of evaluation, the matter of relevancy, the integrative aspects of learning, the inductive method, the creative use of resource material, and the concern for interdisciplinary work all come into play when one sets forth a plan for teaching film and media.

It is the hope of many that preservice training will stress the integrated sum of the training-learning experience for the educator-in-training rather than simply linking together a series of unrelated experiences for him like beads on a string. In short, we teach as we are taught!

A final area of need facing film education relates to educational materials. One simply cannot teach film without the proper materials in hand to do it. (It is hoped that as the prior questions of definition and teacher training are solved, they will contribute to stabilization and further development of materials to service a large body of educators.)

As was true ten years ago, the key problem here is the availability of the filmic material itself in easily accessible, inexpensive format that allows for simple projection of high quality. Films are hard to get and are highly priced as educational materials go. The hardware used to project them remains difficult to work with and the conditions for projection and sound continue to range from minimal to impossible.

The Super 8 Optical Sound Cartridge and supporting projector hold some promise toward solving these problems, as does the somewhat more questionable (at least in terms of fidelity regarding image and sound) EVR Cartridge. But technological development and market uncertainty may delay widespread use of such items until the mid-seventies or eighties.

Another aid in teaching film would be the development of well-chosen extracts from feature films. These have been used extensively in film education in England with profit to student and teacher alike. We need an up-to-date series of these made available to educators at modest cost in a workable format. Full-blown films-on-film would also contribute to the cause of film education if they were carefully developed and shot with quality standards of production in mind. These studies would be especially useful in the study of a genre, a decade, or the work of one director over an extended period of time. Finally, there is need for a variety of printed materials to service the film educator's needs. Disposable, newsletter-type material needs to be freely exchanged so screen educators are kept up-to-date on events, materials, and services. Regional groups are encouraged to develop their own vehicles of communication so persons will be aware of local activities.

There is a need for material of a descriptive character that shares specific experiences in film education. A good bit of prescriptive material is available to teachers indicating what they should do, but too little material has been developed that sets forth clearly and simply what happened when a specific film was taught.

The dialogue among leaders in film education should be documented by publications in which philosophy and approach are spelled out and carefully supported. Difference of opinion when set forth thoughtfully can only serve to enhance and clarify what screen education is all about.

There is also a need for basic reference articles. These include an annotated list of 16mm nontheatrical distributors, a list of annotated books (comprehensive and selective), a guide to 8mm filmmaking hardware for secondary schools, a short film list (comprehensive and selective), and so on. The American Film Institute will try to develop many of these needed pieces through the cooperation of related agencies and teachers at work in the field.

It would be helpful if people at work in film education would make known what kinds of other printed material would assist them. This is true for the beginner as well as for the experienced teacher. Some basic guidelines for the development of educational materials to support film education need to be written. Perhaps such guidelines would indicate a need for more writing on film criticism, on film history or aesthetics, and on practical film education matters. It seems unwise to leave all this to the chance production of the book publishers' marketplace.

I have set the three needs in this order because there seems some logical progression to them. That may be deceiving. It goes without saying that all three needs must be attacked simultaneously. It also goes without saying that if it is necessary to establish a priority category, it is certainly that of teacher training. Nothing is more basic to the educational process than a properly prepared teacher. Through work with teachers the other needs will inevitably be faced as well.

It is my conclusion that, armed with proper definition of the subject, reinforced with appropriate training, and equipped with adequate materials, film study will enter the seventies with the promise of continued growth and development.

Notes

1. Elizabeth W. Pollard, *Teaching Motion Picture Appreciation* (Columbus: Bureau of Educational Research, Ohio State University, 1935), p. 3.
2. Ibid., p. 4.

Ronald E. Sutton is the Executive Director of the National Association of Media Educators in Washington, D.C.

...Plus One

The following is an important statement of certain reservations that the future film teacher should keep in mind.

Film as an Academic Subject: Reservations and Reminders

James F. Scott

The American school teacher has begun to discover the cinema at various levels. Film criticism is finding its way into the established quarterlies, new journals are springing up as further publication outlets, organizations from the Modern Language Association to the National Council of Teachers of English have now hosted conferences that feature the screening of films, and Marshall McLuhan has brought both his medium and his message to the cover of *Newsweek*. Indeed, the film has been found. But whether it will react to this discovery as a grateful refugee or a captured spy remains to be seen. I think the response of the film world will depend largely on the attitude of the educational community towards this new candidate for the curriculum.

Already I sense some uneasiness among film makers and students of long standing. Like Mr. Doolittle of *My Fair Lady*, they resent being made respectable. They do not want someone with two or three symbolic letters

Reprinted from *The Quarterly Journal of Speech* 54:2(April 1968) 154-159.

after his surname to come along and take all the fun out of movies. George C. Stoney, speaking from wide teaching experience, puts the case against film in the schools very well: "About teaching film . . . I have this one great fear: that we will finally make it so acceptably academic that it will become as dull and dead as almost every other subject in the liberal arts curriculum."[1] The same objection is made by Pauline Kael, as she reflects upon her difficulty in making up a film course:

> This was what I had gotten interested in movies to get away from. . . . I remembered how my thumbnails got worn down from scraping the paint off my pencils as the teacher droned on about great literature. I remembered music appreciation with the record being played over and over, the needle arm going back and forth, and I remembered the slide machine in art history and the deadly rhythm of the instructor's tapper. And I knew that I could not present a course of study. . . . It goes against the grain of everything I feel about movies, and against the grain of just about everything I believe about how we learn in the arts.[2]

Maybe there's a trace of caricature in these comments, maybe the average schoolmarm is less a bogey man than Miss Kael allows, but I think this skepticism has merit. It at least discourages the snobbish tomfoolery that we have done film a favor by recognizing its existence. It might even persuade us to take a closer look at a school system which provokes such harsh words from such articulate critics.

Most of us hold, theoretically, that education is a process of discovery, not the assimilation of a fixed heritage. Half a century after Dewey, this is a professional cliché, dutifully repeated every time the teaching order gathers for tea. But we all realize, I imagine, there are forces within the system at odds with this ideal. Our texts still have a way of becoming canonical, even if the canon now includes *Catcher in the Rye* as well as *The Return of the Native* or *Adam Bede*. Though we are all familiar with Cleanth Brooks's rejection of "the heresy of paraphrase," we go on, much like Brooks himself, earnestly grinding up every poem in sight to create those paraphrases we supposedly disapprove of. In practice, it seems, our interest in the neat syllabus, the thoroughly covered lesson, takes priority over commitment to the free play of mind. The urge to prepare the high school students for college, the college student for graduate study, readily displaces the faith in education as a self-validating activity. There follows the inevitable student reaction: grade consciousness, the search for orthodoxy, and the purchase of *Cliff's Notes*. For many young people who feel this pressure, the film is one of the few remaining refuges of the unstructured, spontaneous response. We should not take this away from them just to collect more material for the various qualifying exams.

Perhaps I am putting the prospects a bit too grimly, but I want very much to bring the basic issue into focus. It would be much better to leave cinema out of the curriculum than to include it as only another subject for which we compose handbooks and draw up outlines, and which we then chop into hunks that will fit between one bell and another. Literature sometimes survives this, the novel or the play miraculously living through its dismemberment into fifty page units. But if we take up the film in this same expectation, I think that will be pressing our luck.

I do detect, however, among those considering the film as an academic subject, a willingness to explore new approaches which might neutralize some of these objections. We might eventually persuade ourselves that the whole humanities program needs overhauling, but right now it is more important to reinforce the inclination to experiment that usually characterizes the approach of the academic film buff. Most people working with film in the classroom know they are dealing with a medium especially dear to the American adolescent and are ready to suspend some rules of the pedagogical game. Besides, they also sense that the adolescent, by virtue of his immense exposure to television, is probably better oriented to the visual rhetoric of cinema than the average teacher. This minimizes authoritarian prescripts and helps make teaching a colloquy, not a catechism lesson. But the best intentions still require guidance, which I hope, in a

provisional way, these remarks might help supply.

Apropos of film and the curriculum, I find myself coming back to three points, the first having relevance to the teacher as viewer; the second, to the teacher as theoretician; and the third, to the teacher as exhibitor, projectionist, and program chairman: (1) as to viewing, we should be open to the full visual and sensory experience, not just the verbals and their imagistic ornamentation; (2) as to theorizing, we should proceed inductively and skeptically towards a film aesthetic, regarding all prefabricated systems of film criticism, even those framed by reputed authorities, with some reserve; and (3) as to scheduling and exhibiting, we should experiment with as many different arrangements as possible, taking advantage of all manner of screening situations and teaching strategies. These are merely commonsensical norms, but their implications agitate some rather troubled waters.

"The film," says Ingmar Bergman, "has nothing to do with literature." If so, men of letters must have trouble getting at it. And I fear this is so. Most of our training makes us verbal people, whose intellectual orientation is decidedly bookish. Some of us manage to draw back far enough from the printed page to see what Yeats means in calling poetry "great masses of sound" and to realize that alliteration and assonance imply something other than the piling up of similar letters in a typed line. Furthermore, when it comes to film, we undoubtedly make an effort to appraise the contribution of photography, music, and composition. But the crucial word is *effort*. Our conditioned reflexes impel us to attend to the dialogue, treating everything else as supplementary. The test lies in the films we take seriously. In the majority of cases, I suspect, we define serious films as those in which the people in front of the cameras talk about serious things.

This point was recently brought home to me at a series of educators' screenings which invited comparison of several films, among them one decidedly theatrical work, *A Man for All Seasons*, and a completely musical and painterly creation, *Black Orpheus*. By a count of nearly four to one, the educators preferred the former film, largely, I fear, on grounds that confuse cinema with debate. Not that *A Man for All Seasons* is a bad film: for a stage play that has been adapted to the screen it is unusually effective. Intercut footage of woods and water reinforces the verbal metaphors of land and sea which were unrecognized by many stage audiences; skillful angling of the camera often creates a kind of symbolic decor, as when King Henry's vanity is emphasized in a shot that rings his crown with rays of the setting sun. All this, however, is chiefly for the purpose of heightening the film's forensic values, epitomized in the performance of Paul Scofield. *Black Orpheus,* on the other hand, is an entirely different kind of work, not immediately intelligible through its rhetoric. It is a serious film, as humanly substantial as the collected works of Mircea Eliade, but its form is nonverbal. Meaning reposes not so much in conversational exchanges as in the dynamic interplay of color and costume, the unexplicated significance of astrological emblems, and the emotional force fields achieved through choreography and musical rhythm. *Black Orpheus* brilliantly renders the myth of eternal return, the drama of a people who live on cyclic time. But because the film lacks what we usually call

A Man for All Seasons

Black Orpheus

"issues" its importance seems to have been lost on an audience of language-oriented educators.

Our tendency to devalue films like *Black Orpheus* betokens a deeper problem: we rarely regard expressive movement as a species of statement. Socially this may account for widespread hostility to the watusi and the frug, which are dynamically expressive in themselves, and generally nostalgic longing for waltzes of the 1940s, which existed as an excuse for intimate conversation. Apropos of the cinema, this verbal bias inhibits our ap-

preciating most comedy, even the best work of Chaplin, to say nothing of the Marx brothers or Buster Keaton, all of which depends upon gesture and pose. And beyond that, it invites overvaluation of films such as those of Ingmar Bergman, because of their protracted philosophical dialogues, and the concommitant neglect of directors who depend more upon compositional and rhythmic effects—Resnais, Godard, Antonioni. In thus limiting the range of our artistic sympathies, we pay dearly for our favoritism towards narrative and argument.

If verbalism is one vice of pedagogy, system-making is another. The ambition to organize is intellectually wholesome, but, like the cult of physical fitness, it can become a species of compulsion. Now if, as the psychologists say, we are most susceptible to compulsion during periods of insecurity, what could be more predictable than the present enthusiasm for codifying knowledge of the cinema, reducing its multiple possibilities to a few easily memorized rules. Unfortunately, persons initiating themselves to film study and anxious to make the right beginning often fasten upon the first set of principles cast in their path. The result is a premature synthesis of film aesthetics, which leads to interpretation of today's innovation according to yesterday's precedents, or worse, to a drastically oversimplified description of what yesterday's precedents really were.

One of the most delusively attractive of such principles is the supposition that a chart can be assembled to identify the import of all cinematic strategies—the significance of camera angles and ranges, the dramatic effect of high and low contrast lighting, the meaning of movements towards and away from the camera. According to this approach, low angles, because they elongate an image, always confer stature of authority, while high angles flatten the subject and thus diminish his importance; long range shooting establishes and orients, while close-ups reveal symbolic details or the psychological ambiguities implicit in facial expression; a thrust towards the camera suggests command of the dramatized situation, while movements away from the camera connote weakness, a surrender to circumstance or environment. This line of argument has recently been popularized by Professor Edward Fischer in a series of instructional films designed to give shape to education in the appreciation of cinema. (The films of which I speak are those distributed by OFM Productions: *Elements of the Film, Film as Visual Language, Nature of Film Medium,* and *Film as Art.* A more flexible approach characterizes Professor Fischer's *The Screen Arts: A Guide to Film and Television Appreciation,*[3] but unfortunately this book seems less well known among teachers than the films.) The effort is well meant, the footage from particular films extremely valuable, and some of the comment enlightening, but the controlling assumption of this procedure is unreliable, leading to imprecision and to an unwarranted forcing of meaning.

Black Orpheus

Is it true, for example, that a high camera angle inevitably reduces the stature of the subject? If so, why is this position chosen at the conclusion of *David and Lisa* to study the final embrace of the united lovers? During the course of the film, they have grown into sanity and now have experienced love. If the high angle shot merely smashes them against the surface on which they stand, this must be a colossal photographic botch. But other factors intervene. The take from above is not to diminish the stature of the lovers, but to collect an ample amount of empty space into these closing frames. The emphasis falls not upon their smallness, but their isolation, thus implying their exclusive dependence upon one another, as well as the intimacy of this relationship. No formula, however, would tell us this, only a close look at the ensemble of details in this particular scene. To take another instance, the shooting style in *The Gospel According to Saint Matthew* often runs against the movement-forward-equals-strength formula. Frequently, the Christ figure moves away from the camera, as if forcing the dolly to chase him. Yet this connotes power, not weakness. We see Christ from the perspective of his disciples, who have trouble keeping up with him, both physically and mentally. Christ is the man of vision, moving with broad, swift strides towards new objectives, just occasionally throwing a word over his shoulder to his slightly perplexed followers. He withdraws from the camera, not because the world has beaten him but because he has more important things to do than pose for pictures. Undoubtedly, there are also moments when the effect of these various devices is exactly as Professor Fischer predicts. The armed sentinel, silhouetted atop a steep hill at the opening of *Occurrence at Owl Creek Bridge* is precisely what the low camera angle is supposed to make

him—the epitome of power and anonymous military authority. But the Fischer formula is a little like a roulette system: it might make the game more exciting, but I would not risk much cash on it.

If such schema are treacherous, so too are the inevitable aesthetic fads. One now current is a nostalgic affection for black-and-white photography. This fetish bedevils several astute and competent students of film, including the highly respected Siegfried Kracauer. Writing as late at 1960, Kracauer complains that "natural colors, as recorded by the camera, tend to weaken rather than increase the realistic effect which black-and-white movies are able to produce."[4] This is a case of guilt by association. Kracauer remembers the days when Hollywood was busily turning the greatest story ever told into the longest stories ever filmed, and of course these biblical monstrosities were shot in color. Hence color photography becomes symbolic of everything garish, fantastic, escapist. Once there might have been technical reasons for discouraging the use of color—the slowness of the film stocks, the difficulty of blending the blue tones of daylight with the orange cast of the electric spot floods and fillers. But those days are past. And would Antonioni's portrait of the mods in *Blow-Up* be "more realistic" if it were done in black and white? For the theorist to reject color photography when all the major directors are turning to it is to confirm the view that aestheticians are irretrievably committed to an a priori scheme. Let's not begin our investigation of film by locking ourselves in someone else's ivory tower.

Assuming we break the word barrier as well as avoid the special pleading of film aesthetics, there remain some practical problems of handling film in the curriculum. In the classroom, I would suggest, we could make much more use of short films, running fifteen to twenty-five minutes, which offer adequate exposure to the cinema yet still leave some time for exchange and discussion. With the increasing availability of 16mm prints and the growing willingness of local libraries to purchase them, the academic community has an ever widening range of material to rely on.

I hope, though, we do not restrict ourselves to the study of films we can pull into the classroom. Flexible attitudes are essential to successful pioneering. To neglect the two-hour theatrical film would deform film study in more ways than can readily be named. Again the mushrooming of 16mm distributors puts such films within reach. The museums, the universities, and the high schools, as well as various private organizations, have all begun to conduct series, which provide enough exhibitions to satisfy the demands of anyone's course. The secret is to find out in advance what films will be shown during a given month or a semester and then plan an introduction to film study built around those scheduled for screening. Here we need desperately to improve communication, since duplication and even quadruplication are now the rule more than the exception, as nonprofessional exhibitors vie for the films of demonstrated audience appeal. Yet however confused the booking arrangements, the films do get shown, and perhaps at some time the arrangements themselves will be rationalized and exhibition handled on a city-wide basis.

Most recently, the academic community has been extended another option, this time from the commercial exhibitors who work in 35mm prints. This awakening of the theatrical entrepreneur to the academic market is enormously significant. It promises a regular program of films, screened in the local theatres at reduced prices and managed with professional expertise. To anyone like myself, who has on certain occasions acted as a combination lecturer-ticketman-projectionist and coffee-caterer all in the same evening, the prospect of such cooperation from the professional exhibitors seems appealing indeed. More than that, this plan promises to make films available as soon as they are exhibited commercially, closing up the two or three year gap which usually exists when we depend on the 16mm distributors. It is also important to remember that such things as widescreen projection simply cannot be studied in 16mm. I am not suggesting, however, that we abandon the 16mm distributors, only that we respond cordially to the alternative possibilities as well. My feeling is that the 16mm distributors will probably remain our best source of foreign prints and of prints of films more than ten years old—in other words, the basic stuff of film history courses. On the other hand, it would be tragic to create the impression that film art ended with *Open City* or even with the vintage products of 1960, which already look a little dated. The film is in an explosive state of development, and neglecting the immediately contemporary scene exposes us to the charge of old-fogeyism. Our students are studying expressionist color and skip-frame printing every time they set foot in a movie house or get in front of a television commercial, and we cannot help them with another lecture on *The Caine Mutiny*. As we try to remain relevant at this level, the commercial exhibitor is potentially a valuable ally.

Having thus far thrown emphasis upon exploration and openness, it would be out of character to offer any conclusions. I do not think this is the time for formal summaries. Shrewd guesses and impromptu experiments seem more in order. When Mr. Deasy in Joyce's *Ulysses* asks Stephen if he would like to be a teacher, Stephen replies, "I think I would rather be a learner." This I would recommend as a motto when we approach the study of cinema. At this stage the crucially important thing is to keep the future open to possibility.

Notes

1. George C. Stoney, "Breaking the Word Barrier," *Film Study in Higher Education*, David C. Stewart, ed. (Washington, D.C.: American Council on Education, 1966), p. 82.

2. Pauline Kael, "It's Only a Movie," *Film Study in Higher Education*, David C. Stewart, ed. (Washington, D.C.: American Council on Education, 1966), pp. 127-128.
3. Edward Fischer, *The Screen Arts: A Guide to Film and Television Appreciation* (New York: Sheed and Ward, 1960).
4. Siegfried Kracauer, *Theory of Film* (New York: Oxford University Press, 1960), pp. vii-viii.

James F. Scott is a member of the Department of English at St. Louis University, Missouri.

A Filmography of Films about Movies and Movie-Making

Robert W. Wagner & David L. Parker

A Day with Timmy Page (18 min.). This film shows an eleven-year-old film maker directing an afternoon's shooting in his backyard. Two of his 8mm silents are cut into the film. When the film was made, Timmy had been making films for only ten months, but he had a company of more than forty actors and had made twenty, ten-minute films. Directed by David Hoffman. Contemporary/McGraw-Hill.

A Short History of Animation: The Cartoon (60 min.). Animation 1907-1935, including *Gertie the Dinosaur* by Winsor McKay; Disney's *Flowers and Trees*; and the first appearance of Mickey Mouse in *Steamboat Willie*. Museum of Modern Art.

Abel Gance, Yesterday and Tomorrow (28 min., color). Written and directed by Nellie Kaplan; produced in France in 1962. (English commentary.) The film traces Gance's career from its uncertain beginnings through

This "Filmography" was originally published by the Motion Picture and Education Markets Division of Eastman Kodak Company, Rochester, New York.

his great creative period (1914-1937) to his return to filmmaking in the fifties and sixties. Excerpts are included from *Napoleon*, *La Folie du Docteur Tube*, *Barberousse*, *Mater Dolorosa*, *J'accuse* (silent and sound versions), and *La Fin du Monde* (many are tinted, as Gance originally made them). The excerpts are interspersed with production shots and views of the elderly Gance, who provides a reflective commentary, discussing both his successes and his frustrations. Contemporary/McGraw-Hill.

American Film, The (37 min.). Produced for the White House Festival of the Arts in 1966, narrated by Charlton Heston. Excerpts of American features are used to describe the objectives of each of five talented motion-picture directors: Fred Zinnemann, *High Noon* (b&w); Alfred Hitchcock, *North by Northwest* (color); William Wyler, *Friendly Persuasion* (color); Elia Kazan, *On the Waterfront* (b&w); George Stevens, *Shane* (color). Teaching Film Custodians, Inc.

Animation Goes to School (15 min., color). Illustrates how simple animation techniques are used in school films in various subjects from math to literature. Contemporary/McGraw-Hill; Horace Mann School.

Art Director, The (8 min.). Produced by Twentieth Century-Fox for the Academy of Motion Picture Arts & Sciences Series. This film shows how the art director, working from the script and with the director, designs the set, how it is constructed, and how other forms of background are made. The film ends with multiple exposure effects from *In Old Chicago*. Teaching Film Custodians; Indiana University; University of Iowa; University of Kansas.

Art of the Marx Brothers (40 min.). One reel (10 min.) of selected gags (1934-49) and two excerpts from *Love Happy: The Diamond Thieves* (10 min.), and *The Diamond Chase* (20 min.). British Film Institute.

Artwork in Motion (13 min., color). Explanation and demonstration of basic animation techniques: pop-on, scratch-off, cycle, etc. Produced in 1955 and dated by clothing and camera stock, but still a usable introduction to animation. Calvin Productions, Inc.

Basic Principles of Film Editing (8 min.). An introduction to editing. Compares unedited and edited forms of a dramatic scene from the feature *Pretty Boy Floyd*. Produced by American Cinema Editors, Inc., Department of Cinema, University of Southern California.

Basic Set Construction (8 min.). A straightforward visualization of basic set design, construction, and dressing. Informative documentary. Calvin Productions, Inc.

Before Hollywood, There Was Fort Lee, New Jersey (60 min.). Thomas Hanlon's compilation of rare film clips, stills, and feature excerpts of pre-Hollywood activity: *Perils of Pauline*, 1915 shooting; D.W. Griffith as a film actor; the Gish sisters; Douglas Fairbanks, etc. Teledynamics Corp.

Behind the Scenes of Walt Disney's Studio (27 min., b&w

and color). The late Robert Benchley sees all stages of cartoon feature production at the Disney studio. An excerpt from *The Reluctant Dragon* is included. Audio Film Center.

Biography of a Motion Picture Camera (21 min.). The early history of cinema is reflected here, including the work of Marey, Muybridge, Lumière, and Edison. Produced by Les Films du Cómpas, France. Contemporary/McGraw-Hill; Indiana University; Radim Films.

Best TV Commercials of the Year (30 min.). Produced as a supplement to the book of the same title, edited by Wallace A. Ross, this is a sampling of the winners of the American Television Commercials Festival. Hastings House, New York.

Buster Keaton Rides Again (55 min.). John Spotton's *cinéma vérité* account of the making of *The Railrodder*, Keaton's last film. After a quick survey of Keaton's career to 1933, shows the planning and construction of sight gags for the film, quiet script conference, charming birthday party given for Keaton by the railroad town. Should be seen with *The Railrodder*. Produced by the National Film Board of Canada, 1965. Contemporary/McGraw-Hill.

Cameramen at War (17 min., 35mm). Produced for the British Ministry of Information and compiled by Len Lye, this film shows some of the scenes produced by combat cameramen in 1943 and 1944, and some of the cameramen who made—and recorded—history. Museum of Modern Art.

Cavalcade of Movies (19 min., silent). Review of the silent era beginning with *The Kiss* of May Irwin and John C. Rice in 1896; excerpts from films of Will Rogers, John Barrymore, Mary Pickford, Theda Bara, Chaplin, Fairbanks, and others. Audio Film Center.

Check and Let Me Know (11 min., color). Goes to painful extremes to depict the confusion and wheel-spinning that results when a mishmash of preoccupied film people try to communicate with each other on a specific but not too-well-defined subject. Satire. Calvin Productions, Inc.

Children Make Movies (10 min., color). Produced by the children of the Lillian Wald Recreation Room and Settlement, this film consists of two parts: Part I—*Scratch Film,* and Part II—*Block Building.* The children, ages 5 to 12, made their "scratch" film with a couple of leet of leader, a small straight pin, and some felt-tips for coloring. Part II, inspired by McLaren's *Neighbors,* was made by the children with the help of photographer Kirk Smallman. Contemporary/McGraw-Hill.

Cinematographer, The (10 min.). Produced by Paramount in 1949 for the Academy of Motion Picture Arts & Sciences, this film describes the cinematographer's function in the making of a feature film on a Hollywood lot. Teaching Film Custodians; Indiana University; University of Iowa; University of Kansas.

Citizen Kane: The Snowball Scene; Rosebud (20 min.). Excerpts displaying Orson Welles' remarkable uses of flashbacks and flashforwards in narrative. British Film Institute.

Citizen Kane: Xanadu; The Daily Enquirer (20 min.). Excerpts illustrating Welles' tradition-breaking synthesis of film styles. British Film Institute.

City of Stars (25 min.). Background scenes from Universal Studios of 1925 showing sets from *The Hunchback of Notre Dame* and *Monte Carlo*. Swank Movie Pictures, Inc.

Composition for Photography (10 min.). Demonstrates line, mass, tone, and framing, with elementary examples. Indiana University.

Controlled Photographic Lighting (9 min., color). With the use of a small studio setup, the relation of key, fill, background, and accent lighting is shown. Light ratios, placement, and basic patterns are illustrated. Indiana University.

Costume Designer, The (9 min.). Depicts the research, skill, and sense of the appropriate in designing costumes for feature films. Produced at RKO, with Edith Head, for the Academy of Motion Picture Arts & Sciences Series. Teaching Film Custodians; Indiana University; University of Iowa; University of Kansas.

Creative Person, The—Federico Fellini (30 min.). Impressionistic coverage of the production of *Juliet of the Spirits*. Includes an interview, in English, with Fellini. Produced for National Educational Television in 1967.

Creative Person, The—Richard Williams (30 min.). The Canadian animator is seen working on TV commercials and creating a sequence for *Ivor Pittfalks, Universal Confidence Man* in minute detail, frame by frame, line by line. Excerpts from *The Little Island* and *Love Me, Love Me, Love Me* are examples of the work of an animator who is attempting to give animation full status as an art form. Directed and edited by Robert Morgan. Produced by J.C. Sheers for National Educational Television. National Educational Television.

Culture Explosion, The (60 min.). Art forms (including "underground films") and the current state of cinema are considered in this hour-long television production which relates these forms to the cultural, political, and educational life of Canada, England, and the United States. Actor Peter Ustinov and director Jean Renoir appear. Produced for National Educational Television by the Canadian Broadcasting System. National Educational Television; Indiana University.

Date with Dizzy (10 min.). Drawings by John Hubley, satirizing the TV commercial, are interpreted musically by the Dizzy Gillespie Quintet. Several Hubley animation techniques are shown as they have been applied to the production of TV commercials. Produced by Jim di Gangi. Brandon Films, Inc.

Decision, The Constitution in Action: The Constitution and Censorship (29 min.). Deals with two court cases involving governmental censorship on religious grounds. One involves "The Miracle" sequence from Rossellini's film *Ways of Love,* and the other concerns religious soliciting by a Jehovah's Witnesses minister in Connecticut. Traces the legal proceedings and precedents involved in the banning of "The Miracle" sequence and the eventual reversal of the ban. Presents opposing views on censorship at the close of the film. Produced by the Columbia Center for Mass Communication for National Educational Television. Indiana University.

Dingbat Story, The (15 min., color). Visualizes some of the philosophy of film titling, then proceeds (through the story of an overambitious art department staff trying to rectify a glaring error in a simple title) to demonstrate complex animation techniques and the mechanics of accomplishment. Calvin Productions, Inc.

Directors, The (17 min., color). Based on a special story by Robert Coughlan of *Life* magazine. Through interviews on location, an international cross-section of directorial opinion and style is presented. Includes points of view of thirty-two film directors; features Antonioni, Bergman, De Sica, Fellini, Hitchcock, Huston, Kazan, Kurosawa, Lean, Ray, Resnais, Stevens, Truffaut, Zinnemann. Radim Films.

Doug in Action (10 min., silent; also 8mm). Excerpts from Douglas Fairbanks' *Flirting with Fate, Mark of Zorro,* and *Black Pirate.* Produced by Entertainment Films, Inc. International Film Service.

Editing Synchronous Sound (10 min., b&w and color). Relates camera work to editing and focuses on how to maintain synchronism in shooting and editing "lip-sync" sequences. Indiana University.

Elements of the Film (27½ min., color). One of a series on film appreciation, this episode uses a staged western movie fight to help the viewer develop both a sense of how films are made and a sense of the aesthetics of film. Ann Blyth and Edward Fischer appear as actress and critic. OFM Productions.

Epic That Never Was, The (75 min.). Explores the production and cancellation of Korda's late 1930 epic *I, Claudius* with interviews with its stars, Flora Robson, Emlyn Williams, and Merle Oberon; its author, Robert Graves; the costume designer; and others. Includes thirty minutes of unedited rushes of Charles Laughton directed by Joseph von Sternberg. BBC-TV.

Experimental Film, The (28 min.). Produced by the National Film Board of Canada. Artists Robert Breer and Norman McLaren, and others, talk about their work. Excerpts from *Man Out Walking His Dog, Blazes, Blinkety Blink,* and the complete version of Lipsett's *Very Nice, Very Nice* are included. Contemporary/McGraw-Hill; National Film Board of Canada.

Expressive Society, The (30 min.). Number 5 in the series, "Face of Sweden," produced by the Swedish Institute. Last half is devoted to Ingrid Thulin (seen rehearsing a classic play in repertory, at home with her husband as they discuss film reviews, and at Svenskfilmindustrie refectory) and Ingmar Bergman (rehearsing *Winter Light*; linking him with film tradition of Victor Seaström and Alf Sjöberg). Excerpts from early Seaström silents; Sjöberg's *Miss Julie*; Bergman's *Wild Strawberries, Seventh Seal, Monika*; and others. National Educational Television; Indiana University.

Facts About Film (12½ min., color). One of an audio-visual training series originally released in 1948 and revised in 1959, presenting information on various kinds of motion-picture film, causes of damage, and methods of repair and storage. International Film Bureau, Inc.

Film Maker, The (30 min., color). Producer-director George Stevens in a conducted tour of the pre-production and filming stages of his film, *The Greatest Story Ever Told*. United Artists Corporation.

Film and Reality, The (105 min.). A feature-length compilation made for the British National Film Library by Cavalcanti. The historical development of the documentary film is illustrated by over fifty examples of noted works, including contributions of the Lumière Frères, through Flaherty and Grierson. Examples of the realistic and romantic approaches to documentary are presented. Critic & Film Series. British Information Service; Contemporary/McGraw-Hill.

Film and You (22 min.). The organization of a community film council. Four actual film-viewing situations are shown; includes reactions of adult audiences. Useful for those planning a local film society. Produced by the National Film Board of Canada. Indiana University.

Film as Art (27½ min., color). Actress Jayne Meadows and critic Edward Fischer discuss film editing, film music, and color, using clips from *Teresa, Marty, The Set-Up, Friendship Seven, Nanook of the North, The Little Fugitive, The River,* and *The World of Henry Orient*. OFM Productions.

Film Interlock, The (2½ min., color). An animated description of the interlock process, what it is, its purpose and mechanics. Calvin Productions, Inc.

Film Problems (8 min.). Using the simple situation of a person walking into a room, the film demonstrates with live action and animation the effects created by changes in camera placement, movement, composition, and overlapping action. Indiana University.

Film Research and Learning (14 min.). Depicts work-study situations in which films have been found to reinforce learning. With Professor Walt Wittich. Indiana University.

Film Tactics (22 min.). Five instructors utilize a training film in Navy classrooms. Student reactions dramatize mistakes in film use. A dated but interesting and useful example of a training film and illustrative of Hollywood production (Paramount) of instructional films for the Armed Forces during World War II. Indiana University; DuArt Films, Inc.

Film That Was Lost, The (11 min.). One of John Nesbitt's "Passing Parade" series produced by MGM, this is the story of how the Library of Congress reconstructed early films, many in a state of deterioration, so that the history of the motion picture may be preserved. Films, Inc.

Films of Georges Méliès, The (60 min.). The career of the pioneer French film maker is traced from 1897 through his films *Trip to the Moon* and *The Baron Has Eaten Too Much.* Sketchbooks, photographs of the artist in his studio, and personal recollections of his granddaughter are included. Produced by KQED-TV, San Francisco, for National Educational Television in 1964. National Educational Television.

Flaherty and Film (four 60-min., b&w kinescopes). Frances Flaherty, widow of the father of the documentary film, recalls their experiences making *Nanook of the North, Moana, Man of Aran,* and *Louisiana Story.* One-half hour of film excerpts and one-half hour of interview are devoted to each film. Produced by WGBH-TV, Boston, for National Educational Television in 1961. National Educational Television.

Flicks, I and II, The (30 min. each). *The Flicks I* traces the evolution of film from shadows on the wall to wide-screen color epics. Excerpts include Edison newsreels; Méliès' *Trip to the Moon;* glimpses of Pearl White, Chaplin, Keaton, Laurel and Hardy, W.S. Hart, Ben Turpin, Lon Chaney, Valentino, and Jolson. *The Flicks II* explores animation from cave paintings through the work of Winsor McKay, Disney, Lantz, Hubley, McLaren, Hanna-Barbera, and others. Produced by WTTW-TV, Chicago, for programs 264 and 270 in the series "What's New?" for National Educational Television. National Educational Television.

Flight from Hollywood, The (60 min.). "Runaway production" is surveyed throughout the world, mainly through interviews with film directors and producers, including Otto Preminger, Carl Foreman, and John Huston. Produced by CBS News for "CBS Reports" in 1963. Columbia Broadcasting System.

Four Ways to Drama (33 min.). The translation of a short dramatic incident for radio, television, stage, and screen is presented in four versions to illustrate the problems and techniques involved. The production developed out of a demonstration presented at the University of California at Los Angeles, sponsored by the University and the AETA in 1949. University of California at Berkeley.

German Newsreels (16 min.). Two propaganda newsreels produced for showing to the German people. The first covers the defeat of the British in Greece (1941). The second shows Berlin's welcome to Hitler in 1942 when German victory seemed assured. German narration with English subtitles. Audio Film Center.

Golden Age of Comedy, The (85 min.). Excerpts from comedies of the silent era. Directed by Robert Youngsen, this is a cavalcade of "sight-gags" illustrated by Laurel and Hardy, Ben Turpin, Carole Lombard, Jean Harlow, and the Keystone Kops. Brandon Films, Inc.;

Audio Film Center, Inc.; Contemporary/McGraw-Hill; Twyman Films, Inc.

Great Expectations (6 min.). A. Jympson Harman, of the *London Evening News*, discusses the film *Great Expectations*. He emphasizes the role of camera and editing. Contemporary/McGraw-Hill; Critic & Film Series, British Information Service.

Great Moments from the Birth of a Nation (200 feet, 8mm). Excerpts from Griffith's classic. Blackhawk Films.

Harriet Parsons (33 min.). A discussion of pre-production planning; relates budget, story content, selection of writer and director, and casting to the financial and artistic success of the production. University of Southern California.

Heavy Hammers (2½ min., color). An old show with dated footage, but still useful. Shows results of a loaded narration track and unrelated photography. Calvin Productions, Inc.

Highlights of Horror (12 min.). Excerpts from *The Hunchback of Notre Dame; Phantom of the Opera;* and *Cat and the Canary.* Swank Motion Pictures, Inc.

Historical Still and Motion Picture Projectors (11 min.). Portrays the development of still projectors from the whale-oil lamp through gas, kerosene, and electric illumination. Describes attempts to produce "moving" pictures by zooetrope, slides, and early models of 28mm, 16mm, and 35mm projectors. Produced in co-operation with the Archives and History Committee of the Division of Audiovisual Instruction of the National Education Association. University of Iowa.

History Brought to Life (8 min.). Produced by Paramount for the Academy of Motion Picture Arts & Sciences Series. Features Cecil B. DeMille illustrating the educational values of the theatrical film. Teaching Film Custodians; Indiana University; University of Iowa; University of Kansas.

History of the Cinema, The (9 min., color). Produced and directed by John Halas and Joy Batchelor, two of England's best animation artists, this is a witty history of cinema from cave pictures to CinemaScope. Animation by Harold Whitaker and John Smith; music by Jack King; commentary by Maurice Denham. Contemporary/McGraw-Hill.

History of the Motion Picture, The (26½ min. each). Thirty-one episodes, including silent classics with music scores, from early films to the appearance of sound. Includes excerpts from *Dr. Jekyll and Mr. Hyde* with John Barrymore; *Dracula; Orphans of the Storm; The Black Pirate;* and *The Three Musketeers.* The major themes covered in this material are "Trends in Early Experimental Film"; "Development of the Western"; "Contrasts in Comedy Styles"; "The Horror Film"; and "The Story of the Epics." The examples in each are drawn from the 1920s. Sterling Educational Films, Inc.

History of the Movies (400 feet, 8mm). Shots of Edison's "Black Maria" studio; train entering railway station; early trick films. Blackhawk Films.

Hollywood in Yugoslavia (12 min., also 35mm). Shot during the fifty-third day of filming *Genghis Khan* in Yugoslavia. This witty impression gives an instructive picture of the logistics involved in location work on a large-budget epic. No commentary. Connoisseur Films, Ltd.

Hollywood: The Golden Years (54 min.). Produced for television by David Wolper. A well-documented review of the silent film during Hollywood's "Golden Years" (1919-1929), narrated by Gene Kelly. Includes the development of the story film, referring to stars such as Chaplin, Valentino, Barrymore, Pickford, Garbo, and Fairbanks, and directors such as DeMille and Griffith. Sterling Educational Films, Inc.

Homage to Muybridge (2 min., color). A student-produced film, directed by David Hanson, in which still photographs made by Muybridge are translated into motion. Selected experiments by the man who is sometimes called "the father of the motion picture" are treated in a modest but humorous Victorian interpretation. University of Southern California.

How Motion Pictures Move and Talk (10 min.). Produced in 1940, this is somewhat outdated. Reflects a time when all sound was recorded directly as a photographic image rather than as original magnetic sound.

Useful, however, in the descriptions of the playback systems of optical sound tracks. Produced by Castle-United World. Critic & Film Series, British Information Service.

How to Splice a Film (9 min.). Demonstrates splices and the causes of splice failure. Uses humor, montage, and repetition to emphasize errors and to involve the audience. Splicing sequences are shown from the editor's viewpoint. Michigan State University.

How You See It (8 min.). Explains how "persistence of vision" makes motion pictures possible. An animated presentation of image transmission to the eye, and the relation of image production to projection of a motion picture. Produced by Jam Handy, Inc. Indiana University.

Ideas and Film (11 min., color). The use of motion pictures in communication is discussed. Includes excerpts from industrial films, examples of animation, time-lapse photography, high-speed studies, and applications of motion-picture analyses in the exploration of the world and the space which surrounds it. Sponsored by the Bell & Howell Company (Telcine). Critic & Film Series, British Information Service.

In the Beginning (26 reels). More than 10 years were spent in making motion-picture films from the rolls of paper that were sent to the Library of Congress between 1894 and 1912 by the original producers as proof of copyright. Kemp R. Niver, who developed the method by which the bromide paper prints were re-converted to film, worked with the Library of Congress and the Academy of Motion Picture Arts & Sciences to preserve these records of the early history of film. In 26 reels, 100 films—including the work of companies such as Edison and Selig, and examples of French, British, and Scandinavian producers—make up this significant series. Brandon Films, Inc.

Interpretations and Values (30 min.). Scenes shot for the television film program "Gunsmoke" are shown in un-edited form. The shots are assembled by three different film editors to show how the editorial process involves interpretive values. Produced by American Cinema Editors, Inc. University of Southern California.

Intruders, The (28 min.). Shows location filming for Carl Foreman's *The Victors* in the Italian mountain village of Comtagmia; includes interviews with George Peppard, George Hamilton, Vince Edwards, and other actors; describes the film crew's impact on a small foreign village; offers insight into location shooting of a commercial "blockbuster." By English documentary director, Denis Mitchell, for National Educational Television. National Educational Television.

Jean Renoir (30 min.). The veteran director screens *The Little Match Girl* (1928); discusses it with Arthur Knight; takes audience on a tour of his home; shows memorabilia of his career and art works by his father. Produced by KQED-TV, San Francisco, for National Educational Television. National Educational Television.

Jerry Bressler (32 min.). A discussion of post-production problems, stressing the importance of the editorial process. University of Southern California.

Jerry Wald (25 min.). The late writer-producer discusses problems such as selection of story, the producer's responsibilities, and his relation to members of the cast and the technical staff. University of Southern California.

Jesse L. Laskey (34 min.). Discusses his past film experiences, the early days of Hollywood, and the future. University of Southern California.

Julian Blaustein (29 min.). The producer of *Khartoum* examines the role of the script in making a film and the producer's responsibility for choosing and working with the writer. University of Southern California.

King Vidor (30 min.). Veteran director, King Vidor, revisits sites of the old silent and early sound studios of Hollywood, reminisces about MGM in the twenties. Excerpts from *Our Daily Bread* and *Solomon and Sheba* are included. Produced by KQED-TV, San Francisco, for National Educational Television. National Educational Television.

Let's Go to The Movies (9 min.). Produced for the Academy of Motion Picture Arts & Sciences Series by RKO. Describes the background of the motion picture and the development of showmanship from Edison to

1949. A very general film with excerpts from *Hills of Kentucky, Easy Street, Show of Shows, The Jazz Singer, Night Song,* and *The Great Train Robbery.* Teaching Film Custodians; Indiana University; University of Iowa; University of Kansas.

Life and Death of Rudolph Valentino (60 min.). In this David Wolper production, William K. Everson surrounds a short version of *Son of the Sheik* with clips from the earliest and last screen appearances of Valentino. This is a sympathetic study of an ordinary man trapped by a myth; concludes with newsreel footage of his funeral. Sterling Educational Films, Inc.

Life and Times of John Huston, Esq., The (60 min.). Produced by Allan King and Associates, London, for National Educational Television, this is an intimate portrait of the director, using formal interviews and candid shots of Huston at work and at play. He is pictured directing his first opera, "Mines of Sulphur," at La Scala in Milan, at work with Taylor and Brando on *Reflections in a Golden Eye,* and at his home in Ireland. National Educational Television.

Living Past, The (15 min. each). A series of quarter-hour compilations of newsreel footage from 1896 and after: early U. S. cowboy film; first French cartoon film; Buster Brown comedy; French nickelodeon film; and others. Film Classics Exchange.

Looking Beyond—Story of a Film Council (19 min.). Illustrates the significant functions of the Canadian film council in terms of how these affect the life of rural Canada. The method of forming a typical film council is shown. Useful as a study of adult education via the film medium. National Film Board of Canada.

Lorentz on Film (four 90-min. kinescopes). Six films by pioneer documentary film producer, Pare Lorentz, are discussed by Lorentz and film maker, Charles Rockwell: *The River, The Plow That Broke the Plains, The Fight for Life, Nuremberg,* and two World War II briefing films for pilots. Produced by WGBH-TV in 1961 for National Educational Television. National Educational Television.

Losey Makes "Accident" (9 min.). Follows two days of the filming of *Accident* during the summer of 1966. Shows the setting up of shots in the London studio and on location at Oxford: Dirk Bogarde reading to the children; Sunday afternoon on the lawn; and the last shot of the picture. An interesting document for the viewer who has seen the feature. Hunter Films, Ltd.

Loves of Jeanne Ney, The (4 min., silent). A single scene containing more than forty cuts from the film by G. W. Pabst. Museum of Modern Art.

Making Films That Teach (19 min.). Scripting, shooting, editing, and sound recording of educational film. Emphasizes collaboration between film producer and subject matter specialist. Produced by Encyclopaedia Britannica Films, Inc. Encyclopaedia Britannica Films, Inc.

Making of a Movie, The (21 min.). Background to the production of Otto Preminger's *St. Joan* in 1957. Jean Seberg's tests for the title role, Preminger's methods as an independent producer-director. Museum of Modern Art.

Man I Killed, The (Broken Lullaby) (3 min.). An excerpt of the opening scene of Armistice Day, 1919, in which director Ernst Lubitsch uses natural sound and music with a visible source to counterpoint his use of images. Museum of Modern Art.

Man With the Movie Camera, The (60 min., silent, English subtitles). The work of Dziga Vertov, showing aspects of Soviet life in the 1920s and examples of his "kino-eye" theory of camera. Brandon Films, Inc.

March of the Movies (20 min.). A 1949 "March of Time" release surveying the history of film from *The Great Train Robbery* to *Henry V*, featuring the Museum of Modern Art's film archives. Brandon Films, Inc.

Marlon Brando (30 min.). Produced by Al and David Maysles, this *cinéma vérité* study shows Brando before and during a press conference, self-assuredly interviewing his interviewers. Maysles Films, Inc.

Meet Bela Lugosi (8 min.). Background on the filming of *Dracula*. Manbeck Pictures Corporation.

Meet Oliver Hardy (8 min.). Hardy tells how he and Stan Laurel began working together and points out that it is much more difficult to produce comedy today. Manbeck Pictures Corporation.

Michelangelo Antonioni (60 min.). Produced in 1966 by the Canadian Film Board. Actress Monica Vitti, writer Caesare Zavattini, director Fellini, and others, discuss with Antonioni his career from *Cronaca di un Amore* (1950). Excerpts from *Juliet of the Spirits, L'Avventura, Il Grido, La Notte, Red Desert,* and *Eclipse* are included, together with fragments of Antonioni's own 8mm pre-production studies and out-takes. In French only. Interviews are in Italian with French subtitles. National Film Board of Canada.

Michel Simon (15 min.). Directed and written by Ole Roos in 1964. The late French actor, Michel Simon, relates events which shaped his life and which led him to the theatrical profession. The influence of the early films of Renoir and Jean Vigo's *L'Atalante,* a sequence of which is included, are recounted. Simon tells the story of the production of this film and Vigo's sad destiny. Contemporary/McGraw-Hill.

Moments in Music (10 min.). Musical excerpts from films produced before 1950, including *The Great Caruso, Up in Arms, New Moon, Carnegie Hall, Song to Remember, Road to Rio, Neptune's Daughter,* and *Anchors Aweigh.* Teaching Film Custodians; Indiana University; University of Iowa; University of Kansas.

Movie Magic (14 min.). Demonstrates techniques in animation and the exposing of single-frame images, using models to perform tank maneuvers in a battle scene. Sterling Educational Films, Inc.; Indiana University.

Movie Set in Action (11½ min., color). An elementary example of motion-picture making in progress. Uses a typical western situation to illustrate long shot, medium shot, close-up, indoor and outdoor sets, elementary aspects of lighting and sound, and identification of production personnel such as the director, cameraman, electrician, script girl, makeup man, property man, and actors. Shot on a Columbia Pictures lot. Produced by Fass-Levy Films. Classroom Film Distributors, Inc.

Moviemakers, The (10 min., color). Behind-the-scenes report on the making of the Hollywood feature *Hawaii*. Produced by Professional Film Services for United Artists. Teaching Film Custodians.

Movies from Computers (20 min.). Presents a number of extracts from films made by computer and a brief introduction on how they are produced. Educational Services, Inc.

Movies, The (29 min.). One of a series in which Dr. James Dodds discusses various aspects of twentieth-century American culture. This one examines the motion picture for clues to changes and constancies in American taste and is sociologically oriented. National Educational Television; Indiana University.

Movies Are Adventure (11 min.). Makes the point that movie-going is an experience which can be had in no other way, and that the world is brought to our doorstep by this medium. Produced in 1949 by Universal for the Academy of Motion Picture Arts & Sciences Series. Teaching Film Custodians; Indiana University; University of Iowa; University of Kansas.

Movies Learn to Talk, The (26 min.). Produced for the CBS television program, "The Twentieth Century," this is a well-documented history of the motion picture with historic episodes in the development of the sound film from non-synchronous methods to Vitagraph to photographic sound-on-film. Association Films; contemporary/McGraw-Hill.

Movies March Along (10 min., silent). Excerpts from twenty-four features (1896-1928) with thirty performers, including John Bunny, Fatty Arbuckle, Clara Kimball Young, Chaplin, Fairbanks, Valentino, Lloyd, and Pickford. International Film Service.

Moving with Movies (10 min.). Considers aesthetic effects of film, comparing the movements of lights and objects with an athlete's movements, translating these into emotional tones transmitted to the audience. Contemporary/McGraw-Hill; Indiana University.

Music for the Movies (60 min.). From the series, "Expedition Los Angeles," produced by KABC-TV, Los Angeles, this kinescope features Elmer Bernstein explaining conception, construction, and recording of music for feature films such as *Rat Race, The Great Train Robbery, Summer and Smoke, God's Little Acre, The Magnificent Seven, Men at War,* and *Walk on the Wild Side.* The composer conducts a full orchestra in simulated recording sessions and explains the desired effect of background music. KABC-TV— American Broadcasting Company.

Naked Eye, The (70 min., b&w and color). Louis Clyde Stoumen's technique of translating historic photographs to motion pictures is illustrated in this fluid documentary on photographers from Daguerre to Brady, Eisenstadt, Bourke-White, Weegee, Adams, Stieglitz, Steichen, and others, concluding with a color sequence on Edward Weston. Narrated by Raymond Massey. Contemporary/McGraw-Hill.

National Film Board of Canada Story (30 min.). Presents a tour of the facilities of the National Film Board of Canada. Originally produced for television in the late 1950s. National Film Board of Canada.

✓ **Nature of the Film Medium, The** (27½ min., color). A comparison of stage and screen play, illustrating the psychological effects on the audience of camera movement, camera angles, and editing. Ruth Hussey and critic Edward Fischer explain, using excerpts from *Citizen Kane, Hand in Hand, Requiem for a Heavyweight, Friendship Seven,* and *The World of Henry Orient.* OFM Productions.

New Dimensions through Teaching Films (28 min., color). Shows how instructional films may be used to improve the quality of education in a number of subject matter fields at several grade levels. The setting is an Instructional Materials Center. The situation is a two-day Teacher Institute. Coronet Instructional Films.

Odd Man Out (35 min.). Segments of the film are discussed by British documentary film producer, Basil Wright, with particular emphasis on how the mood of the picture was established. Contemporary/McGraw-Hill; Critic & Film Series, British Information Service.

OK for Sound—20th Anniversary of Talking Pictures (20 min.). Scenes from twenty years of motion-picture entertainment from Edison's laboratory to about 1947. Dominant Pictures Corporation.

Olympia (Part I—117 min.; Part II—95 min., sound). Diving sequence directed by Leni Riefenstahl illustrates filmic time and space created both by editing and by using slow-motion camera techniques (1936-38). Museum of Modern Art; Contemporary/McGraw-Hill.

On Location with David Lean (30 min.). Background on the filming of *Dr. Zhivago.* Produced for MGM by Thomas Craven Associates. MGM.

On Seeing Film and Literature (17 min.). Excerpts and background footage taken during the production of *The Bridge on the River Kwai* are introduced by William Holden in terms of how literature is translated to the screen. University of Southern California.

One Man Went To Mow (10 min.). Extract from Humphrey Jenning's *Fires Were Started,* from condensed version titled *I Was a Fireman.* Demonstrates Jenning's lyrical approach to the wartime documentary. British Film Institute.

✓ **Origins of the Motion Picture** (20 min.). Produced in

1955 by the United States Navy and based on Martin Quigley's book, *Magic Shadows,* this film sketches historical developments in film from the *camera obscura* through the contributions of da Vinci, Kircher, Roget, Plateau, Marey, Edison, and Lumière. The Museum of Modern Art; DuArt Films, Inc.

Our Daily Bread (12 min.). Excerpts from the film directed by King Vidor in 1934. Vidor interrelates acting, cutting, and music in rhythm with a metronome in an exposition of the last 400 feet of the film. Museum of Modern Art.

Overlanders, The (15 min.). A sequence from the film is discussed by Dilys Powell, of the British *Sunday Times,* with particular reference to editing and the construction of the sound track. Contemporary/McGraw-Hill; Critic and Film Series, British Film Institute.

Paris in the Twenties (30 min.). Produced by CBS News for the television series, "The Twentieth Century," this film includes a sequence of Man Ray showing his experimental films of the 1920s and remembering the avant-garde movement of that time. Association Films.

Phantom of the Opera Excerpts (30 min., silent). Excerpts from the feature with Lon Chaney and Mary Philbin, directed by Rupert Julien (1925). Audio Film Center.

Potemkin (10 min., silent). The famous "Odessa Steps" sequence from the film directed by Sergei Eisenstein. Notable example of the concept of montage (1925). Museum of Modern Art.

Pudovkin (68 min.). Distinctive characteristics of the Russian master's editing style demonstrated with excerpts from *Mother* and *End of St. Petersburg;* also documentary scenes of Pudovkin at work with actors. Brandon Films, Inc.

Reclaiming American History from Paper Prints by the Renovare Process (15 min., color). Produced in 1953 by Kemp Niver, who restored paper prints in the Library of Congress. Demonstrates the method of copying these early bromide prints back onto motion-picture film, making it possible for us to see examples of film history dating from 1894. Library of Congress, Film Division.

Rhetoric of the Movie (super 8, silent, color). This is a series of instructional sets designed primarily for teachers of English Language Arts who teach (or plan to teach) movies as a medium of communication. Although elementary in nature, the series can be adapted to a more sophisticated movie course through appropriate narration by an experienced instructor. Each set in the series contains super 8 color movies supplied on fifty-foot reels and a *Teacher's Guide.* Eastman Kodak Company.

Roy Tash Was There (30 min.). Produced by Spaulding Taylor Ltd., this film offers insight into the work of making newsreels. We watch Roy Tash, a newsreel cameraman since 1919, recount incidents surrounding his big stories: birth of the Dionne quintuplets; 1938 collapse of the Niagara Falls Rainbow Bridge; 1939

Royal Tour; etc. Directed by Rene Bonniere for CBC "Telescope." Canadian Broadcasting Company.

Satyajit Ray (13 min.). Indian director seen during actual shooting; discusses casting problems, planning shots, editing, and his attitude toward film. Includes sequence from *Pather Panchali*. Audio Film Center.

Screen Actor, The (8 min.). Produced in 1949 by MGM, this short is designed to show that "actors are people" and presents the viewpoint of the Screen Actors Guild. Teaching Film Custodians; Indiana University; University of Iowa; University of Kansas.

Screen Director, The (10 min.). Produced by Warner Brothers, this one-reeler depicts some of the decisions, pressures, and responsibilities of the Hollywood motion-picture director. Includes a sequence with star actors. Teaching Film Custodians; Indiana University; University of Iowa; University of Kansas.

Screen Writer, The (10 min.). Filmed at Twentieth Century-Fox for the Academy of Motion Picture Arts & Sciences, this film shows the screenwriter adapting a novel to the screen and focuses on the problem of translating verbal to visual and aural images. Teaching Film Custodians; Indiana University; University of Iowa; University of Kansas.

Sergei Eisenstein (50 min.). Produced in the USSR in 1958. This is a biography of the famous Russian film director and includes excerpts from *Potemkin, Old and New, Ten Days That Shook the World, Alexander Nevsky,* and *Ivan the Terrible.* The effects of the Revolution and Communist ideology are evident in this film, which was translated in Britain. Brandon Films, Inc.

Showman, The (53 min.). Film distributor-promoter, Joe Levine, caught candidly by the Maysles brothers' camera as he negotiates for the release of his films, presents an Oscar to Sophia Loren at Cannes, speaks at a reunion of boyhood friends from Boston's west end, argues the art of the film on a David Susskind broadcast, wheels and deals through several months of life. Maysles Films, Inc.

Soundman, The (9 min.). A scene with the late Jack Carson is followed by a description of how the words spoken on the set are recorded, how the tracks are laid out, dubbed, post-synchronized, and finally re-recorded to a combined track for printing in combination with the picture. Includes scenes from the early "talkies" *Tugboat Annie* and *One Night of Love.* Produced by Columbia Pictures for the Academy of Motion Picture Arts & Sciences. Teaching Film Custodians; Indiana University.

Sound Recording and Reproduction (11 min.). Covers optical film recording and playback. Explains "variable area" and "variable density" optical tracks, and describes how sound is recorded optically and played back on a 16mm projection system. Elementary and in certain phases obsolete, but historically useful. Encyclo-

"Dragon Seed" in *The Best Film Plays of 1943-1944.* John Gassner and Dudley Nichols (New York: Crown Publishers, Inc., 1945).

Duet for Cannibals, Susan Sontag (New York: The Noonday Press, 1970).

Easy Rider, Peter Fonda, Dennis Hopper, and Terry Southern (New York: The New American Library, Inc., 1970).

Eight and a Half (8½), Federico Fellini (New York: Ballantine Books, Inc., 1969).

"Entr'Acte" in *A Nous la Liberte and Entr'Acte.* Rene Clair (New York: Simon & Schuster, Inc., 1970).

"The Eternal Return" in *Cocteau: Three Screenplays* (New York: Grossman Publishers, 1971).

Events, Fred Baker (New York: Grove Press, Inc., 1970).

Exterminating Angel, Luis Bunuel (New York: Simon & Schuster, Inc.).

Faces, John Cassavetes (New York: The New American Library, Inc., 1970).

Film, Samuel Beckett (New York: Grove Press, Inc., 1969).

"The Fortune Cookie" in *The Apartment and the Fortune Cookie.* Billy Wilder and I.A. Diamond (New York: Praeger Publishers, Inc., 1970).

"The Four Hundred Blows" in *Four Hundred Blows: A Film by Francois Truffaut* (New York: Grove Press, Inc., 1969).

Freedom to Love, P. Kronhausen and E. Kronhausen (New York: Grove Press, Inc., 1970).

"Gertrude" in *Four Screenplays.* Carl T. Dreyer (Bloomington: Indiana University Press, 1970).

"Going My Way" in *The Best Film Plays of 1943-1944.* John Gassner and Dudley Nichols (New York: Crown Publishers, Inc., 1945).

"The Good Earth" in *Great Film Plays.* John Gassner and Dudley Nichols (New York: Crown Publishers, Inc., 1959).

Grand Illusion, Jean Renoir (New York: Simon & Schuster, Inc., 1968).

Greed, Erich von Stroheim (New York: Simon & Schuster, Inc., 1970).

"Hail the Conquering Hero" in *The Best Film Plays of 1943-1944.* John Gassner and Dudley Nichols (New York: Crown Publishers, Inc., 1945).

"Henry V" in *Film Scripts One.* George P. Garret, O.B. Hardison, Jr., and Jane Gelfann, eds. (New York: Appleton-Century-Crofts, 1971).

"High Noon" in *Film Scripts One.* George P. Garret, O.B. Hardison, Jr., and Jane Gelfann, eds. (New York: Appleton-Century-Crofts, 1971).

Hiroshima Mon Amour, Marguerite Duras (New York: Grove Press, Inc., 1961).

I Am Curious (Blue), Vilgot Sjoman (New York; Grove Press, Inc., 1968).

I Am Curious (Yellow), Vilgot Sjoman (New York: Grove Press, Inc., 1968).

"I Vitelloni" in *Fellini: Three Screenplays*. Federico Fellini (New York: Grossman Publishers, 1970).

If..., Lindsay Anderson and David Sherwin (New York: Simon & Schuster, Inc., 1969).

Ikiru, Akira Kurosawa (New York: Simon & Schuster, Inc., 1968).

"Il Bidone" in *Fellini: Three Screenplays*. Federico Fellini (New York: Grossman Publishers, 1970).

"Il Grido" in *Antonioni: Four Screenplays*. Michelangelo Antonioni (New York: Grossman Publishers, 1963).

I Never Sang For My Father, Robert Anderson (New York: The New American Library, Inc., 1970).

"It Happened One Night" in *Great Film Plays*. John Gassner and Dudley Nichols (New York: Crown Publishers, Inc., 1959).

Ivan the Terrible, Sergei Eisenstein (New York: Simon & Schuster, Inc., 1962).

"The Job" in *Visconti: Three Screenplays*. Luchino Visconti (New York: Grossman Publishers, 1970).

Joe, Norman Wexler (New York: Avon Books, 1970).

Jules and Jim, Francois Truffaut (New York: Simon & Schuster, Inc., 1968).

Juliet of the Spirits, Federico Fellini (New York: Grossman Publishers, 1965; and New York: Ballantine Books, Inc., 1968).

"La Beaute du Diable" in *Rene Clair: Four Screenplays* (New York: Grossman Publishers, 1970).

La Dolce Vita, Federico Fellini (New York: Ballantine Books, Inc., 1961).

L'Age d'Or, Luis Bunuel (New York: Simon & Schuster, Inc., 1968).

La Guerre Est Finie, Jorge Semprin (New York: Grove Press, Inc., 1968).

"La Notte" in *Antonioni: Four Screenplays*. Michelangelo Antonioni (New York: Grossman Publishers, 1963).

Last Year at Marienbad, Alain Robbe-Grillet (New York: Grove Press, Inc., 1962).

La Strada (New York: Ballantine Books, Inc., 1970).

"La Terra Trema" in *Visconti: Two Screenplays*. Luchino Visconti (New York: Grossman Publishers, 1970).

"L'Avventura" in *L'Avventura: A Film by Michelangelo Antonioni*. Robert Hughes, ed. (New York: Grove Press, Inc., 1969).

"L'Avventura" in *Antonioni: Four Screenplays*. Michelangelo Antonioni (New York: Grossman Publishers, 1963).

"L'Eclisse" in *Antonioni: Four Screenplays*. Michelangelo Antonioni (New York: Grossman Publishers, 1963).

Le Jour Seleve, Jacques Prevert and Marcel Carne (New York: Simon & Schuster, Inc., 1970).

Le Petit Soldat, Jean Luc Godard (New York: Simon & Schuster, Inc., 1971).

"Les Belles-de-Nuit" in *Clair: Four Screenplays.* Rene Clair (New York: Grossman Publishers, 1970).

"Les Grandes Manoeuvres" in *Clair: Four Screenplays.* Rene Clair (New York: Grossman Publishers, 1970).

"Les Silence Est d'Or" in *Clair: Four Screenplays.* Rene Clair (New York: Grossman Publishers, 1970).

"Let There Be Light" in *Film: Book 2—Films of Peace and War.* Robert Hughes, ed. (New York: Grove Press, Inc., 1962).

"The Life of Émile Zola" in *Great Film Plays.* John Gassner and Dudley Nichols (New York: Crown Publishers, Inc., 1959).

The Lion in Winter, James Goldman (New York: Random House, Inc., 1966).

Little Faus and Big Halsey, Charles Eastman (New York: The Noonday Press, 1970).

Little Murders, Jules Feiffer (New York: Paperback Library, 1968).

"The Lost Weekend" in *The Best Film Plays of 1945.* John Gassner and Dudley Nichols (New York: Crown Publishers, Inc., 1946).

M, Fritz Lang (New York: Simon & Schuster, Inc., 1968).

"The Magician" in *Four Screenplays of Ingmar Bergman.* Ingmar Bergman (New York: Simon & Schuster, Inc., 1960).

A Man and a Woman, Claude Lelouch (New York: Simon & Schuster, Inc., 1971).

The Married Woman, Jean Luc Godard (New York: Medallion).

Masculine-Feminine, Jean Luc Godard (New York: Grove Press, Inc., 1969).

"Medal for Benny" in *The Best Film Plays of 1945.* John Gassner and Dudley Nichols (New York: Crown Publishers, Inc., 1946).

Metropolis, Fritz Lang (New York: Simon & Schuster, Inc., 1970).

Miracle in Milan, Vittorio De Sica (New York: Grossman Publishers, 1968; and Baltimore: Penguin Books, Inc., 1969).

"Miracle of Morgan's Creek" in *The Best Film Plays of 1943-1944.* John Gassner and Dudley Nichols (New York: Crown Publishers, Inc., 1945).

"Miriam" in *Trilogy.* Truman Capote, Frank Perry, Eleanor Perry (New York: The Macmillan Company, 1969).

"The More the Merrier" in *The Best Film Plays of 1943-1944.* John Gassner and Dudley Nichols (New York: Crown Publishers, Inc., 1945).

Mother, V.I. Pudovkin (New York: Simon & Schuster, Inc., 1970).

"Night and Fog (Nuit et Brouillard)" in *Film: Book 2—Films of Peace and War* (New York: Grove Press, Inc., 1962).

"Night of the Hunter" in *Agee on Film: Five Film Scripts.* James Agee (Boston: Beacon Press, 1960).

"Noa Noa" in *Agee on Film: Five Film Scripts*. James
Agee (Boston: Beacon Press, 1960).

"None but the Lonely Heart" in *The Best Film Plays of
1945*. John Gassner and Dudley Nichols (New York:
Crown Publishers, Inc., 1946).

Oedipus Rex, Pier Paolo Pasolini (New York: Simon &
Schuster, Inc., 1970).

"Ordet" in *Four Screenplays*. Carl T. Dreyer (Bloomington: Indiana University Press, 1970).

"Orpheus" in *Cocteau: Three Screenplays*. Jean Cocteau
(New York: Grossman Publishers, 1971).

"Over Twenty-One" in *The Best Film Plays of 1945*. John
Gassner and Dudley Nichols (New York: Crown Publishers, Inc., 1946).

"The Ox-Bow Incident" in *The Best Film Plays of 1943-
1944*. John Gassner and Dudley Nichols (New York:
Crown Publishers, Inc., 1945).

Pandora's Box, G. W. Pabst (New York: Simon & Schuster, Inc., 1970).

"The Passion of Joan of Arc" in *Four Screenplays*. Carl
T. Dreyer (Bloomington: Indiana University Press,
1970).

"Persona" in *Bergman: Two Screenplays*. Ingmar Bergman (New York: Grossman Publishers, forthcoming).

Pierrot le Fou, Jean Luc Godard (New York: Simon &
Schuster, Inc., 1969).

Potemkin, Sergei Eisenstein (New York: Simon & Schuster, Inc., 1968).

Potemkin, Sergei Eisenstein (New York: Grossman Publishers, forthcoming).

"The Purple Heart" in *The Best Film Plays of 1943-1944*.
John Gassner and Dudley Nichols (New York: Crown
Publishers, Inc., 1945).

Que Viva Mexico, Sergei Eisenstein (London: Vision
Press, 1951).

"Rashomon" in *Rashomon: A Film by Akira Kurosawa*.
Robert Hughes and D. Richie, eds. (New York: Grove
Press, Inc., 1969).

"Rebecca" in *Great Film Plays*. John Gassner and Dudley Nichols (New York: Crown Publishers, Inc., 1959).

"Rocco and His Brothers" in *Visconti: Three Screenplays*.
Luchino Visconti (New York: Grossman Publishers,
1970).

Rules of the Game, Jean Renoir (New York: Simon &
Schuster, Inc., 1970).

Salesman, Albert and David Maysles (New York: The
New American Library, Inc., 1969).

"Satyricon" in *Fellini's Satyricon*. Federico Fellini (New
York: Ballantine Books, Inc., 1970).

"The Secret Sharer" in *Media for Our Time*. Dennis
DeNitto, ed. (New York: Holt, Rinehart & Winston,
Inc., 1971).

"Senso" in *Visconti: Two Screenplays*. Luchino Visconti
(New York: Grossman Publishers, 1970).

The Seven Samurai, Akira Kurosawa (New York: Simon
& Schuster, Inc., 1970).

"The Seventh Seal" in *Four Screenplays of Ingmar Bergman*. (New York: Simon & Schuster, Inc., 1965).

"Shame" in *Bergman: Two Screenplays*. Ingmar Bergman (New York: Grossman Publishers, forthcoming).

"The Silence" in *Bergman's Trilogy*. Ingmar Bergman (New York: Grossman Publishers, 1967) and *Three Films by Ingmar Bergman* (New York: Grove Press, Inc., 1967).

"Simon of the Desert" in *Bunuel: Three Screenplays*. Luis Bunuel (New York: Grossman Publishers, 1969).

"Smiles of a Summer Night" in *Four Screenplays of Ingmar Bergman*. Ingmar Bergman (New York: Simon & Schuster, Inc., 1960).

"Spellbound" in *The Best Film Plays of 1945*. John Gassner and Dudley Nichols (New York: Crown Publishers, Inc., 1946).

"The Southerner" in *The Best Film Plays of 1945*. John Gassner and Dudley Nichols (New York: Crown Publishers, Inc., 1946).

Stagecoach, John Ford (New York: Simon & Schuster, Inc., 1970) and in *Great Film Plays*. John Gassner and Dudley Nichols (New York: Crown Publishers, Inc., 1959).

"Story of GI Joe" in *The Best Film Plays of 1945*. John Gassner and Dudley Nichols (New York: Crown Publishers, Inc., 1946).

"A Streetcar Named Desire" in *Film Scripts One*. George P. Garret, O. B. Hardison, Jr., and Jane Gelfann, eds. (New York: Appleton-Century-Crofts, 1971).

"Sutters Gold" in *With Eisenstein in Hollywood* (New York: International, 1967).

The Swimmer, Eleanor Perry (New York: Stein & Day, Publishers, 1967).

"Temptations of Dr. Antonio" (From Boccacio 70) *Fellini: Three Screenplays*. Federico Fellini (New York: Grossman Publishers, 1970).

"The Testament of Orpheus" in *Cocteau's Screenplays and Other Writings on the Cinema*. Jean Cocteau (New York: Grossman Publishers, 1968).

They Shoot Horses, Don't They? Horace McCoy (New York: Avon Books, 1969).

The Third Man, Graham Greene and Carol Reed (New York: Simon & Schuster, Inc., 1968).

"Thirty Seconds Over Tokyo" in *The Best Film Plays of 1945*. John Gassner and Dudley Nichols (New York: Crown Publishers, Inc., 1946).

"Through a Glass Darkly" in *Bergman's Trilogy*. Ingmar Bergman (New York: Grossman Publishers, 1967) and *Three Films by Ingmar Bergman* (New York: Grove Press, Inc., 1967).

"To Kill a Mockingbird" in *Screenplay of To Kill a Mockingbird, With a Word from Harper Lee*. Horton Foote, ed. (New York: Harcourt Brace Jovanovich, Inc.).

"Tom Jones" in *Tom Jones: Film Script Based on the Novel by Henry Fielding*. John Osborne (New York: Grove Press, Inc., 1965).

"A Tree Grows in Brooklyn" in *The Best Film Plays of 1945*. John Gassner and Dudley Nichols (New York: Crown Publishers, Inc., 1946).

The Trial, Orson Welles (New York: Simon & Schuster, Inc., 1970).

"Twelve Angry Men" in *Film Scripts One*. George P. Garret, O. B. Hardison, Jr., and Jane Gelfann, eds. (New York: Appleton-Century-Crofts, 1971).

Un Chien Andalou, Luis Bunuel (New York: Simon & Schuster, Inc., 1968).

"Vampyr" in *Four Screenplays*. Carl T. Dreyer (Bloomington: Indiana University Press, 1970).

"Variety Lights" in *Fellini: Early Screenplays*. Federico Fellini (New York: Grossman Publishers, 1969).

"Viridiana" in *Bunuel: Three Screenplays*. Luis Bunuel (New York: Grossman Publishers, 1969).

"Vivre Savie" (Jean Luc Godard) in *Film Culture #26* (Winter 1962).

"Watch of the Rhine" in *The Best Film Plays of 1943-1944*. John Gassner and Dudley Nichols (New York: Crown Publishers, Inc., 1945).

✓ *Weekend*, Jean Luc Godard (New York: Simon & Schuster, Inc., 1971).

"White Nights" in *Visconti: Three Screenplays*. Luchino Visconti (New York: Grossman Publishers, 1970).

"The White Sheik" in *Fellini: Early Screenplays*. Federico Fellini (New York: Grossman Publishers, 1970).

"Wild Strawberries" in *Four Screenplays of Ingmar Bergman*. Ingmar Bergman (New York: Simon & Schuster, Inc., 1960).

"Wilson" in *The Best Film Plays of 1943-1944*. John Gassner and Dudley Nichols (New York: Crown Publishers, Inc., 1945).

"Winter Light (The Communicants)" in *Bergman's Trilogy*. Ingmar Bergman (New York: Grossman Publishers, 1967) and *Three Films by Ingmar Bergman* (New York: Grove Press, Inc., 1967).

Woman in the Dunes, Hiroshi Teshigahara (New York: Phaedra, Inc., 1966).

✓ "A Woman Is a Woman" (Jean Luc Godard) in *Cahiers du Cinema in English*. Vol. 12 (December 1967).

Selected Bibliography

Historical

Brownlow, Kevin. *The Parade's Gone By*. New York: Alfred A. Knopf, Inc., 1968. A stunning compendium of nostalgia and technical detail of the days of the silent film.

Goodman, Ezra. *The Fifty Year Decline and Fall of Hollywood*. New York: MacFadden-Bartell Corp., 1961. Just what it says.

Jacobs, Lewis. *The Rise of the American Film*. New York: Teachers College Press, 1968. A first rate history.

McGowan, Kenneth. *Behind the Screen*. New York: The Delacorte Press, 1965. Subtitled "the history and technique of the motion picture," it covers these areas in great depth.

An earlier version of this bibliography appeared in *Screen Education News* 3:1 (January-February 1970) 4-5.

Ramsaye, Terry. *A Million and One Nights.* New York: Simon & Schuster, Inc., 1954. One of the most useful histories available. It goes up to 1925.

Renan, Sheldon. *An Introduction to the American Underground Film.* New York: E. P. Dutton & Co., Inc., 1967. A useful account of a wide range of underground films and short biographies of underground film makers.

Rotha, Paul, and Richard Griffith. *The Film Till Now.* New York: Funk and Wagnalls, Inc., 1949. The book that is the keystone of any film library. A classic.

Theoretical

Arnheim, Rudolph. *Film as Art.* Berkeley and Los Angeles: University of California Press, 1964. An interesting though somewhat dated book. It contains many insights, by one of our foremost aestheticians, into why a film might be considered a work of art.

Bluestone, George. *Novels into Film.* Los Angeles: University of California Press, 1966. A fascinating study of the changes undergone by a work of art when it is transferred into another medium.

Eisenstein, Sergei. *Film Form and the Film Sense.* New York: Meridian Books, 1949. A somewhat difficult book with a superlative passage on Dickens.

Huss, Roy, and Norman Silverstein. *The Film Experience.* New York: Delta Books, 1968. An extraordinary description of the rhetoric of film.

Jacobs, Lewis. *Introduction into the Art of the Movies.* New York: The Noonday Press, 1960. A useful anthology containing among its offerings a piece by Vachel Lindsay.

Montagu, Ivor. *Film World.* Baltimore: Penguin Books, Inc., 1964. A sometimes trying, often prejudiced book which is nevertheless useful in its analysis of the economics of filmmaking.

Spottiswoode, Raymond. *A Grammar of the Film.* Berkeley and Los Angeles: University of California Press, 1959. A book which is frequently difficult to read but often illuminating, especially in its exploration of the syntax of film.

Stephenson, Ralph, and J. R. Debrix. *The Cinema as Art.* Baltimore: Penguin Books, Inc., 1967. A well-written and informative book discussing a wide range of films.

Talbot, Daniel. *Film: An Anthology.* Los Angeles: University of California Press, 1966. A useful collection of seminal articles about film.

Truffaut, Francois. *Hitchcock*. New York: Simon & Schuster, Inc., 1967. A definitive study of a great director.

Practical

Hall, Stuart, and Paddy Whannel. *The Popular Arts*. New York: Pantheon Books, Inc., 1964. An attempt to "discern what is of value in the mass media."

Kuhns, William, and Robert Stanley. *Exploring the Film*. Dayton, Ohio: Pflaum/Standard, 1968. A good introduction to film teaching for the novice film teacher. Excellent illustrations.

Mallery, David. *The School and the Art of Motion Pictures*. Boston: National Association of Independent Schools, 1964. A listing of films used by the author and various interesting and perceptive comments about them.

McAnany, Emile G., S.J., and Robert Williams, S.J. *The Filmviewer's Handbook*. Glen Rock, New Jersey: Paulist/Newman Press, 1965. A useful assemblage of film teaching materials.

Pincus, Edward. *Guide to Filmmaking*. New York: Signet, 1969. Very complete coverage of the technical knowledge necessary for filmmaking written in an easy-to-read style.

Sheridan, Marion C., Harold H. Owen, Ken Macrorie, and Fred Marcus. *The Motion Picture and the Teacher of English*. New York: Appleton-Century-Crofts, 1965 (Available from NCTE. Stock No. 45203 $1.95.). A seminal work which, even though uneven, offers many insights for the novice film teacher.

Smallman, Kirk. *Creative Filmmaking*. London: Collier Books, 1969. Probably the best all-around introduction to the making of films, with lucid explanations of the aesthetics of technical effects.

Taylor, Theodore. *People Who Make Movies*. New York: Avon Books, 1967. A discussion of various jobs and duties of the many people involved in the making of a film.

Critical

Agee, James. *Agee on Film*. Boston: Beacon Press, 1958. Arthur Knight called Agee "the best movie critic this country ever had."

Alpert, Hollis. *The Dreams and the Dreamers*. New York: The Macmillan Company, 1962. A critic with a particular aptitude for examining the people who make films and revealing meaning through that examination.

_____, and Andrew Sarris, eds. *Film 68/69.* New York: Simon & Schuster, Inc., 1969. A collection of the best film criticism from 1968-1969.

Crist, Judith. *The Private Eye, The Cowboy, and the Very Naked Girl.* New York: Holt, Rinehart & Winston, Inc., 1968. A critic who doesn't apologize for American films.

Crowther, Bosley. *The Great Films.* New York: G. P. Putnam's Sons, 1967. Fifty years of great films discussed by the "dean of American film critics."

Kael, Pauline. *Kiss Kiss Bang Bang.* New York: Bantam Books, Inc., 1967. A reviewer for *Book Week* said "Reading her is better than going to the movies." See also *I Lost It at the Movies.*

Kauffmann, Stanley. *A World on Film.* New York: Harper & Row, Publishers, 1966. An excellent series of reviews from the former critic for the *New Republic.*

Schickel, Richard, and John Simon, eds. *Film 67/68.* New York: Simon & Schuster, Inc., 1968. A collection of the best film criticism from 1967-1968. This collection is to be continued each year.

Index

*n indicates that entry is found in a note on that page

Baby Doll, Tennessee Williams (New York: New Directions Publishing Corp., 1956).

"Beauty and the Beast" in *Cocteau: Three Screenplays.* Jean Cocteau (New York: Grossman Publishers, 1971).

Belle du Jour, Luis Bunuel (New York: Simon & Schuster, Inc., 1970).

Bicycle Thief, Vittorio De Sica (New York: Simon & Schuster, Inc., 1968).

"Big Sleep" in *Film Scripts One.* George P. Garret, O.B. Hardison, Jr., and Jane Gelfann, eds. (New York: Appleton-Century-Crofts, 1971).

"The Blood of a Poet" in *Cocteau's Screenplays and Other Writings on the Cinema.* Jean Cocteau (New York: Grossman Publishers, 1968).

Blow-Up, Michelangelo Antonioni (New York: Simon & Schuster, Inc., 1970).

Blue Angel, Josef von Sternberg (New York: Simon & Schuster, Inc., 1968).

"Blue Hotel" in *Agee on Film: Five Film Scripts* (Boston: Beacon Press, 1960).

Blue Movie, Andy Warhol (New York: Grove Press, Inc., 1970).

"The Bride Comes to Yellow Sky" in *Agee on Film: Five Film Scripts* (Boston: Beacon Press, 1960).

Butch Cassidy and the Sundance Kid, William Goldman (New York: Bantam Books, Inc.).

The Cabinet of Dr. Caligari, Robert Wiene (New York: Simon & Schuster, Inc.).

Carnal Knowledge, Jules Feiffer (New York: The Noonday Press, 1971).

"Casablanca" in *The Best Film Plays of 1943-1944.* John Gassner and Dudley Nichols (New York: Crown Publishers, Inc., 1945).

Children of Paradise (Les Enfants du Paradu), Marcel Cerne (New York: Simon & Schuster, Inc., 1968).

"China is Near" in *Bellocchio's China is Near.* Marco Bellocchio (New York: Grossman Publishers, 1969).

Closely Watched Trains, Jiri Menzel (New York: Simon & Schuster, Inc., 1970).

Coming Apart, Milton Moses Ginsberg (New York: Lancer Books, Inc., 1969).

"Christmas Memory" in *Trilogy.* Truman Capote, Frank Perry, Eleanor Perry (New York: The Macmillan Company, 1969).

"The Defiant Ones" in *Film Scripts One.* George P. Garret, O.B. Hardison, Jr., and Jane Gelfann, eds. (New York: Appleton-Century-Crofts, 1971).

Danish Blue, Gabriel Axel (New York: Grove Press, Inc., 1970).

David Holzman's Diary, L.M. Kit Carson and Jim McBride (New York: The Noonday Press, 1970).

"The Doctor and the Devils" in *The Doctor and the Devils and Other Scripts.* Dylan Thomas (New York: New Directions Publishing Corp., 1970).

"Double Indemnity" in *The Best Film Plays of 1945.* John Gassner and Dudley Nichols (New York: Crown Publishers, Inc., 1946).

Screenplays in English

"A Nous la Liberte" in *A Nous la Liberte and Entr'Acte*. Rene Clair (New York: Simon & Schuster, Inc., 1970).

"African Queen" in *Agee on Film: Five Film Scripts*. James Agee (Boston: Beacon Press, 1960).

Alice's Restaurant, Arthur Penn and Venable Herndon (New York: Doubleday & Co., Inc., 1970).

The All American Boy, Charles Eastman (New York: The Noonday Press, 1971).

"All That Money Can Buy" in *Great Film Plays*. John Gassner and Dudley Nichols (New York: Crown Publishers, Inc., 1959).

Alphaville, Jean Luc Godard (New York: Simon & Schuster, Inc., 1968).

"An American Tragedy" in *With Eisenstein in Hollywood* (New York: International, 1967).

"Among the Paths to Eden" in *Trilogy*. Truman Capote, Frank Perry, Eleanor Perry (New York: The Macmillan Company, 1969).

"The Apartment" in *The Apartment and the Fortune Cookie: Two Screenplays*. Billy Wilder and I.A. Diamond (New York: Praeger Publishers, Inc., 1970).

National Film Board of Canada, 680 Fifth Avenue, New York, New York 10019.

NBC News, 30 Rockefeller Center, New York, New York 10019.

OFM Productions, 1229 South Santee Street, Los Angeles, California 90015.

Radim Films, 220 West 42nd Street, New York, New York 10036.

Standard Oil, 910 Pennsylvania Avenue, Pittsburgh, Pennsylvania 15222.

Sterling Educational Films, Inc., 241 East 34th Street, New York, New York 10016.

Swank Motion Pictures, Inc., 201 South Jefferson Avenue, St. Louis, Missouri 63103.

Swedish Institute, 49 Egerton Crescent, London S.W. 3, England.

Teaching Film Custodians, Inc., 25 West 43rd Street, New York, New York 10036.

Teledynamics Corporation, 729 Seventh Avenue, New York, New York 10019.

Twyman Films, Inc., Box 665, Dayton, Ohio 45401.

United Artists Corporation (UA/16) 729 Seventh Avenue, New York, New York 10019.

University of California, Media Center, Berkeley, California 94720.

University of Iowa, Radio-Television-Film Division, Iowa City, Iowa 52240.

University of Kansas, Bureau of Visual Instruction, Lawrence, Kansas 66044.

University of Southern California, Department of Cinema, Los Angeles, California 90007.

Robert W. Wagner and David L. Parker are members of the Department of Photography and Cinema at Ohio State University.

Columbia Broadcasting System, 485 Madison Avenue, New York, New York 10022.

Connoisseur Films, Ltd., 554 Wardour Street, London W. 1, England.

Contemporary/McGraw-Hill, 330 West 42nd Street, New York, New York 10036.

Coronet Instructional Films, 65 E.S. Water Street, Chicago, Illinois 60611.

Dominant Pictures Corporation, a subsidiary of United Artists Television, Inc., 555 Madison Avenue, New York, New York 10022.

DuArt Films, Inc., 245 West 55th Street, New York, New York 10019.

Eastman Kodak Company, Audio-Visual Services, 343 State Street, Rochester, New York 14650.

Educational Testing Service, 20 Nassau Street, Princeton, New Jersey 08540.

Educational Services, Inc., 37 Chapel Street, Newton, Massachusetts 02158.

Encyclopaedia Britannica Films, Inc. (EBF), 425 North Michigan Avenue, Chicago, Illinois 60611.

Film Classics Exchange, 1926 South Vermont Avenue, Los Angeles, California 90007.

Film Images, Inc., 220 West 42nd Street, New York, New York 10037.

Films Incorporated, 1144 Wilmette Avenue, Wilmette, Illinois 60091.

Hastings House, 151 East 50th Street, New York, New York 10022.

Horace Mann School, Columbia University, 246th Street, Riverdale, New York 10471.

Hunter Films, Ltd., 280 Chartridge Lane, Chesham, Bucks, England.

Indiana University, Audio-Visual Center, Bloomington, Indiana 47405.

International Film Bureau, 332 South Michigan Avenue, Chicago, Illinois 60604.

International Film Service, Inc., Greenvale, Long Island, New York 11548.

KABC-TV-American Broadcasting Company, Los Angeles, California 90027.

Library of Congress, Film Division, Washington, D.C. 20540.

Metro-Goldwyn-Mayer, 1350 Avenue of the Americas, New York, New York 10019.

Manbeck Pictures Corporation, 3621 Wakonda Drive, Des Moines, Iowa 50321.

Maysles Films, Inc., 1697 Broadway, New York, New York 10019.

Michigan State University, Audio-Visual Center, East Lansing, Michigan 48823.

Museum of Modern Art, Department of Film, 11 West 53rd Street, New York, New York 10019.

National Educational Television (NET), 10 Columbus Circle, New York, New York 10019.

paedia Britannica Films, Inc.

Sound Recording for Motion Pictures (9 min., color). Contrasts ideal sound studio conditions with acceptable synchronous sound recording on location. Includes acoustical set treatment, microphone placement, control of extraneous noise, including sources of electrical hum and interference. Indiana University.

Splicing Techniques (3½ min., color). A demonstration using the Griswold splicer. Uses animation to show a cross-section of film, how a splice is made, and typical mechanical errors. Calvin Productions, Inc.

Staging for Television (30-min. kinescope). Verne Weber demonstrates the use of modular flat units; specially tailored furniture and curtains; and the integration of maps, charts, and display devices into sets. Includes a series of production stills of various settings for educational television programs. Produced in 1959 by National Educational Television. Indiana University.

Swedish Film Classics (40 min.). A survey of the silent Swedish film. Includes archival excerpts from the work of Sjostrom and Stiller. Swedish Institute.

Teenage Movie Award Winners (27 min., color). Excerpts from award-winning films made by teenagers in the competition sponsored by the University Film Foundation and Kodak. Dr. Louis Forsdale of Columbia University presents background information on their production. Eastman Kodak Company.

Television Directing (two 30-min. kinescopes). Features Allan Beaumont. Part I deals with motivating and positioning subjects for interviews and panel discussions and for demonstration-teaching programs. Part II deals with problems of camera rehearsal: building shot sequences, use of dissolves, and integration of pre-filmed material. Produced in 1959 by National Educational Television. Indiana University.

Television Lighting (30-min. kinescope). Using diagrams, lighting equipment, and a miniature set and figures, Greg Harvey demonstrates use of key, back, fill, and set lighting. Produced in 1959 by National Educational Television. Indiana University.

Test Shots for Hamlet (5 min., color). Two tests made in 1933 for a planned but never realized production are all that remain of John Barrymore's *Hamlet*, the most famous of his stage roles. Museum of Modern Art.

Thirty Years of Fun (85 min.). Excerpts from silent films (1895-1925) feature the work of Chaplin, Keaton, Langdon, and Laurel and Hardy. Produced by Twentieth Century-Fox in 1962. Directed by Robert Youngsen. Brandon Films, Inc.

This Theatre and You (8 min.). Produced in 1949 by Warner Brothers for the Academy of Motion Picture Arts & Sciences, this is the story of a small-town exhibitor and his role in bringing entertainment to the community. Teaching Film Custodians; Indiana University; University of Iowa; University of Kansas.

Three-Ten to Yuma (38 min.). John Freeman, editor of *The New Statesman,* analyzes the psychological overtones of myth and morality in this Delmer Daves western. A British Film Institute "Critic and Film" production. Cinema 16.

Top Hat, Extracts from (7-10 min. each). Five complete musical production numbers from the influential 1935 film with Fred Astaire and Ginger Rogers: "White Tie and Tails," "Isn't This a Lovely Day?" "No strings," "Cheek to Cheek," and "The Piccolino." Each is available on a separate reel. British Film Institute.

Toy That Grew Up, The (17 min.). Also available in a forty-minute version in French under the title *Naissance du Cinema.* Produced by Les Filmes du Compas. The film begins with the Thaumatrope of the Belgian physicist, Plateau, and studies of persistence of vision; it then considers the animation work of Emile Reynaud and the beginnings of the animated cartoon. Indiana University; Radim Films.

Twelve Angry Men (25 min.). Number four in the British Film Institute's "Critic and Film" series, this film presents Arbot Robertson's provocative viewpoints on writing and characterization. Excerpts from the United Artists release are included. Contemporary/McGraw-Hill.

Understanding the Movies (17 min.). A series of sequences made available by Loews, Inc., from MGM pictures. Illustrates aspects of directing, acting, photography, editing, art, and music. Teaching Film Custodians; Indiana University; University of Iowa; University of Kansas.

Unique Contribution, The (29 min., color). Produced by Encyclopaedia Britannica Films, Inc., this series of clips from EBF instructional films illustrates the "unique contribution" which the motion picture makes in science, education, and information. The clips are linked by on-camera comments by Maurice Mitchell, former president of EBF. Indiana University.

Van Gogh—From Darkness into Light (20 min., color). Examines the technical skills involved in building sets and filming locales for the MGM film *Lust for Life.* Emphasizes the problem of matching photographic colors to those used by Van Gogh. Contemporary/McGraw-Hill; Indiana University.

Vicious Circle, The (15 min., color). Satirical handling of the subject of production approval. Depicts woes of producer who attempts to satisfy the script preferences of individual department heads in a large corporation, rather than calling for the necessary, all-inclusive, production conference before attempting a detailed treatment and script. Calvin Productions, Inc.

Visual Language of the Film (27½ min., color). Actress Ann Blyth and critic Edward Fischer discuss the "language of film" in terms of composition, camera angles, use of lighting, and the effects of lenses of different focal lengths. OFM Productions.

Voice That Thrilled the World, The (20 min.). Examines the development of the motion picture from Eastman and Edison, including excerpts from Barrymore's *Don Juan,* Jolson in *The Jazz Singer,* Arliss in *Disraeli,* Muni in *Émile Zola* and *Louis Pasteur,* Cooper in *Sergeant York;* and Cagney in *Yankee Doodle Dandy.* Dominant Pictures Corporation.

Western Hero, The (The Cowboy) (30 min.). Produced by CBS for "The Twentieth Century" TV series. A tongue-in-cheek survey of movie cowboy heroes from W.S. Hart through Autry and Rogers. Very funny early sound westerns included. Walter Cronkite gives a left-handed analysis of the perennial appeal of the cowboy. Association Films.

When Comedy Was King (81 min.). Written and produced by Robert Youngsen, this tribute to the visual gag ranges from the Sennett films of 1914 to the Roach comedies of 1928. Includes the work of Chaplin, Keaton, Laurel and Hardy, Turpin, Arbuckle, Beery, Swanson, Normand, Clyde, Conklin, Swain, the Keystone Kops, and others. Brandon Films, Inc.; Audio Film Center; Contemporary/McGraw-Hill; Twyman Films, Inc.

William Thomas (28 min.). A discussion of film exploitation, with emphasis on roles of the distributor and the exhibitor. University of Southern California.

Window on Canada: An Interview with Norman McLaren (31 min.). Noted experimentalist, Norman McLaren of the Canadian Film Board, describes various techniques he uses in his animation experiments. Illustrative films included are *C'est L'Aviron, Boogie Doodle,* and *La-Haut Sur Cos Montagnes.* The work of a Chinese student working under McLaren's direction on a UNESCO grant is also shown. Contemporary/McGraw-Hill.

World Heritage Films, The (28½ min., videotape/kinescope). Hollis Alpert, *Saturday Review* film critic, and Margaret Twyman, director of community relations for the Motion Picture Association of America, discuss school utilization of MGM revivals, *Captains Courageous, Kim, Julius Caesar, Little Women, A Tale of Two Cities, The Good Earth,* etc., with educators. MGM.

World of Darryl Zanuck, The (60 min.). One of the NBC "Project 20" productions. The career of Zanuck is traced from *Forty Second Street* through the filming of *The Longest Day* and *Cleopatra* battle scenes with director Joseph L. Mankiewicz and production crew. Produced by NBC News. NBC News.

World of Sophia Loren, The (60 min.). An NBC "Project 20" production. This is a rambling impression of the weekly round of events in the life of a film star who has become an institution. Produced by NBC News. NBC News.

World Theatre (60 min. each, color). A series of seven hour-long cultural documentaries on the arts (including film) in Greece, France, Japan, Nigeria, and Sweden. Sequences by famous directors include the hour on India by Satyajit Ray. Standard Oil.

Worlds of Dr. Vishniac (20 min., color). Special cine-microphotography by Dr. Roman Vishniac and a discussion of how he produces some of the most spectacular and scientifically useful motion pictures ever made in the field of the invisible. Educational Testing Service.

Yank Comes Back (43 min.). Cameramen follow Burgess Meredith as he visits British cities, mines, and farms to gather material for a motion picture. British Information Service; Indiana University.

You Only Live Once (10 min.). Excerpts from Fritz Lang's film. Designed to show a film in the making, this short program consists of uncut "takes," followed by a sequence from the film as finally edited. Shows studio craftsmen at work before and after the take. Museum of Modern Art.

Your Name Here Story, The (10 min., color). Satirical description of the "all-purpose film." Created to meet the demands of film buyers for specially tailored motion pictures—without the often-difficult-to-explain costs of creative writing and personalized production. Visualizes how stock footage and sound can be edited to realize a "quickie-cheapie." Calvin Productions, Inc.

Sources of Films about Movies and Movie-Making

Academy of Motion Picture Arts & Sciences, 9038 Melrose Avenue, Hollywood, California 90069. (Also, see Teaching Film Custodians.)

Association Films, 600 Madison Avenue, New York, New York 10022.

Audio Film Center, Inc., 34 MacQuesten Parkway So., Mt. Vernon, New York 10550.

Blackhawk Films, Davenport, Iowa 52808.

Brandon Films, Inc., 221 West 57th Street, New York, New York 10019.

BBC-TV, London, England.

British Film Institute, 81 Dean Street, London W. 1, England.

British Information Service, Central Office of Information, Westminster Road Bridge, London S.E. 1, England. (In U.S., see Contemporary Films, Inc.)

Calvin Productions, Inc., 1106 Truman Road, Kansas City, Missouri 64106.

Canadian Broadcasting Company, Box 500 Terminal A, Toronto 1, Canada.

Carousel Films, 1501 Broadway, New York, New York 10036.

Cinema 16, 175 Lexington Avenue, New York, New York 10017.

Classroom Film Distributors, 5620 Hollywood Boulevard, Los Angeles, California 90028.